Nick Nairn
New Scottish Cookery

Nick Nairn

New Scottish Cookery

To everybody at Lochend

The recipes in this book are drawn from various sources. Some are reworkings of recipes previously published in *Wild Harvest*, *Wild Harvest 2* and *Island Harvest*, changed to reflect not only my new attitude to diet and healthy eating, but also in acknowledgement that most people do not have the time or desire to reproduce complicated 'restaurant' dishes. Other recipes have come from my column in the *Sunday Herald* or were written especially for the book.

It would not have been possible for me to carry out all the writing, editing, testing and re-writing without some serious help, so huge thank yous to all involved, in no particular order: the ever wonderful Maxine Clark, home economist and stylist extraordinaire; my consistently level-headed, organized and good humoured assistant Nadine Carmichael; star chefs Derek Blair of Nairns restaurant, John Webber of Nairns Cook School and Colin Halliday of Nairns Anywhere; Gareth Morgans for his quite superb photography.

Last, but by no means least, I must thank the team from my publishers of the last seven years, BBC Worldwide: the boss, Nicky Ross, for her continued faith in my ability to deliver on time, my editor, Sarah Miles, for her patience, perfectionism and enthusiasm, Janet James for her wonderful design work and Julie Tochel for helping pull it all together.

I hope that this book reflects my continued passion for good food and commitment to a healthy diet. My philosophy on food remains unchanged – buy the best seasonal produce (preferably Scottish), cook it properly and know when to stop. For those of you who would like to do more than just read the book, I highly recommend Nairns Cook School (www.nairnscookschool.com) for hands-on cooking and Nairns restaurant (www.nairns.co.uk) for a great night out.

Published by BBC Books, BBC Worldwide Limited, Woodlands, 80 Wood Lane, London W12 0TT

First published in hardback 2002 and in paperback 2004
Reprinted in paperback 2005, 2006
Reprinted in hardback 2006
© Nick Nairn 2002
The moral right of the author has been asserted.

Some of the recipes contained in this book are based on recipes that first appeared in *Wild Harvest* (BBC Books, 1996) and *Wild Harvest 2* (BBC Books, 1997), photographs by Graham Lees, and *Island Harvest* (BBC Worldwide, 1998), photographs by Jean Cazals. Other recipes first appeared in the *Sunday Herald*, photographs by Stephen Kearney and Martin Hunter.

New photography for this edition: Gareth Morgans © BBC Worldwide 2002, except page 7 © Craig Easton

Hardback ISBN 0 563 53453 2
Paperback ISBN 0 563 52151 1

Commissioning Editors: Nicky Ross and Rachel Copus
Project Editors: Sarah Miles and Julie Tochel
Copy-editor: Deborah Savage
Designer: Janet James
Art Director for jacket: Pene Parker
Art Director for new photography: Lisa Pettibone
Production Controller: Kenneth McKay
Home Economist: Maxine Clark
Stylist: Sue Rowlands

Printed and bound in Italy by L.E.G.O. spa
Colour separations by Kestrel Digital Colour, Chelmsford

For more information about this and other BBC Books, please visit our website on www.bbcshop.com or telephone 08700 777 001.

contents

introduction

I came to cooking at a relatively late stage in my life. My mum was a great cook; she always had warming broths, stews and fantastic home-baking on the go. I was extremely fortunate that I ate well; wild salmon, venison and pheasant were all regulars on the menu, albeit simply cooked with no added onions, garlic or spices – my dad was not one for 'fancy food'. After leaving school I joined the Merchant Navy as a navigator, to spend seven happy years bobbing around the world's oceans, and it was during this time that my taste buds were awakened. I vividly remember tasting satay, freshly barbecued over charcoals on the seafront in Singapore and the amazing flavours simply blew me away. It was then that I realized there was more to cooking than mince and tatties. However, it wasn't until I was studying for my naval exams in Glasgow that a lack of funds forced me into cooking for myself. So I went out and bought a frying pan, wooden spoon and a cookery book and, thus armed, rustled up chicken breasts stuffed with bananas, hazelnuts and grapes in a curried cream (it was the eighties after all!). The results were a revelation, more than good enough to eat and from then on I was hooked. I had discovered something that I was good at. A dinner party obsession ensued and, after a time, this led me to believe I could open my own restaurant. Armed with the naïvety of youth combined with a not inconsiderable amount of hard graft, my first wife, Fiona, and I opened my first restaurant, Braeval, in a converted watermill in June 1986.

We started simply but, as my skills and confidence grew, the food became more and more refined until, by the early 1990s, we were regarded as one of the top places to eat in Scotland. A chance encounter with restaurant customers Colin Cameron of BBC Scotland and television producers Hamish Barber and Muriel Gray led to my first series, *Wild Harvest*, where I travelled around Scotland meeting producers of the most wonderful raw materials. I met divers, farmers, fishermen and mushroom gatherers, all with one thing in common – a passion for the wonderful produce available all over Scotland. Seeing the amazing quality of this natural harvest at first hand led me to be increasingly dissatisfied with complex cooking and encouraged me to continue my set, no-choice menu, allowing me to prepare the best possible food depending on the produce available that day. This practice helped me develop my own cooking style, using the produce as the inspiration instead of finding the ingredients to suit a recipe idea.

The secret of good food is simplicity. This of course demands not only good cooking technique, but also the confidence to know where to stop in order to allow the produce to speak for itself.

I had spent the best part of a decade living and breathing Braeval and, up until this point, my cooking was confined to 'restaurant food' since 18-hour shifts meant I rarely cooked at home. Over the following

Above: A fishing boat returns to Oban, on the west coast of Scotland, at dusk.

years, things changed dramatically and I started doing increasingly varied work, which got me out of the kitchen and opened my eyes to a whole new world. There was not only life outside the kitchen, but for me, a whole different style of cooking.

In 1997, I filmed my third television series, *Island Harvest*, and, not being one for taking the easy route, opened Nairns restaurant in the same year. Nairns Anywhere, my catering company, and Nairns Cook School followed soon after. All this, combined with the continuing television work, writing cookery books and the ever-increasing food consultancy work, means I no longer cook professionally for a living. This change in lifestyle has brought me back to home-cooking and most of my 'cheffy' recipes of the past years have been simplified and refined. Holly, my present wife, has developed a herb and salad garden that supplies the school and restaurant; having access to such fresh, high-quality produce means my recipes and cooking are simpler than ever. These days I love nothing more than getting home from work, when Holly and I select vegetables from the garden and then decide what to cook for dinner. It keeps my imagination going, but more than anything it reinforces the keep-it-simple ethos of my Scottish cooking.

So what is new Scottish cooking? Historically, Scottish cooking is difficult to define as we have no real tradition of gastronomy, unlike our neighbours in continental Europe, where food has always played an important part in their culture. In Scotland, we still suffer a bit of a hangover from the post-war intensive farming industry, when food was seen simply as fuel to get you through the day. It is only in the past 15 years that we have begun to value the fact that we have the most wonderful produce available in the world, a fact well known on the continent, to where, sadly, a lot of our produce is exported.

It is my opinion that modern Scottish cooking is as much defined by its produce as it is by the various cooking styles of the Mediterranean, oriental and Indian restaurants in our communities. We have been influenced by the changing fashions of British cookery, from *nouvelle cuisine* to fusion cooking, and continue to be inspired by travel, magazines and cookery books. We are still very much in the process of forming our own definitive style, but one thing is certain – our cooking has a truly international flavour. Throughout all of this, however, the star is the produce and we have a talent for picking key parts of various cooking styles and using these techniques and flavours to bring out the best in our own ingredients.

Yet a glimpse at traditional Scottish cooking reveals how the diet of Scots in the past was heavily influenced by the seasons, by region and, of course, by poverty. Some of Scotland's most famous dishes – haggis, Scotch broth and porridge – have developed from the cheapest and most basic ingredients – oatmeal, barley and sheeps' entrails. Scottish flair did, however, manage to transform these staples into wonderfully tasty dishes, which are enjoyed all round the English-speaking world.

When it comes to the humble potato, no nation (aside perhaps from the Irish) is as inventive in its use as Scotland. This is illustrated by the myriad range of Scottish potato dishes such as Kailkenny (made with kale or cabbage), Clapshot (a blend of mashed spuds and turnip), Rumbledethumps (mashed potato layered with cabbage) and Stovies (see page 173). The list goes on.

Historically, however, Scottish poverty-driven cooking wasn't all gruel and oatcakes. The abundance of fish and wild game meant that in the eighteenth century modern luxuries, such as wild salmon, oysters and game birds, were often found on the tables of Scottish peasants. Preservation of food without refrigeration has also left its mark on traditional Scottish cooking, with the various processes of smoking, salting and curing leaving a legacy in the form of smoked salmon, kippers, salt herring and smoked haddock. These are now some of the ingredients that regularly contribute to my new Scottish cooking.

The Scottish regions have all contributed their own individual flavours to Scottish cooking: salt ling, myriad shellfish and blood pudding from the islands; grouse with bread sauce (an invention of the Scots, not the English!), soft fruits, smoked fish and Aberdeen Angus from the north east; venison, lamb and barley from the Borders. The more refined areas of Edinburgh, Glasgow and the central belt of Scotland are responsible for a range of pies, cakes and pastries.

This book on Scottish cooking is a very personal collection of recipes, developed over the years. It's quite a diverse compilation, but the one thing the recipes have in common is that they all work well with

**Opposite:
Roasted Root
Vegetables
(see page 176)**

Scotland's produce. Many are drawn from my first books, *Wild Harvest* and *Wild Harvest 2*, but all have been reworked to reflect the changing philosophy of my cooking. I've reached a stage in my life where I've realized I'm not invincible and health is of paramount importance and I recognize the need to have a balanced healthy diet. To achieve that balance, I eat plenty of fresh fruit and vegetables, try not to include too much salt and use unsaturated fats where possible. I'm also a great believer in 'a little of what you fancy does you good', so there's room in my diet for a drop of butter sauce here and there.

You'll find meals for all occasions here, from the everyday Carrot, Ginger and Honey Soup (see page 22), Perfect Steak and Chips (see page 137) and simple puds like Hot Whisky Cream with Frozen Berries (see page 205), to the more adventurous Shellfish and Saffron Broth with Herb Potato Dumplings (see page 28), Scallops with Oriental Salad and Sweet Chilli Dressing (see page 89) and Hot Raspberry Soufflés (see page 191). Some are traditional – Cullen Skink (see page 31), Bashed Neeps and Chappit Tatties (see page 175) and Cranachan (see page 186) – but mainly it's a varied collection of recipes, which for me reflects the diversity of Scottish cooking today.

I've created these recipes using the great produce that surrounds me but, if you can't access Scottish produce, they'll still work well using your best local produce. I love cooking and most of all I love cooking with Scottish produce and here in this book you'll find the flavours and textures unique to Scottish cooking today. There's nothing precious about the recipes and they're certainly not rocket science, but hopefully they'll be a source of inspiration in your kitchen for years to come.

Cook's notes

In most of my recipes I use freshly ground sea salt, preferably Maldon. I prefer it above processed salt and coarse sea salt, because the soft flakes give lovely frissons of flavour in your mouth and have the delicious iodine taste of the sea. Always taste before seasoning as most of us have a tendency to oversalt our food and too much salt really is detrimental to your health. You will find freshly ground pepper in most savoury recipes – in general I prefer to use black pepper for meat, game and poultry and white pepper for fish and shellfish.

Eggs are large unless otherwise stated. Buy fresh farm eggs from chickens allowed to run around free. The difference in quality between these and even supermarket free-range eggs is huge – the yolks are a brilliant orange colour and the flavour is exceptional. Butter is unsalted unless otherwise stated.

Spoon measurements are level. A tablespoon is equivalent to 15 ml for liquids and 15 g for solids and a teaspoon is equivalent to 5 ml for liquids and 5 g for solids. Conversions are approximate and have been rounded up or down. Follow one set of measurements only; do not mix metric and imperial. Oven temperature and cooking times may vary according to the equipment and ingredients used.

And one final word – do wash all fruit and vegetable produce before preparation. I'll sign off now and leave you to get on with it…happy cooking!

**Opposite:
Hot Whisky Cream
with Frozen Berries
(see page 205)**

scotland's larder

Vegetables and Herbs

ASPARAGUS

Scottish asparagus is sublime. Generally grown in the north-east, the season is shorter in Scotland than in England – beginning early May and ending in late June. If you can, find a local producer like Eassie Farm, near Glamis, Angus (see page 257). Growers often advertise when they are picking in local papers; alternatively, farmers' markets are a great place to buy. Sizes vary from thin Sprue to big fat Jumbos and prices vary accordingly. For eating on its own, opt for medium-sized spears; the fat Jumbos are perfect for soup and stir-frys or salads are the ideal way to serve the thinner spears.

POTATOES

Potatoes love Scotland's damp climate, so we have a wonderful array of potato varieties on offer. Always look out for new-season Ayrshires, which pop into the shops just prior to the influx of Jersey Royals, and those late-season gems, Pink Fir Apples. Supermarkets now seem to carry a greater variety – Sainsbury's have the delicious Anya potatoes, which are perfect for warm salads.

ROOT VEGETABLES

We may not have the best climate in the land but it has to be said our 'dreich' weather (that's grey and wet to non-Scots) is ideal for growing root vegetables. Farmers' markets are a great stop for carrots, turnips, celeriac and beetroot or, if you've got space, try growing your own.

WILD MUSHROOMS

The Highlands are a haven for wild mushrooms, where a wide variety can be found. If you are going to pick your own, take a guide book as not all are edible. Look out for woodland bluets, chanterelles and saffron milk caps. If picking your own isn't possible, try Strathspey Mushrooms (see page 257), who supply the best selection of fresh and dried wild mushrooms.

Fish and Shellfish

A great variety of fish is landed all around the coasts of Scotland and thankfully it's no longer all shipped off to the continent. From the ubiquitous haddock to John Dory, halibut, turbot and monkfish, we have a great range of extensively farmed or wild fish. Find a good fishmonger – I recommend MacCallums of Troon (see page 257) or The Fish People (see page 257). If you find yourself near Peterhead or Aberdeen, rise early and head to the fish market – it's a tourist attraction in itself.

ARBROATH SMOKIES

As the name suggests, Arbroath, on the east coast of Scotland, is home to these small haddock, which are hot-smoked (smoked and cooked simultaneously) as opposed to the standard cold-smoking. They have a wonderful, deep, earthy, smoky flavour which, to me, is very Scottish in essence. For the best, try Spinks (see page 257), who supply some of the major supermarkets. Arbroath smokies are a delicious addition to risottos and soups, and make smashing fishcakes – just be careful to remove the bones when flaking off the flesh, as they are smoked whole to help retain moisture.

HOT-SMOKED SALMON

Smoked at a higher temperature than traditional smoked salmon, the salmon is lightly cooked and the result is a flavourful, flaky textured, smoked fish. I find it extremely versatile and, as it is already cooked, it's a good flavourful ingredient to add in at the end of a recipe. My favourite is from Salar on South Uist (see page 257).

SALMON

Scotland has a thriving salmon farming industry, but unfortunately the quality is variable. As a basic rule look out for the Tartan Quality Mark, though for the best go for Orkney organic salmon, from Aquascot (see page 256), which is also available in major supermarkets. Fishing for salmon is still possible in many areas, especially Speyside, but yield is low and it can be a very expensive hobby.

SHELLFISH

Scottish shellfish is second to none – look to the Western Isles for the best lobster, langoustines and prawns. These should still be lively when you buy them, otherwise they've been out of the water too long. For the freshest langoustines and lobster, try MacCallums of Troon (see page 257), whose new establishment offers tanks with live lobster, langoustines and oysters. If you see creel-caught langoustines, snap them up as they are superior even to the best tiger prawns. Creel-caught means that the langoustines have been hand-hauled by small baited boats and not dredged, as the majority of langoustines and scallops have been. Dredged shellfish is caught, as the name suggests, by scraping the bottom of the seabed. Scallops and langoustines are scraped up, along with gunk and sand from the seabed and anything else that happens to be lingering down there. The general result is suffocated langoustines, choked with sand – a far cry from the lively creel-caught specimens. The same goes for scallops – always buy hand-dived as dredged ones are often full of sand and get damaged in the process. A word of warning, however: avoid buying scallops that have been soaked in water – they are like small sponges and absorb all the water, leaving you with not very tasty waterballs.

SMOKED HADDOCK

The north-east of Scotland produces wonderful smoked haddock. The apotheosis of smoked haddock is finnan – an on-the-bone version from the village of Findon, which you will find about five miles down the coast from Aberdeen. As it's cold-smoked, it's quite different in flavour and texture to the Arbroath smokies (see page 14).

SMOKED SALMON

When buying smoked salmon, pay particular attention to the wording on the label. Scottish smoked salmon can mean salmon from Chile, Norway or wherever, but smoked Scottish salmon will always be Scottish fish. Quality varies from the pale pink pappy fish, which is mass-produced and really only fit for sandwiches, to full-flavoured smoked salmon from individual small producers, which each have their own unique characteristics. The best smoked salmon is dry-salted before undergoing a slow curing process. It is then smoked slowly at a very low temperature. Smoked salmon is not to be confused with hot-smoked salmon (see page 14).

Above:
Scallops with Oriental Salad and Sweet Chilli Dressing (see page 89)

Meat, Game and Poultry

BEEF

Without a doubt pure-bred, native, grass-fed beef is the best there is. In Scotland these hardy wee beasts spend most of the time outdoors, feeding on grass, which makes some of them not far from being organic. Aberdeen Angus, Highland, Shorthorn or Galloway are my preferred breeds. Properly treated and hung for at least 21 days, this is the tastiest beef you can buy. Find a good butcher – I've been a customer of Jonathan Honeyman at The Aberfoyle Butcher (see page 256) for over 15 years now and I know I'm sure to get nothing but the very best quality meat there.

GAME

The standard of our seasonal game is prized the world over. Venison, hare, rabbit, grouse, pigeon and mallard all live in their natural habitat, making them as close to organic as you can get. It's possible to get game of some sort all year round. Roe deer bucks are in season from the beginning of May until late October and does from late October until the end of February. Red stags are in season from the beginning of July until late October and red and sika hinds from late October until mid-February. Sika stags have the longest season, from the end of July until the end of April. Lastly, fallow deer bucks are available from the beginning of August until the end of April, and hinds from late October until mid-February. It is always possible to get rabbit and wood pigeon, but many have restricted seasonal availability – the farmed grouse season starts on the 'glorious' 12 August, ending in mid-December, partridge runs from the beginning of October until the end of January, and hares from the beginning of July until the end of March. If you are keen on finding out more about game, try to lay your hands on Ian McAndrew's great game guide book – *Ian McAndrew on Poultry and Game* (Pyramid, 1990). Shooting your own game can be rewarding, but these days my pacifist wife prefers me to use a good game supplier. Try Burnside Farm Foods (see page 256) for a good selection of game and Fletchers (see page 256) are a must when it comes to sourcing deer. For a great range of smoked game, try the Rannoch Smokery (see page 256), who do the best smoked venison, amongst other things.

LAMB

I always opt for Scottish hill lamb, which is often very close to being organic and has a wonderful flavour and texture. The Argyllshire Scottish black-face breed are a firm favourite.

PORK

There is more free-range pork becoming available, which is really full of flavour. For bacon, try Puddledub Pork and Fifeshire Bacon's drycure by Tom Mitchell (see page 256) – it's the best quality around.

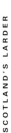

POULTRY

It's always worth paying that little bit extra for free-range or organic birds as they have a far superior flavour to intensively reared broilers. Look out for corn- or maize-fed varieties. Farmers' markets are a great place for poultry or try Burnside Farm Foods (see page 256) – they offer good quail, guinea fowl and organic chickens. Linda Dick is synonymous with quality poultry in Scotland and you'll find her birds in a few select east coast stores, including Crombies (see page 256).

Dairy

CHEESE

Iain J. Mellis Cheesemongers (see page 257) are dedicated to quality cheeses and stock a wide array of the world's greats, including my personal favourite – the Tobermory truckle from the Isle of Mull Cheese company (see page 257).

CREAM

The milk from grass-fed cattle has a far superior flavour to that of ordinary milk and there are many, many independent producers in Scotland using such milk to produce superb-quality dairy products. I recently visited the Isle of Skye and tasted fantastic crème fraîche from Auchmore Dairy (see page 257), which is absolutely worth making an effort to find, especially as they also sell a good selection of cheeses, yoghurts and ice-creams. If you find yourself in the Borders, visit one of the many creameries there for top-quality dairy products. Visit Loch Arthur Creamery (see page 258) for delicious organic hand-churned butter and award-winning cheeses; Cream O'Galloway is also worthy of a day out for its delicious ice-cream.

EGGS

If you can, buy your eggs direct from farms who allow their hens to run wild; the difference in flavour is noticeable, even compared with free-range supermarket varieties. Farmers' markets are also a good bet for fine fresh eggs, including ducks' eggs, with their lovely deep orange yolks.

Soft Fruits

BLAEBERRIES

These are tiny berries, often found growing wild in Scotland, particularly in moorland areas. They are very similar in taste to blueberries, so feel free to substitute with these if you can't get your hands on the real thing, but blaeberries have a more intense flavour, perfect for making jam. They're quite a delicate berry and burst easily, so picking your own usually means you'll end up with interestingly stained hands.

If you're serious about your berry picking, you could invest in a blaeberry rake, which makes for a much cleaner job!

BRAMBLES

Generally this refers to berry-wielding shrubs, but the Scots tend to be referring to blackberries when using this term.

RASPBERRIES

England is famous for its strawberries, but few people realize that in Scotland, raspberries are the national fruit. Scottish raspberries are widely recognized as being among the most flavoursome in the world. They were first grown commercially here following the First World War, when returning soldiers were given small plots of land to cultivate and chose to grow raspberries as their favoured crop. The cool climate in Scotland is perfect for rearing the fruit. Central Scotland is ripe for berry-picking and in the summer, head for the Blairgowrie area, which produces the best raspberries I know. There are plenty of pick-your-own farms in the area, and in July and August there are plenty of students doing just that.

STRAWBERRIES

June to September sees the season for open-grown strawberries and this is the only time to eat them for their full flavour. Buy locally produced varieties and keep Scotland's berry industry afloat. The flavour of Scottish strawberries in season is sublime, and knocks Spanish imports out of the water (these are harder and more sour, having been cultivated to travel). Recently I came across a variety called Everest, grown in Tayside. They were very red, really big and juicy and had bags of taste. Keep your eyes peeled.

Whisky and Liqueurs

I love whisky and different occasions require different favourites. There are four main malt-producing regions – Islay, the Lowlands, the Highlands and, of course, Speyside. Speyside produces many of my favourites – among them 12-year-old Cragganmore and Macallan, with its sherry barrel flavour. If I'm in a reflective mood, I'd opt for a big, peaty Islay malt, perhaps Bowmore, Caol Ila, Laphroaig, or Talisker from Skye. My local distillery, Glengoyne, provides my favourite everyday malt, which is easy and balanced. For cooking, I'd recommend using a blended whisky for a really rich, smoky flavour. Malts can be used, but go easy as they can easily overpower the other ingredients. I enjoy many blends, but for everyday drinking I would choose Chivas Regal, which has a lighter flavour than many others, but still has enough complexity without being overpowering. Drambuie is a great Scottish liqueur that must not be forgotten – pour over sliced, segmented oranges for the simplest of desserts.

Right:
Cranachan
(see page 186)

We Scots have a big thing about soups. Traditionally these are broths, based around a good meat stock, often featuring barley and root vegetables, the best known being Scotch broth – I've given my version of this on page 37. However there is no end to the Scots' inventiveness when it comes to soup-making so anything goes. Everything from a sheep's head to a bunch of nettles can be used to good effect.

I've included a couple of my favourite traditional Scottish soups – Cullen Skink (see page 31), made from smoked haddock and potatoes, and Partan Bree (see page 30), featuring brown crab – but I've also included lighter, more modern soups, whose flavour relies more on cooking technique than on stock. Soups such as Carrot, Ginger and Honey Soup (see page 22) and Parsnip, Parmesan and Chilli Soup (see page 26) fall into this category.

Whilst I was brought up on warming broths – even my mum's tomato soup was based around a ham stock and lentils – it is stockless soups, which extract the maximum amount of flavour from often humble vegetables, that I find myself making most often. I'm conscious not only of their flavour and affordability, but also see them as a good way of ensuring that I eat as many as possible of my five portions of fruit and veggies a day.

As viewers of *Ready Steady Cook* may have noticed, I have been noted as being able to produce a soup from virtually any combination of ingredients, but be reassured that all the recipes here are tried and tested winners.

soups

carrot, ginger and honey soup

Fabulous colour. Easy to make. Tastes great. Cheap. What more do you want?
Using Scottish heather honey really makes a difference to this unusual soup, as it has
a fragrance quite unlike ordinary honey, and is less processed into the bargain.

Serves 6

25 g (1 oz) butter
200 g (8 oz) onions, thinly sliced
2.5 cm (1 in) root ginger, peeled
750 g (1 lb 10 oz) carrots, grated
2 tablespoons clear heather honey
1 tablespoon lemon juice
1 teaspoon freshly ground sea salt
Freshly ground pepper
4 tablespoons lightly whipped
double cream
1 tablespoon chopped chives

Melt the butter in a large saucepan on a medium-to-low heat. Add the onions and stir well to coat.

Using the flat edge of a heavy knife, crush the ginger (this releases the oils) and roughly chop. Add to the onions, cover the pan and let everything sweat for 10 minutes, without letting the onions brown.

Now add the grated carrots, the honey and the lemon juice and season with the salt and a few turns of pepper. Stir well. Pour in 1 litre (1¾ pints) of boiling water, bring to the boil, reduce the heat and leave to simmer for 45 minutes. You may have to add a little more water during this time to allow for evaporation.

Remove the pan from the heat and liquidize the contents (with a hand-held blender or in a liquidizer) until smooth and creamy.

Check the seasoning, reheat if necessary and serve, garnishing with the cream and chives.

If you are making the soup ahead and want to freeze it, allow the soup to cool completely before pouring it into a tub with a well-fitting lid and freezing for up to 3 months. The soup will keep well for up to 3 days in the fridge.

wild mushroom soup

To achieve an intense wild mushroom flavour and a thick, rich texture, make the soup using mushrooms that are a few days old and have started to darken a bit. I usually buy up any older (and cheaper) baskets when they're available. The best variety of mushrooms I have used is Paris Browns, which are fairly readily available, but ordinary chestnut mushrooms are also ideal. Dried Highland ceps are quite different from French and Italian ones; they are less dry, with a spongier texture. The depth of flavour from the mushrooms is so intense that no stock is needed, making this an excellent vegetarian soup.

Serves 6

50 g (2 oz) butter

200 g (8 oz) onions, thinly sliced

1 garlic clove, crushed

600 g (1 lb 5 oz) Paris Browns (or chestnut mushrooms), roughly sliced

3 teaspoons dried ceps, preferably Highland ceps

30 ml (1 fl oz) light soy sauce

$\frac{1}{2}$ teaspoon salt

Freshly ground pepper

Single cream, to serve

Chopped fresh chives, flatleaf parsley, basil or tarragon, to garnish

Sliced, sautéed mushrooms, to serve (optional)

Melt the butter in a large saucepan and gently soften the onions and garlic for 10 minutes, until soft. Add the mushrooms and the dried ceps and stir to coat. Now add the soy sauce, the salt and a generous amount of pepper and, finally, 1 litre (1¾ pints) of boiling water.

Bring back to the boil, reduce the heat and then simmer for 40 minutes, until the mushrooms are tender. Liquidize the soup and check the seasoning.

If serving immediately, garnish with a squiggle of cream and some greenery (chives, flatleaf parsley, basil or tarragon), or drop on a few sliced, sautéed mushrooms. If making ahead, cool completely and store covered in the fridge for up to 2 days, or freeze for up to 3 months.

cauliflower and mull cheddar soup

I've taken the classic combination of cauliflower and cheese and made it into a smooth, light soup, made a bit more special by the bite and acidity of one of the world's great cheeses, the fabulous Tobermory truckle from the Island of Mull.

Serves 6

50 g (2 oz) butter
1 onion, finely chopped
1 garlic clove, crushed
1 large cauliflower
140–175 g (5–6 oz) Mull Cheddar, grated, plus extra to garnish
Freshly ground sea salt and freshly ground pepper
1 tablespoon chopped fresh parsley, to garnish

Heat the butter in a large pan. Add the onion and garlic and leave to cook on a medium heat for 8 minutes, until they become soft and clear.

Whilst the onion and garlic are softening, chop the cauliflower as finely as possible. Add the chopped cauliflower to the onions and pour in 1 litre (1¾ pints) of boiling water. Bring back to the boil, reduce the heat and simmer for 20 minutes.

When the cauliflower is tender, add the Mull Cheddar. Whizz the soup well in a liquidizer to give it a really smooth texture; a food processor is not fast enough to give the velvety smooth texture this soup requires.

Check and adjust the seasoning and reheat if necessary. Ladle into warm soup bowls and garnish with some more grated cheese, a sprinkle of parsley and perhaps a little Herb Oil (see page 242).

If you plan to freeze the soup, liquidize it without the cheese and add this later, when you reheat the soup. The soup will keep for up to 3 days in the fridge and 3 months in the freezer.

parsnip, parmesan and chilli soup

A modern twist to a traditional idea: soups made from root vegetables have been a Scottish staple for centuries. The chilli combines well with the flavour of the parsnips to make an intriguingly warming soup, best enjoyed in autumn or winter — which just happens to be when parsnips are at their best. The Parmesan ensures a gloriously rich finish to this excellent soup.

Serves 6

50 g (2 oz) butter
200 g (8 oz) onions, thinly sliced
900 g (2 lb) parsnips, peeled and finely sliced across the diameters
1 red chilli, finely chopped
1 teaspoon freshly ground sea salt
50 g (2 oz) Parmesan cheese, grated
Snipped fresh chives, to garnish

Melt the butter in a large saucepan and sweat the onions for 6–8 minutes, until they are soft.

Add the parsnips, chilli and salt and stir to coat everything in butter. Add 1 litre (1¾ pints) of boiling water, bring back to the boil, then reduce the heat. Simmer for 40 minutes.

Stir the Parmesan into the soup and then liquidize. Check and adjust the seasoning and reheat if necessary. Garnish with the fresh chives.

You can refrigerate this soup for up to 3 days, or put it in the freezer minus the Parmesan, where it will keep for up to 3 months.

artichoke and smoked bacon soup

Definitely my favourite use for Jerusalem artichokes. These are rather unassuming, knobbly roots (not to be mistaken for globe artichokes) and a bit of a pain to peel, but they have a knockout smoky flavour that works a treat with smoked bacon.
There are now lots of small independent bacon producers in Scotland, many of whom supply by mail order. I only buy dry-cured bacon, which is far superior to brined.

Serves 8

900 g (2 lb) Jerusalem artichokes
A squeeze of lemon juice
100 g (4 oz) smoked bacon
2 tablespoons sunflower oil
50 g (2 oz) butter
250 g (9 oz) onions, thinly sliced
1 teaspoon freshly ground sea salt
Freshly ground pepper
A pinch of snipped fresh chives or chopped fresh parsley, to garnish

Peel the artichokes with a potato peeler and then place immediately in a bowl of cold water with a squeeze of lemon juice added in (to prevent them from turning brown).

Chop the bacon into matchsticks. Then heat a large pan and pour in the sunflower oil. Rapidly add the bacon and fry until nicely crisp, stirring with a wooden spoon. Remove 1 tablespoon of the bacon bits and leave aside to use as a garnish.

Add the butter and, as soon as it starts to foam, the onions, and stir until everything is well coated. Reduce the heat and sweat for 8 minutes.

Meanwhile, thinly slice the artichokes (a mandolin slicer is perfect for this or use the coarse face on a box grater). Once they are all sliced, add them straight away to the onions and bacon, followed by 1.2 litres (2 pints) of boiling water. Season with the salt and a generous amount of pepper.

Bring back to the boil before reducing the heat to a simmer. Cook for 35 minutes, until the artichokes are tender.

Liquidize the soup and check the seasoning. Serve immediately, garnished with a few snipped chives or chopped parsley and the reserved bacon.

Alternatively, allow the soup to cool before freezing (it keeps for 3 months frozen or 3 days in the fridge).

shellfish and saffron broth with herb potato dumplings

For the very finest flavour, shellfish from the west coast of Scotland really cannot be beaten. This is an incredibly delicious but expensive soup: if you win the Lottery it's the first thing you should make! Simon Hopkinson is responsible for creating the absurdly delicious green paste used here – I usually have it to hand in the fridge and have also discovered that it freezes well.

Serves 4

1 litre (1³/₄ pints) Fish Stock (see page 237)

300 ml (½ pint) Quick Tomato Sauce (see page 249)

Shells, crushed, and whites of 4 eggs

A pinch of saffron strands

Freshly ground sea salt and freshly ground pepper

200 g (8 oz) potatoes, cooked and mashed

50 g (2 oz) plain white flour

1 small lobster, cooked, meat removed and cut into chunks

12 langoustines, cooked and shelled

450 g (1 lb) fresh mussels, cooked and shelled

8 large scallops, with corals removed

FOR THE GREEN PASTE (this makes a lot!)

8 garlic cloves

6 green chillies, seeded

100 ml (3½ fl oz) creamed coconut

85 g (3 oz) coriander leaves, stalks and roots

25 g (1 oz) mint leaves

2 teaspoons ground cumin

1 teaspoon sugar

1 teaspoon salt

75 ml (2½ fl oz) lime or lemon juice

First make the broth – this involves clarifying it, but it's easier to do than you think! Put the fish stock and tomato sauce into a large saucepan with the crushed egg shells and egg whites. Now bring slowly to the boil, whisking vigorously with a balloon whisk, until a crust forms.

Stop whisking just before it boils and allow the crust to rise to the top of the pan. Turn off the heat and let it settle for a couple of minutes, then raise the heat and let the crust rise again. Do this three times.

Line a sieve with a bit of muslin or a J-cloth, place over a clean saucepan and pour the broth through it, keeping the crust back. The broth will be crystal clear! Add the saffron strands to the stock and simmer for 10 minutes, then taste it and season with salt and pepper.

Meanwhile, make the green paste. Roughly chop the garlic, chillies and coconut and whizz in the blender with all the other ingredients. Spoon into a storage jar to keep in the fridge (cover with a layer of olive oil).

Next, make the dumplings. Beat the potato with the flour and 2–3 tablespoons of the green paste until well mixed. Break off into tiny lumps and roll into balls. Place on a greased tray.

Drop the dumplings into the broth and poach them for a minute or two, until they float to the surface. Then scoop them out and keep warm.

Next, add the seafood to the broth for 1 minute to heat through and then return the dumplings to the pan. Carefully ladle the soup into warm bowls, making sure that each person gets a fair share of the seafood and the dumplings!

partan bree

'Partan' is a traditional Scottish name for crab and 'bree' means gravy. So this is 'crab gravy', a name that doesn't do this gorgeous soup justice. Using rice to thicken the soup was a big thing in Victorian times and it still works for me.

When buying crabs, look for a big heavy monster, which will mean less work and more meat. Failing that, you could use frozen or pasteurized crabmeat but you won't get the same intensity of flavour as when using fresh.

Serves 6

One 1.8 kg (4 lb) cooked brown crab or 450 g (1 lb) white crabmeat

600 ml (1 pint) Chicken Stock (see page 236) or Fish Stock (see page 237)

50 g (2 oz) long-grain rice

600 ml (1 pint) full-cream milk

1 teaspoon anchovy essence or Thai fish sauce

8 drops of Tabasco sauce

Freshly ground sea salt and freshly ground pepper

450 ml (16 fl oz) single cream

A pinch of ground mace

Cayenne pepper and snipped fresh chives, to garnish

Remove both the brown and white meat from the crab – you should have about 450 g (1 lb) – setting aside the larger pieces of white meat from the claws for garnishing the soup (don't worry about this if you're using frozen crabmeat). Put all the pieces of crab shell into a pan with the chicken or fish stock, bring to the boil and leave to simmer for 15 minutes.

Meanwhile, put the rice and the milk into another pan, bring to the boil and simmer for 15–20 minutes, until the rice is tender.

Strain the crab-flavoured stock through a muslin-lined sieve into another pan. Stir all the crabmeat, except the claw meat, into the rice and milk mixture and liquidize until smooth. Then stir this into the pan containing the stock, together with the anchovy essence or fish sauce, Tabasco and some seasoning to taste. Bring gently to the boil, stir in the cream and the mace and continue heating until not quite boiling.

Spoon the soup into warmed bowls and garnish with the reserved claw meat, a sprinkling of cayenne pepper and a few snipped chives.

cullen skink

Another traditional Scottish soup and one that's stood the test of time. It's vital to use top-quality, undyed smoked haddock to get a true flavour.

**Serves 6 as a starter
or 4 as a main course**

50 g (2 oz) butter

1 onion, chopped or sliced

1 bay leaf

1 blade of mace (optional)

600 ml (1 pint) milk

150 ml (¼ pint) double cream

350 g (12 oz) small, even-sized
new potatoes

450 g (1 lb) undyed finnan haddock fillets

Freshly ground sea salt and
freshly ground pepper

2 tablespoons finely chopped fresh chives

Melt the butter in a large saucepan. Add the onion and cook gently for about 7 minutes, until soft but not browned. Then add the bay leaf and mace, if using, and pour in the milk and 300 ml (½ pint) water. Drop in the potatoes, bring to the boil and simmer for 10–15 minutes, until the potatoes are almost cooked.

Cut the haddock into large pieces and add to the pan. Simmer for about 10 minutes or less, until the fish is cooked and the potatoes completely tender.

Lift the fish out of the pan, cool a bit, peel off the skin and then flake into large chunks. Remove the bay leaf and mace from the soup. Using a potato masher, lightly crush the potatoes into the soup and stir in the flaked fish and double cream. Bring back to the boil. Taste to see if you need any salt (the fish is quite salty) and add pepper. If the soup is too thick, thin it with some more hot milk.

Stir in the chives and serve piping hot in warmed soup bowls. This soup shouldn't be frozen because of the cream content, but keeps for up to 48 hours in the fridge.

spicy salmon broth

I normally make this soup using a blend of fish stock and mussel juices; however, I well know that folks at home don't have ready access to that kind of kit, so I experimented using a fish stock cube – not great. I then tried my personal favourite – a chicken stock cube – and found that it made a really good soup; perhaps not acceptable to 'pescatarians' (I know, it was a new one on me too, it means fish-eating vegetarians!) but plenty good enough for me. The base can be made up in advance and freezes well; add the salmon just prior to serving. Be careful not to overcook the salmon, it needs only a couple of minutes. You can check by breaking one of the pieces open – it should still be nice and pink inside.

Serves 4

1 tablespoon vegetable oil

2.5 cm (1 in) piece of root ginger, peeled and cut into matchsticks

2 large garlic cloves, sliced into slivers

1 large fresh red chilli, seeded and cut into matchsticks

1 whole bird's eye chilli

1 lemon grass stalk, chopped very finely

1.2 litres (2 pints) Fish Stock (see page 237) or Chicken Stock (see page 236)

3 tablespoons Thai fish sauce

1 tablespoon light soy sauce

Juice of 1 lime

4 spring onions, finely shredded

175–200 g (6–8 oz) salmon fillet, cut into 5 mm (1/4 in) slices

3 tablespoons roughly chopped fresh coriander

Freshly ground pepper

Heat the oil in a large pan and add the ginger, garlic, chillies and lemon grass. Cook over a low heat until softened (approximately 8 minutes).

Next, add the stock and splash in the fish sauce, soy sauce and lime juice. Bring to the boil and then turn down the heat and simmer for 10 minutes.

Add the spring onions and cook for 3 minutes. Slip in the fish, with the coriander, and simmer for 2 minutes, or until the fish is cooked. Taste and season with pepper only – the fish and soy sauce will add sufficient salt – it should be quite punchy! Ladle into warm bowls and serve.

pea, apple and curry soup

Scottish orchards produce a good crop of apples, though many people don't realize this, and in our garden, late-season peas are available at the same time as the early apples: perfect for this soup. This is a most surprising combination of flavours that is unlikely-sounding but very tasty. The sweetness of the peas is offset by the mild acidity and fruitiness of the apples. Curry paste deepens the flavours and adds a warm, spicy note.

Serves 6

50 g (2 oz) butter

175 g (6 oz) onions, thinly sliced

1 garlic clove, crushed

2 cm (³/₄ in) piece of root ginger, peeled and crushed

1 tablespoon mild curry paste

Freshly ground sea salt and freshly ground pepper

3 Granny Smith apples, cored and grated but not peeled

280 g (10 oz) fresh peas or good-quality frozen petits pois

Crème fraîche, to serve

Melt the butter in a large saucepan and add the onions, garlic, ginger, curry paste and a little seasoning. Cook gently for 8–10 minutes, until softened.

Add the apples and cook for a further 4 minutes. Stir in the peas and 1.2 litres (2 pints) of boiling water, bring back to the boil, cover and simmer for 5 minutes.

Now purée in a liquidizer and then pass through a conical strainer or a fine sieve. You can refrigerate at this point, or freeze (it keeps well for up to 2 months).

To serve, heat through gently and check and adjust the seasoning if necessary. Serve immediately, with a good-sized blob of crème fraîche on each bowl.

plum tomato, basil and olive oil soup

Although this soup originates from the Mediterranean, it is perfectly suited to the especially good Scottish greenhouse-grown tomatoes that are available from late August until mid-October. At home we're lucky enough to have a greenhouse to grow our own tomatoes and we often have a glut, which is when I make big batches of this soup for freezing to enjoy throughout the winter.

Serves 6

50 ml (2 fl oz) olive oil, plus extra to serve

140 g (5 oz) red onions, finely sliced

1 garlic clove

950 g (2 lb 2 oz) plum tomatoes, roughly chopped

1 heaped teaspoon sugar

2 tablespoons *fino* (dry) sherry

Freshly ground sea salt and freshly ground pepper

3 teaspoons chopped fresh basil

Basil sprigs, to garnish

Take a large saucepan with a tightly fitting lid, add the olive oil, red onions and garlic and cook over a low heat until softened but uncoloured, which should take approximately 10 minutes.

Add the plum tomatoes, sugar, sherry and a little salt and pepper. Cover and cook over a low heat for 45 minutes.

At this stage you may have to add a little more water to achieve the correct consistency for liquidizing.

Add the chopped basil to the soup and then liquidize in batches. Check and adjust the seasoning and either reheat as necessary and serve immediately, garnished with a sprig of basil and a drizzle of olive oil, or cool and store in the fridge for up to 48 hours. If frozen it will keep for up to 3 months.

asparagus soup

Make this in season (May–August), when asparagus is good, plentiful and cheap. Scottish asparagus has a later, shorter season than English, but the flavour compares with the best from south of the border.

Serves 4

700 g (1 lb 9 oz) asparagus
50 g (2 oz) butter
1 large onion, finely chopped
200 g (8 oz) potatoes, peeled and finely sliced
1.2 litres (2 pints) Chicken Stock (see page 236) or Marinated Vegetable Stock (see page 239)
½ teaspoon salt
Freshly ground pepper

Trim off any woody ends from the asparagus and, using a potato peeler, remove any tough skin layers. Cut off the top 4 cm (1½ in), including the tips, and blanch for 4 minutes in boiling, salted water (allow four tips per person). Remove from the water with a slotted spoon and refresh immediately in cold water. Drain and put to one side, for the garnish. Roughly chop the remaining stalks.

Melt the butter in a large pan. Add the onion and potatoes and sweat for a few minutes. Add the stock and the salt, bring to the boil and cook for 15 minutes, or until the potato has broken down. Add the asparagus stalks and cook for 8 minutes, until tender. Add lots of pepper, then liquidize the soup.

To serve, reheat the garnish tips in boiling water, then drain. Reheat the soup, then divide between four bowls, garnish with the asparagus tips and serve.

The soup will keep for up to 24 hours in the fridge and 2 weeks in the freezer.

my scotch broth

I've been reasonably faithful to this, a soup most Scots were brought up on, though I've replaced the traditional lamb with beef and left out the split peas. It's as if the nineties had never happened.

Serves 4

450 g (1 lb) shin of beef
Freshly ground sea salt and freshly ground pepper
50 g (2 oz) pearl barley
1 potato, cut into 5 mm (¼ in) dice
1 carrot, cut into 5 mm (¼ in) dice
1 celery stick, cut into 5 mm (¼ in) dice
1 onion, cut into 5 mm (¼ in) dice
1 leek, cut into 5 mm (¼ in) dice
2 tablespoons chopped fresh parsley

Put the shin of beef and 1.2 litres (2 pints) of cold water into a large pan. Add some seasoning, bring to the boil and then cover and simmer very slowly for about 2 hours, until the meat is very tender.

Lift the meat on to a plate and set aside to cool slightly.

Put the pearl barley in the pan, bring back to the boil and simmer for 10 minutes. Add the potato and simmer for 10 minutes. Then add the carrot, celery, onion and leek and simmer for a further 15 minutes. If, at this stage, the soup looks a bit too thick, add a little more water and bring back to a simmer.

Cut the cooked shin of beef into 5 mm (¼ in) dice and add to the soup, with the chopped parsley. Check the seasoning and serve – it tastes even better if it's left to cool and reheated the next day. It also freezes well for up to 2 months.

I believe that a complete dish is only as good as the raw materials used in its making, and nowhere is this more true than with fish and shellfish. It's vitally important that the fish is as fresh as possible and to that end it's essential to make friends with your fishmonger. Always try to see the whole fish before it's filleted as you will be able to check for the signs of freshness – bright shiny eyes, firm skin and the odour of the sea. When deciding what dish to cook, always start by sourcing the fish and finding the recipe to suit; you'll find plenty of inspiration in this chapter.

Scotland has a thriving salmon farming industry, mainly situated on the west coast and the Northern Isles. These salmon range in quality, so choose carefully – look out for a shiny firm texture with no oiliness or flabby, gaping flesh. The best farmed salmon in Scotland is sublime and a personal favourite because of its versatility.

Sadly many Scots only ever eat anonymous fish fillets that have been dipped in batter and deep-fried, although there is an increasing awareness of the huge range of Scottish fish and shellfish and an acknowledgement that the deep-fat fryer is not essential in the success of Scottish cooking. Restaurants such as the Loch Fyne oyster bar, near Inverary, and Crannog in Fort William have shown that spanking-fresh seafood simply cooked is a sure-fire hit with Scots and visitors alike. Scots are now more willing to experiment with fish and shellfish, but despite the growing numbers of restaurants offering the best, many are still finding it difficult to source good-quality fish and shellfish to cook at home. One of the main problems is the huge amount of quality Scottish fish that ends up in large trucks bound for continental Europe, the other is the reluctance or inability of supermarkets to set up direct-supply chains with local Scottish fish merchants.

It is not all doom and gloom, however, and there are without doubt signs that consumer-led demand for quality fish has increased the standard and variety of fish for sale across Scotland. You can play a part in ensuring this continues by settling for nothing less than fresh, quality Scottish fish in your shopping basket.

fishy

hot-smoked salmon with mango and avocado salsa

This is one of my most tried and tested starters – it's perfect as a dinner party opener for a big number of guests, as all the prep is done in advance. The biggest number I've prepared for at one time was 600, for the dinner to celebrate the opening of the Scottish Parliament. I like to mould this into a neat tower using a scone cutter. This aids pre-preparation, but it doesn't make it taste any better so, when I serve this at home, I simply break off a piece of hot-smoked salmon and sit it next to a dollop of salsa – end of story.

Serves 4 as a starter

250 g (9 oz) hot-smoked salmon

FOR THE SALSA
1 ripe avocado
1 red chilli, seeded and finely chopped
1 tablespoon chopped fresh coriander
¼ red onion, finely chopped
1 ripe mango, peeled and chopped into 1 cm (½ in) dice
1 tablespoon Thai fish sauce
Freshly ground sea salt and freshly ground pepper
Juice and grated zest of 1 lime

TO SERVE
100 g (4 oz) baby salad leaves, iceberg lettuce or purslane
1 teaspoon olive oil
Lemon juice
Herb Oil (see page 242, optional)
Balsamic Syrup (see page 242, optional)

To make the salsa, halve the avocado and remove the stone. Halve again and remove the skin before chopping it into 1 cm (½ in) chunks. Place in a mixing bowl and add the chilli, coriander, red onion, mango, fish sauce, a pinch of salt and the lime juice and zest. Mix well and leave at room temperature for about 30 minutes, to allow the flavours to develop.

Lightly dress the salad leaves in the teaspoon of olive oil, a small squeeze of lemon juice and a pinch of seasoning.

To serve in the formal way, set a 7.5 cm (3 in) scone cutter or food ring in the centre of each plate. Flake the salmon into large pieces and, using about 85 g (3 oz) per ring, press into the base of each ring, banking it up the sides of the ring so that it will hold. Spoon the salsa on top of the salmon and press down lightly. The towers are ideal for preparing in advance: simply prepare to this stage and place on a tray in the fridge until needed. When ready to serve, remove the ring carefully and garnish with a small handful of the lightly dressed salad leaves. Drizzle round the herb oil and the balsamic syrup, if using.

To serve informally, flake the salmon and divide between the serving plates. Place some salsa alongside the fish and drizzle round the herb oil and balsamic syrup, if using. Serve with the salad in a bowl on the side.

poached salmon with sorrel butter sauce

When you start with a really good piece of salmon (my current favourite is organic Orkney salmon) it only needs the simplest of cooking methods. Here it is poached in a delicately flavoured liquid called a court-bouillon, which keeps it moist, tender and full of flavour with the benefit of no added fat. It's especially good for cooking fish to serve cold. The leftover poaching liquid will give you a soup base, perfect for making Spicy Salmon Broth (see page 33).

Serves 4

4 skinless salmon fillets, each weighing 140–175 g (5–6 oz)

FOR THE COURT-BOUILLON

½ lemon, sliced

1 small onion, sliced (optional)

1 carrot, sliced

1 celery stick, sliced

1 bay leaf

10 peppercorns

A handful of bruised parsley stalks (you can add other herb stalks, but too much can be overpowering)

FOR THE SORREL BUTTER SAUCE

2 shallots, very finely chopped

3 tablespoons dry white wine

2 tablespoons white wine vinegar

6 peppercorns, lightly crushed

1 tablespoon double cream

175 g (6 oz) chilled butter, diced

Freshly ground salt and freshly ground pepper

100 g (4 oz) fresh sorrel leaves, tough stalks removed, leaves roughly chopped

Put all the court-bouillon ingredients into a large saucepan with 1.2 litres (2 pints) of water and bring slowly to the boil. Turn off the heat and allow it to cool.

For the butter sauce, put the shallots, white wine, wine vinegar and peppercorns into a small pan and boil rapidly until reduced to about 2 tablespoons of liquid. Stir in the double cream. Reduce the heat to low. (This is important – if you let the sauce get too hot it will curdle; if it's getting a bit hot, just remove the pan from the heat and dip the base in cold water. But be careful, if it gets too cold the butter will solidify and the sauce will split – the temperature is correct when you can stick your finger in and it feels warm but not hot.) Now whisk in the butter furiously, adding it in three separate big dollops, whisking each dollop until it melts into the sauce. Season with a little salt and pepper, pass through a fine sieve into another pan and keep warm at the back of the stove or dip the pan in a bowl of warm water.

When ready to cook, strain the court-bouillon and pour into a wide sauté pan, just deep enough to cover the salmon fillets. Bring up to barely simmering and slip in the fillets. Poach for about 5 minutes until opaque and just set.

Meanwhile, stir the sorrel into the warm butter sauce and heat through again. Lift the salmon out of the court-bouillon with a fish slice; drain well if serving hot. Take four warmed plates, place a salmon fillet in the centre of each, pour round the sorrel butter sauce and serve. Don't let this sauce hang around – the sorrel loses its colour quickly once heated.

salmon fishcakes with wilted greens

This dish was a classic at my first restaurant, Braeval, proving that food doesn't have to be 'fancy' to be good. I believe fishcakes deserve the best ingredients possible and shouldn't be regarded as an opportunity to clear all the leftovers out of your fridge. I've found that coating the fishcakes with breadcrumbs is easier to do if the patties are frozen first and, of course, cooking them from frozen makes them an ideal standby dish.

Serves 4–8

50 g (2 oz) butter

450 g (1 lb) salmon fillet, skinned and boned

1 tablespoon lemon juice

Freshly ground sea salt and freshly ground pepper

1 long red chilli, seeded and finely chopped

450 g (1 lb) Perfect Mashed Potatoes (see page 165)

3 tablespoons flatleaf parsley, chopped

4 spring onions, finely chopped

100 g (4 oz) plain flour, sifted and seasoned

2 eggs

250 g (9 oz) fresh white breadcrumbs

Sunflower oil, for deep-frying

Wilted Greens (see page 175), to serve

Vegetable Butter Sauce (see page 240), to serve (optional)

Preheat the oven to 230°C/450°F/Gas 8. Use half the butter to grease a roasting tin big enough to hold the salmon fillets comfortably. Dot the remaining butter over the fish in pinch-sized lumps. Sprinkle the lemon juice over and add salt and pepper and the chopped chilli. Bake the fish for approximately 5 minutes, until just cooked, allowing the fish to be slightly undercooked in the centre. Once out of the oven, allow the fish to stand for 5 minutes, then flake. Reduce the oven temperature to 150°C/300°F/Gas 2.

Put the mashed potato (this can be hot or cold) into a large mixing bowl and add the fish, parsley and spring onions. Fold together with a wooden spoon until the fish is well mixed through. Taste and adjust your seasoning if required. With floured hands, shape the mixture into eight patties by taking handfuls and moulding on greaseproof paper. Arrange the fishcakes on a tray and freeze for a couple of hours, until they are solid enough to handle.

To finish the fishcakes, put the flour on a shallow plate, beat the eggs in a shallow bowl and spread the breadcrumbs out on a tray. Dust each fishcake with flour, then dip into the beaten egg and, finally, roll in the breadcrumbs, covering them thoroughly. At this stage you can freeze them or cook them straight away.

To cook straight away, heat a heavy-based pan or deep-fat fryer, one-third full of sunflower oil, to 180°C/350°F. Place the fishcakes in the pan and deep-fry them for 4–5 minutes, until nicely golden in colour. If cooking from frozen, place the deep-fried fishcakes on a baking sheet covered with a double thickness of kitchen paper. Place the tray in a low oven (150°C/300°F/Gas 2) for approximately 45 minutes – this allows them to defrost and to warm through completely.

Serve with the wilted greens, and some vegetable butter sauce for a real treat!

fresh fettuccine with smoked salmon and avruga

What did we do before Avruga? The delicious smoky flavour of the grey/black herring roe is a wonderful (and affordable) caviar substitute and perfect with smoked Scottish salmon, which is usually darker and smokier with a slightly chewier texture than the usual pale 'London smoke'. I use an American gadget called a microplane grater to remove the yellow rind effortlessly from the lemon, leaving behind the bitter pith – it has become my favourite kitchen gadget!

Serves 4 as a starter

1 quantity Pasta Dough (see page 250)

150 ml (¼ pint) double cream

Finely grated rind and juice of 1 small lemon

Freshly ground sea salt and freshly ground pepper

2 tablespoons Avruga caviar

250 g (9 oz) smoked salmon, finely shredded

Chopped fresh chervil or parsley, to garnish

Knead the pasta dough to form into a ball shape. Knead it briskly for 1 minute – it should be quite stiff and hard to knead. Wrap in clingfilm and leave to rest in a cool place for at least 30 minutes before using.

Now unwrap the pasta dough and cut in half. For each piece, flatten with a rolling pin to about 5 mm (¼ in) thickness. Fold over the dough and pass it through the pasta machine at its widest setting, refolding and rolling 10 times (not changing the setting) until you have a regular shape. It is important to work the dough until it is nice and shiny, as this gives it a good texture. Repeat with the second piece of dough.

Now roll and cut the pasta. With the pasta machine at its widest setting, pass each piece of dough through the rollers. Do not fold but repeat this process, decreasing the roller setting grade by grade with each pass, down to the penultimate setting, then pass the pasta through the fettuccine (spaghetti-like) cutters on the machine. Hang over a clean suspended broom handle to dry or toss in semolina flour and leave in loose piles on a tea towel until ready to cook.

To make the sauce, put the cream, lemon rind and a little salt and pepper in a saucepan and bring to the boil. Boil for 2–3 minutes, until thickened, and then stir in lemon juice to taste and set aside.

Bring a huge pan of salted water to the boil and throw in the pasta – it is cooked as soon as the water comes to the boil again. Drain well and toss with a tablespoon of the sauce.

Reheat the sauce and stir in the Avruga caviar. Wind the pasta around a carving fork into four bundles, drop on to four warm plates, top each with a mound of smoked salmon and spoon the sauce over and around. Finish off with a scattering of the chervil or parsley. Serve immediately.

seared salmon with avocado salsa

This simple, elegant starter is one of the few dishes that I can claim totally for my own. As with all simple dishes, it relies on the finest quality ingredients to make it really sing. Scotland has an extensive salmon-farming industry but the quality is variable: look for the Tartan Quality Mark or, my favourite, organic Orkney salmon. The salsa and butter sauce can be made in advance, which allows you time to concentrate on cooking the salmon to perfection. This means crisp on the outside, underdone and yielding on the inside.

Serves 4 as a starter

2 tablespoons sunflower oil

4 thin, skinless salmon escalopes, weighing about 85 g (3 oz) each

A few drops of lemon juice

Freshly ground sea salt and freshly ground pepper

4 tablespoons Vegetable Butter Sauce (see page 240), to serve

FOR THE SALSA

1 large ripe avocado

1 red chilli, seeded and finely chopped

1/4 red onion, finely chopped

3 tablespoons chopped fresh coriander

1 tablespoon Japanese pickled ginger, finely chopped (optional)

2 ripe plum tomatoes, peeled, seeded and chopped into 1 cm (1/2 in) dice

2 teaspoons Thai fish sauce

Juice and grated zest of 1 lime

To make the salsa, halve the avocado and remove the stone. Halve again and remove the skin before chopping it into 1 cm (1/2 in) chunks. Place in a mixing bowl and add the chilli, red onion, coriander, pickled ginger, if using, tomatoes, fish sauce, a pinch of salt, some pepper and the lime juice and zest. Mix well and leave at room temperature for about 30 minutes for the flavours to develop.

Heat the oil in a large, heavy-based, non-stick frying pan until the oil smokes. Carefully place the salmon escalopes in the pan and turn the heat up to full. Cook for 1½ minutes on one side only, until the edges start to turn opaque. If the pan isn't big enough to allow all the escalopes to fit comfortably, cook them in two batches and then remove to a warm metal tray, seared-side up.

To serve, season the escalopes with lemon juice, a little salt and freshly ground pepper. Then divide the salsa between four serving plates and place an escalope on top. They are delicious served just like this; however, a tablespoon or two of warmed vegetable butter sauce drizzled around the salsa turns this into something quite special.

roast fillet of monkfish with rösti potatoes, spinach and red wine sauce

This dish is loosely based on steak and chips. The meaty texture of monkfish lends itself well to this treatment. Monkfish has a huge head and a big muscular tail (this is the bit you want). The head could be used to make stock but, personally, I don't rate it much. Get your fishmonger to fillet and skin the tail for you and also to remove the centre bone, leaving you with two roughly triangular long strips of fillet. The sauce needs a light and fruity wine and I usually use a Beaujolais.

Serves 4

2 monkfish tails weighing about 450 g (1 lb) each, skinned and boned to give four 100–140 g (4–5 oz) fillets

Freshly ground sea salt and freshly ground pepper

3 tablespoons sunflower oil

4 portions Rösti Potatoes (see page 166)

1 tablespoon olive oil

200 g (8 oz) spinach leaves, washed, with the tough stalks and damaged pieces removed

A squeeze of lemon juice

FOR THE SAUCE

300 ml (½ pint) Beaujolais or other light red wine

450 ml (16 fl oz) Fish Stock (see page 237)

25 g (1 oz) butter, chilled and diced

Preheat the oven to 150°C/300°F/Gas 2.

To make the sauce, pour the wine into a medium-sized, stainless steel saucepan and place it over a high heat, reducing it until it's nearly gone. Add the fish stock and reduce it by two-thirds. Add the diced cold butter and shake the pan over the heat until all the butter has melted and the sauce is dark and glossy. Keep it warm.

Next, heat a frying pan until it's hot. Season the monkfish fillets all over with a little salt and freshly ground pepper. Add the sunflower oil to the hot pan and lightly fry the fish fillets for about 2 minutes on each of their three sides, depending on their thickness, until lightly browned. Lift the pan to a warm place and leave the fish to relax for 5 minutes.

Place the rösti potatoes on a tray and put in the oven to heat them through for 4–5 minutes.

Heat a large pan until it's hot, add the tablespoon of olive oil, then dump in the spinach and stir-fry it until it's wilted (this will take about 2 minutes). Season with pepper and the lemon juice.

To serve, have four warm plates ready and divide the spinach between them. Place a portion of rösti potatoes on top of each pile. Remove the monkfish fillets from the pan, pouring any juices into the sauce. Carve each fillet into three pieces and place atop the potatoes. Spoon the sauce around and serve.

seared monkfish with mussels, fettuccine, curry and coriander

Monkfish is landed all around Scotland, on both the east and west coasts. Here the meaty texture of the monkfish is a perfect foil for the squidgy mussels and the coriander has a natural affinity for both the pasta and the fish. Add the curry paste cautiously, however, since it should be very much a background flavour.

Serves 4

750 g (1 lb 10 oz) live mussels, soaked for 30 minutes

125 ml (4 fl oz) white wine

200 g (8 oz) fettuccine

Freshly ground sea salt and freshly ground pepper

Lemon juice

2 tablespoons sunflower oil

1 monkfish tail, skinned and boned to give 450 g (1 lb) piece of fillet

12 tablespoons chopped fresh coriander

FOR THE SAUCE

25 g (1 oz) butter

2 shallots, finely diced

1/2 teaspoon medium curry paste

4 button mushrooms, finely sliced

175 ml (6 fl oz) double cream

Scrub the mussels well, scrape off any barnacles and pull out the beards that protrude from between the two halves of the shell. Discard any that won't close when lightly tapped on the work surface.

Choose a pan, with a tight-fitting lid, large enough for the mussels to half fill it. Heat the pan until hot, add the mussels, then the wine. With the lid on, shake the pan. Cook until all the mussels have opened (it should take about 3 minutes). Once they're ready, set a sieve or colander over a bowl and pour in the mussels. Strain the juice caught in the bowl and reserve 300 ml (1/2 pint) of the liquid. Shell the mussels and put to one side, discarding any that have not opened.

For the sauce, melt the butter in a saucepan. Add the shallots and the curry paste and cook for 2 minutes over a medium heat. Add the mushrooms and cook for a further 2 minutes. Now add the reserved mussel juice and reduce over a high heat until the liquid becomes thick and foamy (this takes 10–15 minutes).

Meanwhile, cook the fettuccine according to the packet instructions, drain and set aside.

Add the cream to the sauce and bring back to the boil. Season with pepper and a touch of lemon juice (you shouldn't need any salt, since the mussel juices are quite salty). Keep the sauce warm.

To cook the monkfish, heat a frying pan until it is very hot. Add the sunflower oil and fry the monkfish fillet until it is nicely browned on all sides (this will take about 8 minutes). Season with salt, pepper and a squeeze of lemon juice. Remove the pan from the heat and leave to rest in a warm place.

Next, put the pre-cooked fettuccine in a pan, add the mussels and coriander and then pour on the sauce. Heat it through gently and check the seasoning.

To serve, divide the pasta and mussel mixture between four warm serving plates. Carve the monkfish into 12 slices, laying three slices of monkfish on each plate and devour immediately.

steamed monkfish and summer vegetable stew

I devised this for *The Beechgrove Garden*, a Scottish gardening programme, to make the most of all the wonderful baby vegetables that were growing in the garden at the time. This recipe is proof that healthy doesn't have to be boring! Best prepared for just two people, it's cooked in minutes and looks so fresh and appetizing. You can substitute any other kind of fish for the monkfish and you can vary the vegetables according to season. The secret of success is to ensure that the fish is cut into even-sized pieces so that it cooks uniformly. You may have to adjust the cooking times for denser- or lighter-fleshed fish.

Serves 2

200 g (8 oz) prepared monkfish fillet (get the fishmonger to do this for you or buy it ready prepared)

25 g (1 oz) butter

2 new carrots, scraped and diced small

2 small white turnips, peeled and diced small

85 g (3 oz) fresh shelled or frozen peas

85 g (3 oz) asparagus, peeled and cut into 2.5 cm (1 in) pieces

6 ripe cherry tomatoes (kept whole)

2 tablespoons chopped fresh parsley

Freshly ground sea salt and freshly ground pepper

Cut the monkfish into 1 cm (½ in) thick slices, cover and chill.

Take a medium-sized deep-fry or sauté pan and add 150ml (¼ pint) of water and the butter. Bring to the boil and, when the butter is melted and the liquid rolling, throw in the diced carrots and turnips. Cover and simmer for 2–3 minutes, until almost tender. Uncover, add the peas and asparagus, cover and cook for 1 minute.

Uncover and lay the monkfish on top, slam on the lid and cook for 3 minutes. Lift the lid, scatter the tomatoes and parsley on top, cover again and cook for a final minute. Whip off the lid, taste the collected juices and season with a little salt and pepper.

Don't hang around – serve this right away with loads of crusty bread. (You could add a dash of cream at the end if you must, but the flavour of all those fresh veg and the juices from the fish are delicious enough!)

seared monkfish with curried lentils

Puy lentils come from a specific area in France, are tiny and a beautiful slatey greenish-grey. They have a lovely earthy flavour and tend not to disintegrate during cooking.
All lentils have an affinity with curry spices (just think of Indian dhal) and these are no exception. Use any type of firm-fleshed fish for this dish – halibut and cod could both be a good substitute for monkfish.

Serves 4

200 g (8 oz) Puy lentils

50 ml (2 fl oz) olive oil

25 g (1 oz) carrot, very finely diced

25 g (1 oz) celery, very finely diced

25 g (1 oz) leek, very finely diced

1 garlic clove, crushed and then finely diced

2 cm (3/4 in) piece of root ginger, peeled, crushed and then finely diced

1 teaspoon mild curry paste (or more if you like your curries)

300 ml (1/2 pint) Chicken Stock (see page 236) or Fish Stock (see page 237)

3 ripe vine tomatoes, roughly chopped

3 tablespoons chopped fresh coriander or chervil

Freshly ground sea salt and freshly ground pepper

2 tablespoons sunflower oil

4 monkfish tail fillets, weighing about 140 g (5 oz) each (or any other firm-fleshed fish)

A squeeze of lemon juice

2 tablespoons crème fraîche

First, cook the Puy lentils in boiling water for 20–30 minutes, or until tender. Drain them in a colander and spread on a tray to dry.

Warm the olive oil in a saucepan and sweat the carrot, celery, leek, garlic and ginger until soft. Add the curry paste and some seasoning and cook for 2–3 minutes. Stir in the lentils, then add the stock and bring to the boil.

Add the tomatoes and 2 tablespoons of the chopped coriander or chervil. Check the seasoning. Simmer for 30 seconds, or until you have a loose sauce – not too wet, not too dry. Then remove from the heat.

Put the sunflower oil in a very hot frying pan or ribbed cast iron pan and add the monkfish fillets. Fry until well browned on both sides. If you leave them for 3–4 minutes before turning to cook the other side, this should prevent sticking.

Now remove the monkfish fillets from the pan. They should be brown on the outside but still soft in the centre. Leave them to rest on a baking tray and season with salt, pepper and the lemon juice.

Stir the crème fraîche into the lentils, which should be looking nice and rich by now. Divide the lentils between four warmed serving bowls, making sure the sauce is evenly distributed. Cut each piece of fish into three slices and place on top of the lentils. Serve garnished with the rest of the chopped coriander or chervil.

skate with caper salsa

Delicate poached skate is the perfect foil for the clean, sharp-tasting flavours of caper salsa. The skate should be very fresh – if it's not it will smell of ammonia, in which case reject it. I like to use dry-salted capers rather than the brined ones, as they have a much cleaner flavour and texture. However, they must be rinsed well to get rid of the salt before using. Capers are an acquired taste; if you've never tasted them before, now's the time to try – just pop one in your mouth, give it a good chew and savour the musky exotic perfume that is unique to really good capers. The sauce is best used on the day of making but will keep for 2–3 days in the fridge.

Serves 4

600 ml (1 pint) court-bouillon
(see page 42)

4 skate wings, weighing about
900 g (2 lb) in total

FOR THE CAPER SALSA

1 teaspoon freshly ground sea salt

2 garlic cloves, finely chopped

3 tablespoons chopped fresh parsley

3 tablespoons chopped fresh mint

3 tablespoons chopped fresh basil

1–2 tablespoons salted capers,
rinsed and chopped

75 ml (2½ fl oz) really good
extra-virgin olive oil

2 tablespoons lemon juice

Freshly ground pepper

First, make the caper salsa. Pound the teaspoon of salt and the garlic in a pestle and mortar until creamy. (You can also do this with the side of a knife, crushing the garlic gradually into the salt – use a piece of greaseproof paper to stop your chopping board smelling too much!) Stir in the remaining ingredients and season with pepper.

Pour the court-bouillon into a wide, shallow pan and add the skate wings in a single layer, cover and bring slowly to the boil. Just before the water boils, turn down the heat and cook at a bare simmer for 8–10 minutes, until cooked through. Carefully lift out of the pan, drain well and place on four warm plates. Reserve the poaching liquid and freeze for future use as a fish stock. Serve the skate with the caper salsa.

fillet of cod with spring onion mash and avruga butter sauce

Cod is landed all around the Scottish coast, but I try and only buy cod caught in the Atlantic as North Sea cod stocks are very depleted. This is, in essence, a very posh fish pie, and sticks with the comfort theme. If you don't feel extravagant, skip the Avruga caviar and double the amount of chives in the sauce. This dish highlights cod's star qualities – large translucent flakes of firm-textured flesh. If you can't get cod, substitute hake, ling or even salmon.

Serves 4

2 large baking potatoes, weighing about 700 g (1 lb 9 oz) in total, peeled and quartered

3 tablespoons olive oil

2 tablespoons milk

3 spring onions, finely sliced

Freshly ground sea salt and freshly ground pepper

150 ml (¼ pint) Vegetable Butter Sauce (see page 240)

4 cod fillets, weighing about 140–175 g (5–6 oz) each, skinned

25 g (1 oz) butter

1 tablespoon lemon juice

175 g (6 oz) young, tender spinach leaves

2 tablespoons Avruga caviar (optional)

2 teaspoons chopped fresh chives (4 teaspoons if not using Avruga caviar)

Preheat the oven to 230°C/450°F/Gas 8.

Boil the potatoes in salted water for about 20 minutes, until just tender. Drain and dry out in the pan over a low heat for a further 5 minutes, then mash them. Add 2 tablespoons of the olive oil, the milk, spring onions and seasoning. Beat everything in with a wooden spoon until nice and fluffy. Cover with foil or clingfilm and keep warm.

Heat and season the vegetable butter sauce and keep warm. Heat a large saucepan ready for the spinach.

Place the cod fillets on a well buttered baking dish. Season with a little salt and pepper. Dot the top of the cod with pinch-sized pieces of butter and squeeze over half the lemon juice. Pour in 2 tablespoons of water, to prevent the butter from burning. Put the cod into the oven for 6 minutes, until it is just cooked (the fillets should look translucent, not cracked).

While the cod is cooking, pour the remaining olive oil into the preheated pan, add the spinach and stir-fry until slightly wilted. Season it with a little salt, pepper and the rest of the lemon juice.

Remove the cod from the oven and allow to rest for 2 minutes. Take the warmed vegetable butter sauce from the heat and stir in the Avruga, if using, and the chives at the last minute.

To serve, lay out four warmed serving plates and divide the spinach between them. Place a dollop of mash on top, flattening it slightly. Place a cod fillet on top of each one and spoon over the vegetable butter sauce. I cannot exaggerate my unalloyed enthusiasm for this dish.

goujons of sole with green mayonnaise

This is a recipe for real fish fingers or 'goujons', as they say in France. Really fresh white fish fillets cooked this way are not only irresistible, but healthier than you would think, provided you cook them in clean oil at the correct temperature.

Serves 4

450 g (1 lb) thick sole fillets, skinned

4 tablespoons plain flour, seasoned

2 eggs, beaten

140 g (5 oz) Natural Dried Breadcrumbs (see page 246)

Sunflower oil, for deep-frying

FOR THE GREEN MAYONNAISE

About 140 g (5 oz) mixed fresh herbs, watercress or spinach

300 ml (½ pint) mayonnaise

Freshly ground sea salt and freshly ground pepper

Lemon wedges, to serve

Cut the fillets across the grain diagonally into thick 'fingers'. Have three dishes containing the seasoned flour, beaten egg and breadcrumbs ready. Toss the fingers in the seasoned flour and shake off the excess. Next, dip the sole fingers in batches into the beaten egg, turning them around until well coated. Give them a bit of a shake and then dunk them in the breadcrumbs, tossing them about until evenly coated. At this stage you can lay them on a tray (as long as they don't touch), cover them with clingfilm and refrigerate until you are ready to cook.

Now make the green mayonnaise. Pick over the herbs, watercress or spinach, and strip the leaves from the stalks – you should end up with about 85 g (3 oz). Wash and dry them well on kitchen paper. Dollop the mayonnaise into a liquidizer or food processor and add the herbs, watercress or spinach. Blitz until smooth and creamy and green. Taste and season then pour into a serving dish.

Before you cook the goujons, get everything organized. Have a large plate or tray with a wad of kitchen paper and a slotted spoon handy and have your serving dish warming. Preheat the oil in a deep-fat fryer to 190°C/375°F. Fry a few goujons at a time until crisp and golden. Drain each batch on the kitchen paper. Keep them warm in a low oven with the door slightly ajar (they will go soggy if it's closed) while you cook the rest.

Serve with the green mayonnaise for dipping and dunking and with juicy lemon wedges for squeezing over.

baked sole with spring onions and ginger

A modern marriage of quality Scottish ingredients and Asian flavours. Whole fish cooked on the bone is always tastier than fillets, as the bones give up both flavour and moisture during cooking. My number one choice for this dish would be Dover sole – expensive, but very tasty; number two: witch sole – not particularly easy to find; number three: lemon sole – widely available and delicious.

Serves 4

4 whole soles, weighing about 300–350 g (10–12 oz) each, cleaned and gutted

75 ml (2½ fl oz) sunflower oil

Juice and finely grated zest of 1 lime

1½ tablespoons Japanese light soy sauce

2 tablespoons dry sherry

Freshly ground sea salt and freshly ground pepper

4 spring onions, cut into 7.5 cm (3 in) pieces and then shredded lengthwise

2.5 cm (1 in) piece of root ginger, finely grated

2 garlic cloves, lightly crushed and then finely diced

1 small red chilli, seeded and very finely diced

Preheat the oven to 230°C/450°F/Gas 8.

Trim the fins of the soles with scissors. Take four large sheets of foil and lift the edges of each piece to form a large well in the centre.

Mix the sunflower oil, lime juice, soy sauce and sherry together. Spoon a tablespoon of the mixture into each piece of foil and lay a sole on top, dark-side up. Season each one well with a little salt and pepper. Now scatter over the lime zest, shredded spring onions, ginger, garlic and red chilli and then divide the remaining liquid between the parcels. Fold over the edges of the foil and scrunch them together well to seal.

Place on one or two large baking trays and bake for 10–15 minutes, until the fish are cooked through. Serve in the foil, with egg noodles or Perfect Basmati Rice (see page 249).

sole and courgette gratin

As with all simple dishes, this relies on top-quality raw materials, so ask the fishmonger
for a whole fish that you can check for freshness, then ask him to fillet it. Pre-cut fillets
can hang around the shop and lose their freshness.

I grow courgettes in my greenhouse and I always seem to have a surplus, so I am
constantly on the lookout for good ways to use them up.

Serves 4

3 teaspoons butter

4 skinless lemon sole fillets, weighing
about 140 g (5 oz) each

Freshly ground sea salt and
freshly ground pepper

1 teaspoon lemon juice

2 medium courgettes, very
thinly sliced lengthwise

25 g (1 oz) Parmesan cheese, finely grated

150 ml (¼ pint) double cream

2 tablespoons chopped fresh
chives or chervil

Preheat the oven to 240°C/475°F/Gas 9.

Heavily grease a gratin dish with the butter and arrange the sole fillets in it,
overlapping them slightly. Season well and sprinkle with the lemon juice. Lay the
courgettes over the sole and season lightly. Scatter with the grated Parmesan
and pour over the double cream.

Pop this into the hot oven and bake for 10 minutes, until golden and bubbling.
Sprinkle with the chopped herbs and you're ready. I like this with Perfect
Mashed Potatoes (see page 165) with a spoonful of Pesto (see page 251), some
olive oil and roughly torn basil leaves stirred through.

seared john dory
with noodles

Instant noodles are simple to prepare and a great vehicle for the punchy Asian flavours used here. And these in turn provide the perfect accompaniment for a nice piece of translucent, straight-from-the-boat John Dory; you could use any other firm-fleshed white fish as a substitute.

Serves 4

1 chicken stock cube

200 g (8 oz) medium egg noodles

3 tablespoons olive oil

1 red chilli, seeded and finely chopped

½ red pepper, finely diced

3 spring onions, finely chopped

1 garlic clove, finely chopped

1 tablespoon Thai fish sauce

1 tablespoon lime juice

1 teaspoon of cornflour, mixed with 3 tablespoons of the stock

Freshly ground sea salt and freshly ground pepper

1 tablespoon diced Japanese pickled ginger

2 tablespoons roughly chopped fresh coriander

2 tablespoons sunflower oil

8 John Dory fillets, weighing about 85 g (3 oz) each, skinned

Cook the noodles first. Bring a large pan of water to the boil, add the stock cube and whisk to dissolve, then drop in the noodles. Remove the pan from the heat and stir with a fork and cover. Leave to stand for 4 minutes, stir again, then drain in a colander, reserving 300 ml (½ pint) of the stock.

Warm the olive oil in a large shallow pan, add the chilli, red pepper, spring onions and garlic and soften for 2 minutes. Add the noodles and toss well to coat with the spicy oil.

Stir in the fish sauce, the reserved stock, lime juice, cornflour mix and some seasoning. Toss well, then add the Japanese pickled ginger and chopped coriander. Keep warm.

Put the sunflower oil in a hot frying pan or ribbed cast iron pan, then add the fish fillets and cook for 2 minutes over a fierce heat, until they start to curl. Turn the fish over and cook for 1 minute, then transfer to a baking sheet and season.

To serve, divide the noodles between four bowls, spoon round the juices and place two John Dory fillets on top.

baked fillet of halibut with cabbage, smoked bacon and a tarragon cream sauce

Halibut is widely landed in Scotland and is an absolutely topping fish – it has a beautiful texture and flavour, it's easy to fillet and the bones make good stock – no scales to get everywhere either! It has sufficient flavour to partner the robust cabbage and bacon, which is all you really need for this dish, though I'd go for rösti potatoes too.

Serves 4

1 small Savoy cabbage

2 rashers smoked back bacon

1 tablespoon olive oil

Freshly ground sea salt and freshly ground pepper

25 g (1 oz) butter

4 skinless halibut fillets (steaks will do), weighing 140–175 g (5–6 oz) each

A few drops of lemon juice

2 tablespoons dry white wine

4 portions of Rösti Potatoes (see page 166), to serve (optional)

FOR THE TARRAGON CREAM SAUCE

15 g (½ oz) butter

2 shallots, sliced

4 button mushrooms, finely sliced

1 bay leaf

3 tarragon sprigs, leaves and stalks separated

300 ml (½ pint) white wine

300 ml (½ pint) Fish Stock (see page 237)

150 ml (¼ pint) double cream

Preheat the oven to 230°C/450°F/Gas 8.

To make the sauce, melt the butter in a pan over a low heat. Sweat the shallots and mushrooms until they are soft. Add the bay leaf and tarragon stalks, increase the heat to full and add the white wine. Reduce until it's nearly all gone. Add the fish stock and reduce again until it's nearly all gone. Then add the cream and bring to the boil. Pour the sauce into a fine sieve, forcing it through with the bottom of a ladle into a small clean pan. Season, adding lemon juice to taste.

Now cook the cabbage and bacon. Heat a medium-sized saucepan until hot. Peel off the coarse outer leaves of the cabbage and discard them. Give the centre part a good wash, then cut it into quarters lengthwise. Cut out the root part of each quarter, then finely shred the remaining cabbage with a sharp knife.

Cut the bacon into matchsticks. Pour the olive oil into the now-hot saucepan and stir-fry the bacon matchsticks until crisp. Add the cabbage and stir-fry it for 5–6 minutes, splashing in 3 tablespoons of water to help steam the cabbage, until it is tender. Season with a little salt and pepper and keep warm.

For the halibut, use half the butter to grease the base of a roasting tin. Place the fillets into the tin, season them with salt, pepper and a little lemon juice and dot the remaining butter over the fish. Now pour the 2 tablespoons of wine into the pan to prevent the butter from burning.

Whack the roasting tin into the middle of the hot oven and place the rösti potatoes, if using, on a baking sheet at the bottom of the oven. Set the timer for 6 minutes, and get four warmed serving plates ready.

Place four good-sized piles of the cabbage and bacon combo into the centre of each plate. Chop the tarragon leaves and add to the sauce before pouring it around each pile of cabbage and bacon. When the timer pings, the fish should be just cooked through and no more. Place a fillet on top of each pile, finishing with an individual portion of rösti potatoes, if using. Spoon over the juices left in the roasting tin for extra flavour and hand the plates out to the lucky guests.

baked hake with celeriac purée, red wine sauce and crispy parma ham

Hake is similar to cod, though its superior flavour and softer texture warrant further attention. It is landed all around Scotland but, sadly, most of it is exported to continental Europe, where it is a prized delicacy and not just 'for your cat', as I have seen in some fishmongers.

Deep-fried Parma ham is a garnish of the moment. I've used it with risottos, salads and game but I think it works best with a robust fish dish such as this one. You can deep-fry it up to 12 hours in advance.

This recipe may seem elaborate but, with a bit of planning, the actual cooking and serving should be really quite straightforward. The purée can be made the day before and reheated at the last minute and so can the sauce, if you don't add the butter until just before serving. Baking is the easiest way to cook fish. Just get it in the baking dish ready to bang in the oven.

Serves 4

Sunflower oil, for deep-frying
4 slices Parma ham
25 g (1 oz) butter
4 hake fillets, weighing about 175 g (6 oz) each, skinned
2 teaspoons lemon juice
4 tablespoons water or white wine
Freshly ground sea salt and freshly ground pepper
Celeriac Purée (see page 181), to serve

FOR THE RED WINE SAUCE
150 ml (¼ pint) red wine
1 teaspoon black treacle or dark brown sugar
300 ml (½ pint) Fish Stock (see page 237)
25 g (1 oz) cold butter, diced

Pour 2 cm (¾ in) of sunflower oil into a medium-sized saucepan or deep-fat fryer and heat to 180°C/350°F. Deep-fry the Parma ham slices, two at a time, for about 30 seconds, until nice and crisp. Drain them on kitchen paper and set aside.

Now make the red wine sauce. Bring the wine to the boil in a saucepan, add the treacle or sugar and boil until it is reduced by about three-quarters, to a thick and foamy syrup. Add the stock and boil until reduced to about 150 ml (¼ pint). Then add the diced butter, a few pieces at a time, swirling the pan as the butter melts. The sauce needs to be dark and glossy, so don't be tempted to whisk in the butter as this would make it too foamy. Keep swirling until the butter has been incorporated, then season the sauce and keep warm. If it begins to look as if it might split, heat it up a bit and give the pan a good swirl until you have a glossy sauce. Keep warm.

Preheat the oven to 230°C/450°F/Gas 8.

Heavily grease a baking dish with some of the butter and place the hake fillets in it. Sprinkle them with the lemon juice, dot generously with the rest of the butter and season. Add the water or wine to the baking dish and bake for 5–6 minutes.

Meanwhile, warm through the celeriac purée and have four warm plates ready.

When the fish is cooked, remove from the oven and baste with its juices. Put some celeriac purée in the centre of each plate, then put the hake on top. Spoon the sauce around the purée and place a piece of the Parma ham on each fish fillet. The soft fish, crispy ham, rich purée and glossy sauce complement each other beautifully. Serve with Wilted Greens (see page 175) and boiled new potatoes on the side.

tuna pâté with melba toast

This is a forgotten classic that deserves to be revived. You can jazz it up with grated lemon rind, a bit of mustard, anchovy essence, chopped parsley, chopped dill, chopped capers or even chopped olives – just whatever takes your fancy. I have it on good authority that this pâté used to be served in the scooped-out shells of lemons – life is just *too* short for lemon-scooping, but tasting the pâté again makes me wonder why it was ever forgotten!

Serves 4–6

2 large cans tuna in oil, drained

100 g (4 oz) butter, cubed and softened

100 g (4 oz) cream cheese, softened

Juice of 1 lemon

Freshly ground sea salt and freshly ground pepper

FOR THE MELBA TOAST

2 sfilatino breads or small ciabatta loaves

Put the tuna in a bowl and flake with a fork. Beat the butter and cream cheese together in another bowl – you can do this in a food processor if you like. Tip in the tuna and beat well to mix. Add as much lemon juice as you like to balance the richness of the butter and cream cheese. Season well with salt and pepper.

Cover and allow the flavours to develop in a cool place for a couple of hours. Whatever you do, though, don't serve this straight from the fridge – it won't spread and it will have lost its taste, as most things do when served really cold.

To make the melba toast, preheat the oven to 180°C/350°F/Gas 4. Take your sharpest serrated bread knife and cut the loaves in half across the middle. Then slice each half horizontally as thinly as possible. Arrange the slices in a single layer on a baking sheet. Bung in the oven and bake for 5–10 minutes, until golden and crisp (watch them like a hawk as they can burn easily).

Pile the tuna pâté into a large bowl and pass round for everyone to help themselves to a dollop and a couple of pieces of melba toast.

baked mackerel with curry spices

Mackerel is fished all around Scotland and is dirt-cheap in summer. While filming in Scotland, I once saw mackerel shoaling through a sound – there were so many you could almost have walked on them. Mackerel loves spices – I'm sure this is because it is an oily fish with a firm texture, a perfect vehicle for this spicy mix. Baking a spanking-fresh mackerel is one of the best ways to cook this cheap and underrated fish. Try to buy mackerel that is less than 24 hours old – it must be very fresh – old mackerel is only fit for bait!

Serves 4

4 tablespoons curry paste (Thai, Indian, whatever is your favourite)

3 tablespoons olive oil

Juice of 2 lemons

4 medium-sized mackerel, weighing about 350 g (12 oz) each, cleaned

Freshly ground sea salt and freshly ground pepper

4 tablespoons chopped fresh coriander

Lemon wedges, to serve

Preheat the oven to 200°C/400°F/Gas 6.

Mix the curry paste with the olive oil and half the lemon juice.

Make deep diagonal slashes down both sides of each fish and spread these cuts with the curry paste.

Take four double-thickness squares of foil that will easily wrap each fish, and lay a fish on top of each square. Pour over the remaining lemon juice, season and sprinkle with the coriander. Loosely wrap the foil around the fish, sealing tightly. Place the foil parcels on a baking sheet and bake in the oven for about 15 minutes.

Take the fish out of the oven, place on warm plates and let each person open their own parcel. Serve with lemon wedges and plain boiled potatoes or Perfect Basmati Rice (see page 249).

smoked haddock and puy lentil tart

Scottish smoked haddock is superb and I am pleased that it is now easy to get the undyed variety, which is vastly superior to the glow-in-the-dark stuff from days of yore. The earthy flavour of the lentils combines with the smoked fish to give a nice contrast of tastes and textures. For an even richer, more luxurious tart you could substitute hot-smoked salmon for the haddock.

Serves 8

1 quantity Savoury Shortcrust Pastry (see page 252)

50 g (2 oz) Puy lentils

300 ml (½ pint) double cream

750 g (1 lb 10 oz) undyed smoked haddock, skin and bones removed, to give 450 g (1 lb)

3 eggs, beaten

25 g (1 oz) Parmesan cheese, grated

3 tablespoons chopped fresh flatleaf parsley

Freshly ground sea salt and freshly ground pepper

Roll out the pastry, use to line a greased 25 cm (10 in) flan tin and bake blind in an oven preheated to 200°C/400°F/Gas 6 (see page 252). Remove from the oven and reduce the oven temperature to 190°C/375°F/Gas 5.

Cook the lentils in boiling water for 20–30 minutes, until tender. Drain and cool.

Bring the cream to the boil in a saucepan large enough for the fish and then add the haddock. Cover and poach gently for 3 minutes. Remove from the heat and tip the contents of the pan into a large sieve set over a mixing bowl, then leave to one side. Break up the fish with a fork and leave to cool.

When cool, mix the eggs into the cream and then add the lentils, Parmesan, parsley and flaked fish. Check and adjust the seasoning but go easy on the salt. Dump the whole lot into the pastry case and bake for 25 minutes, until just set. Cut into wedges and serve warm, with Tomato Salad (see page 180).

lasagne of smoked haddock and peas

In Scotland, there are grim November days when it seems to get dark two hours after you get up. On days like these, this dish is perfect, as what you need is some comfort food, and this is as good as it comes. Try to avoid the radioactive-looking, orange-dyed smoked haddock. It may be easily found in a dark fridge, but there's little to recommend the flavour. Fresh egg pasta is best for this, bought or home-made.

Serves 2

4 fresh lasagne sheets
(see Pasta Dough, page 250)
150 ml (1/4 pint) Vegetable Butter Sauce
(see page 240)
2 pieces of smoked undyed haddock fillet,
weighing about 175 g (6 oz) each, skinned
100 g (4 oz) good-quality frozen peas
2 tablespoons chopped fresh chives
Lemon juice
Freshly ground sea salt and
freshly ground pepper

It can be difficult to divide the portions when this is cooked in a single pan so, if possible, cook each portion separately in a small pan.

Cook the pasta in a large pan of boiling, salted water until *al dente*, then drain. Warm some vegetable butter sauce in each small pan until nearly boiling. Add the fish and simmer very gently for 3–4 minutes, until almost tender. Turn the fish over carefully halfway through as it will not be completely covered by the sauce.

Now add the peas and the cooked pasta to each pan and warm through for 2–3 minutes. Add most of the chives and a few drops of lemon juice, then check the seasoning and heat for a minute longer.

Now put the contents of each pan into a shallow, heated serving bowl, rearranging the fish and pasta nicely and scattering over the remaining chives. Serve immediately, and forget that it's winter.

salt and pepper squid with stir-fried vegetables

Dry-frying salt and Sichuan peppercorns together produces a really wonderful aromatic flavour – the amount here (enough for about 20 portions) is about the minimum quantity it is practical to make, but it does keep well in a screw jar for several weeks. The mixture is used to coat the squid prior to deep-frying. Don't be tempted to use frozen squid tubes, which have all the flavour and texture of rubber. When frying, don't overcrowd the pan or the pieces will stick together and become overcooked and rubbery. Serve with lemon wedges or a dipping sauce.

Serves 4 as a starter

300 g (10 oz) cleaned squid
2 tablespoons freshly ground sea salt
2 tablespoons Sichuan peppercorns
2 tablespoons black peppercorns
Sunflower oil, for deep-frying
6 tablespoons self-raising flour

FOR THE STIR-FRIED VEGETABLES
50 g (2 oz) mangetout
50 g (2 oz) red pepper
2 tablespoons sunflower oil
2 spring onions, chopped
1 teaspoon finely chopped root ginger
1 teaspoon finely chopped garlic
50 g (2 oz) fresh beansprouts
2 teaspoons Thai fish sauce
Juice of 1/2 lime
1 tablespoon chopped fresh coriander

Slice the squid across into thin rings and separate the tentacles, if large.

Heat a dry, heavy-based frying pan over a medium heat. Add the salt and stir it around for a couple of minutes, until it begins to look a bit grey. Tip it into a bowl, reheat the pan and then add the Sichuan and black peppercorns and toss them around until they darken slightly and start to smell aromatic. Grind the salt and peppercorns to a fine powder in a coffee grinder or a pestle and mortar.

Preheat 5 cm (2 in) of sunflower oil in a heavy-based saucepan or deep-fat fryer to 190°C/375°F.

For the stir-fried vegetables, cut the mangetout and the red pepper into strips about the same thickness as the beansprouts. Heat a large frying pan or wok until very hot. Add the oil, spring onions, ginger and garlic and stir around for a few seconds. Then throw in the mangetout and red pepper and stir-fry for 1 minute. Take the pan off the heat and stir in the beansprouts, fish sauce, lime juice and coriander and keep warm.

Mix the salt and pepper powder with the flour, place it in a plastic bag and add the squid. Give the bag a good shake so that all the pieces of squid become evenly coated in the highly seasoned flour. Then deep-fry 5–6 pieces at a time in the hot oil for 30–45 seconds, until crisp and golden. Lift out with a slotted spoon on to a paper-lined tray and keep warm in a low oven.

Place the salt and pepper squid on four warmed plates, pile a little of the stir-fried vegetables alongside and serve at once.

Note: If you want to make a Thai dipping sauce simply combine 1 green chilli, seeded and finely chopped, with 1 tablespoon of Thai fish sauce, 1 tablespoon of lime juice, 1 tablespoon of caster sugar and 2 tablespoons of water.

crab and parmesan soufflé

White meat from Scottish brown crabs is every bit as good as that from the more famous crabs of Devon and Cornwall. However, for this, I often use frozen crabmeat – it's nearly as good as fresh and a lot easier than cracking crustaceans open with your bare hands.

Serves 6

25 g (1 oz) butter (plus a little to line the ramekins)
300 ml (½ pint) full-cream milk
25 g (1 oz) plain white flour
3 egg yolks
50 g (2 oz) Parmesan cheese, grated
Freshly ground sea salt and freshly ground pepper
A squeeze of lemon juice
25 g (1 oz) Natural Dried Breadcrumbs (see page 246)
5 egg whites
175 g (6 oz) frozen (or fresh) white crabmeat, thawed and drained

Take six 150 ml (¼ pint) ramekins (size 1) and put them in your fridge before starting. This makes it easier to line them with butter.

To make the soufflé base, melt the butter in a small pan but don't let it brown. In a separate pan, warm the milk. Add the flour to the butter and mix well with a wooden spoon for 2 minutes. Grab a whisk, add the milk and bring to a simmer, whisking all the time. Cook for a further 10 minutes – the mix will get very thick – and then remove from the heat. Allow it to cool slightly before beating in the egg yolks, the Parmesan, the seasoning and the lemon juice. Leave it to one side covered with clingfilm. (If you have any problems with lumps, force the mixture through a sieve using the back of a ladle and hey presto – no more lumps.)

Remove the ramekins from your fridge. Grease the insides with butter, then coat them with breadcrumbs (it helps if the butter is at room temperature). Place the ramekins on a baking sheet and return to the fridge until you need them. You can prepare to this stage up to 24 hours in advance.

When ready to serve, preheat the oven to 200°C/400°F/Gas 6. Place the egg whites in the mixing bowl of an electric food mixer and whisk at full speed, adding a pinch of salt. Continue whisking until the whites are nice and light and you can shape them into a soft peak. (A soft peak bends gently. If it stands straight and stiff, it's a 'stiff' peak.) Do not overwhisk here; if in doubt, stop. Place the soufflé base in another bowl and mix in the crabmeat with a wooden spoon (if preparing ahead, it helps to warm the soufflé base to room temperature). Now mix one-quarter of the egg whites into the soufflé base and work well with your spoon to loosen up the mix. Fold the remaining whites in gently so as not to knock out too much air – it's the trapped air that makes the soufflé rise. A plastic spatula is best for this part.

Spoon the mix into the ramekins, bringing it level with the top but taking care not to get any on the rims. Give each ramekin a tap on the bottom – there's no need to smooth the tops. Place in the oven and set the timer for 12 minutes (depending on your oven you may need an extra 3–4 minutes). The soufflés should be well risen and golden on top and may be a bit cracked but this is OK. Serve on their own or with Speedy Hollandaise Sauce (see page 240) poured over.

crab, leek and parmesan tart

The Scots are keen on tarts of all kinds, sweet and savoury. Here, the sweetness of white crabmeat perfectly offsets the soft, delicate flavour of the leeks. Parmesan seems to have been made to go with crab, too. All in all, this is something of a treat – and so simple to make.

Serves 6–8

6 eggs

300 ml (½ pint) double cream

2 tablespoons olive oil

3 leeks, finely shredded

3 spring onions, sliced

100 g (4 oz) Parmesan cheese, grated

Cayenne pepper

500 g (1 lb 2 oz) frozen (or fresh) white crabmeat, thawed and drained

Freshly ground sea salt

FOR THE PASTRY

100 g (4 oz) butter

175 g (6 oz) plain white flour

50 g (2 oz) Parmesan cheese, grated

A pinch of salt

1 egg, beaten

First, get the pastry made and chilled. Rub the butter, flour, Parmesan and a pinch of salt together in a mixing bowl until the mixture has the consistency of fine breadcrumbs. Then add the egg and bring it all together into a dough. Knead this lightly three or four times with floured hands. Cover in clingfilm and refrigerate for an hour before use.

Preheat the oven to 200°C/400°F/Gas 6. Roll the pastry out 3 mm (⅛ in) thick and use to line a greased 25 cm (10 in) metal flan tin, 3 cm (1¼ in) deep. Fill with greaseproof paper and baking beans and bake blind for 11 minutes. Remove the beans and paper and bake for another 8–9 minutes, until lightly golden. Leave to cool. Reduce the oven temperature to 180°C/350°F/Gas 4.

Meanwhile, whisk the eggs and the cream together. Heat the olive oil in a pan and sauté the leeks and spring onions until softened, but not coloured. Allow to cool slightly and fold into the egg mix. Add the Parmesan, cayenne pepper and crabmeat, mix well, season and turn out into the pastry shell. Place the tart in the oven and bake for 35–45 minutes, until just firm. Leave to cool slightly before portioning.

Serve in wedges with dressed salad leaves or Tomato Salad (see page 180).

spaghetti with crab, chilli, garlic, parsley and lemon

For a dish as simple as this, fresh Scottish crab is unbeatable, though you could use frozen or pasteurized crabmeat. If you go to the trouble of cooking your own crab, make sure it's as big and firm as possible. Brown crabs are best, preferably ones that have big claws and feel heavy when you pick them up. The bigger they are, the easier it is to ferret out the delicious sweet flesh. I cook crabs in a court-bouillon, or flavoured cooking liquid, as I think it improves the taste. I also cook them for a much shorter time than most people, who recommend 30 minutes or more of boiling.

Serves 4

1 crab, weighing about 1 kg (2 lb 4 oz) or 200 g (8 oz) crabmeat

FOR THE COURT-BOUILLON
1 celery stick, roughly chopped
1 small onion, roughly chopped
1 carrot, roughly chopped
1 garlic clove, lightly crushed
1 bay leaf
1 small bunch of fresh parsley

FOR THE SPAGHETTI
100 ml (3½ fl oz) olive oil
1 or 2 small red chillies, seeded and very finely chopped
1 garlic clove, finely chopped
Juice and grated zest of 1 lemon
200 g (8 oz) spaghetti or linguine
Freshly ground sea salt and freshly ground pepper
3 tablespoons chopped fresh parsley

The first thing is to cook the crab. Make sure it's alive when you buy it, then ask your fishmonger to kill it for you. If you cook it alive, the legs will fall off and overcook. Place the crab in a large pan with all the court-bouillon ingredients. Cover with cold water and bring to the boil over a high heat. Once boiling, simmer for 10 minutes and then turn off the heat. Leave the crab to cool completely in the cooking water. It will be just cooked, and the meat nice and moist.

Now comes the fiddly bit. Fish out the crab and reserve the cooking liquid. Place the crab face down on a chopping board and give its back a good bash with the heel of your hand. This should open it up. Pull off the claws and give them a good bash with the back of a heavy knife or an old rolling pin. Pick out all the meat from the claws, legs and body including the brown meat (the handle of a small teaspoon is useful for this), taking care to leave behind the feathery-looking gills or 'dead man's fingers'. You should have approximately 200 g (8 oz) of crabmeat.

The rest of the dish is straightforward. Place the olive oil, chilli, garlic and lemon zest in a large saucepan and warm through until just simmering. Then remove from the heat and leave to stand for 10 minutes (or you can let it cool completely and reheat it when you're ready to serve).

Meanwhile, cook the spaghetti or linguine in a large pan of boiling, salted water until *al dente* and then drain. Add the lemon juice to the olive oil and chilli mixture and season well, then add the pasta and warm through for 1–2 minutes. Add the crabmeat and mix well, then add the chopped parsley, mixing again.

Divide between four warm serving bowls. I love it with a salad of herbs on top and a glass of chilled Sancerre on the side.

FISHY

75

grilled scottish lobster

There are no better lobsters than those from the cold unpolluted waters off the Scottish coast. You can always tell Scottish lobster from Canadian or Maine lobster because the live ones have such a beautiful deep blue, almost black colour. The beauty of this dish is that it can all be prepared in advance and only needs a last-minute grilling. Classically, the lobsters are cleaved in two alive and grilled immediately. Cooking them lightly before-hand seems to relax the flesh and make them tender and juicy. It needs only the simplest of accompaniments – a lobster mayonnaise or a blob of Hollandaise (see page 240).

Serves 2

2 live Scottish lobsters, weighing about 750 g (1 lb 10 oz) each

50 g (2 oz) butter

Freshly ground pepper

FOR THE LOBSTER MAYONNAISE

I egg yolk

1 tablespoon Dijon mustard

300 ml (½ pint) Lobster or Shellfish Oil (see page 245) or 300 ml (½ pint) sunflower oil and extra-virgin olive oil

1 tablespoon lemon juice

Freshly ground sea salt

To prepare the lobsters, half-fill a large pan with water and bring to the boil. Plunge the live lobsters into the pan, cover with the lid and cook for 7 minutes – this kills them in the most humane way. Remove the lobsters and place them into a bowl of iced water. Allow to cool for 15 minutes.

Lift the lobsters out of the water. Pull off the claws, crack them open and lift out the flesh and reserve it. Place the lobster body and tail on a board and cut in half lengthwise. Pull out the plastic-like stomach sac behind the head and discard. Remove the meat from the shells, rinse out and place the shells on a tea towel to drain.

Next, make the lobster mayonnaise. Mix the egg yolk and mustard together in a small bowl. Very gradually whisk in the lobster or shellfish oil, or sunflower and olive oil mix, so that the mixture becomes thick and glossy. You may have to add a little hot water to thin the mayonnaise. Add the lemon juice and season with a pinch of salt. Keep covered in the fridge until ready to serve.

When almost ready to serve, preheat the grill to the highest setting. Place the lobster shells, cut-side up, in the grill pan, fill with the lobster meat taken from the claws and body, and dot with the butter. Season with pepper and shove under the grill for about 2 minutes, until browned and heated through. Serve with a salad and the lobster mayonnaise.

filo basket of mussels with bacon and brie

A great combination of crunchy filo, soft mussels, salty bacon and gooey, melting Brie, this dish was once so popular at my first restaurant, Braeval, that I got fed up with cooking it and stopped making it. However, I still get constant requests for the recipe, so here it is. Use Scottish rope-grown mussels – my favourites are from Loch Etive – and remember to soak them in water for 30 minutes prior to cooking to flush out any grit.

Serves 6

FOR THE FILO BASKETS

18 x 15 cm (6 in) square sheets of filo pastry (cut from 3 large leaves)

50 g (2 oz) melted butter

FOR THE MUSSEL FILLING

2.25 kg (5 lb) live mussels, soaked for 30 minutes in cold fresh water

300 ml (½ pint) dry white wine

50 g (2 oz) butter

1 onion, finely chopped

2 garlic cloves, crushed and finely chopped

Juice of ½ a lemon

150 ml (¼ pint) double cream

Freshly ground sea salt and freshly ground pepper

A pinch of sugar

4 rashers smoked back bacon, grilled and cooled on kitchen paper, then chopped into small pieces

100 g (4 oz) ripe Brie, rind removed, cut into 6 squares

For the filo baskets, preheat the oven to 190°C/375°F/Gas 5. Take three squares of the filo pastry, place the first one on a flat surface (a chopping board will do) and brush with a little melted butter. Turn the next square through 30 degrees and place it on top of the first before brushing it with the butter. Turn the remaining one a further 30 degrees (thus creating a 'star' shape) and brush again with the butter.

Ease the star, butter-side down, into an individual 7.5 cm (3 in) metal tartlet tin or ramekin, the star points facing up. Push down well and prick the bottom with a fork. Repeat for the five other baskets. You should now have six filo-lined ramekins or tins. Put them on a baking sheet and bake them for 5–6 minutes, until they are slightly golden and hold their shape. Remove them from the oven and lift the baskets out of the tins. Turn the baskets upside-down, replace them on the baking sheet and return to the oven to cook for a further 4–5 minutes, until evenly brown. Leave to cool on a wire rack. These will keep for up to 12 hours.

To prepare the mussels, scrub them well, scrape off any barnacles and remove the beards that protrude from between the two halves of the shell. Discard any that do not close when lightly tapped on the work surface.

For the mussel filling, choose a pan with a tight-fitting lid. Heat it dry, then put in the drained mussels. Add 100 ml (3½ fl oz) of the wine, put the lid on and cook until the mussels open (it takes about 5 minutes). Do not overcook. Discard any that don't open in this time. Drain in a colander over a bowl. Shell the mussels. Strain the juice carefully through double muslin or in a chinois strainer and retain. Add some water, if necessary, to make it up to 450 ml (16 fl oz).

Melt the butter in a saucepan and sweat the chopped onion and garlic until soft. Add the mussel juice and the rest of the wine. Reduce it to a fifth of the original volume. Now add the lemon juice, cream, seasoning and sugar and reduce again until it is very thick and sticky. Add the bacon and mussels and heat through, checking your seasoning as you go.

TO SERVE

200 g (8 oz) salad leaves

2 tablespoons Vinaigrette (see page 241)
or your own salad dressing

Divide the mixture between the filo baskets. Top each one with a square of Brie and pop them into a hot oven for 3 minutes.

Serve the baskets on individual plates, surrounded by dressed salad leaves.

steamed mussels with fresh green flavourings

Scotland is now a major producer of rope-grown mussels which, as they are grown clear of the beach, aren't as gritty as beach mussels; my favourites are from Loch Etive. This is really a variation on classic *moules marinières*, an easy dish spiked with lively green herbs and oriental flavourings. I like to use a microplane grater for the ginger and garlic here – it makes short work of them, grating them almost to a purée. I would even use it on the lemon grass, which tends to be very tough and stringy. If presenting this dish as a main course, serve with noodles.

**Serves 4 as a starter
or 2 as a main course**

1.3 kg (3 lb) live mussels, soaked in cold
fresh water for 30 minutes

4 spring onions, trimmed

1 tablespoon groundnut or sunflower oil

1 cm (½ in) piece of root ginger, peeled
and finely chopped

1 garlic clove, very finely chopped

1 lemon grass stick, very finely chopped

Finely grated zest and juice of 1 lime

1 green chilli, seeded and finely sliced

150 ml (¼ pint) light dry white wine

2 tablespoons (or more) roughly chopped
fresh coriander

Freshly ground pepper

Scrub the mussels well, scrape off any barnacles and pull out the beards protruding from between the two halves of the shells. Discard any that won't close when they are lightly tapped on the work surface.

Cut the green tops off each spring onion and slice the greens into long fine shreds. Thinly slice the remaining white parts lengthwise. Heat the oil in a large pan. Add the white parts of the spring onions, the ginger, garlic and lemon grass and stir-fry for 2–3 minutes. Add the lime zest, chilli and white wine. Boil for 4–6 minutes to evaporate the alcohol.

Fling the mussels into the pan. Cover tightly and cook over a high heat for 3–4 minutes, shaking the pan every now and then, until the mussels have opened. Discard any that remain closed.

Add the coriander, lime juice and most of the shredded green tops of the spring onions to the pan and turn everything over once or twice. Ladle the mussels into warmed bowls and serve sprinkled with the remaining spring onion shreds.

If you are serving this with cooked noodles, remove the mussels from the pan with a slotted spoon after you have added the coriander and spring onion tops and then add the noodles to the sauce. Warm them through, divide them among the bowls and then spoon the mussels on top. Season with a liberal amount of freshly ground pepper and serve.

shellfish risotto with ginger and coriander

This risotto is a happy marriage of Italian know-how, the best of Scottish ingredients and a little Asian flavouring. The first method removes the mystique from making risotto and allows you to pre-cook, then finish it at the last moment. However, I've given the classic method as well for purists.

Shellfish and ginger work well together and the coriander adds a fresh, zingy touch. Any shellfish combination will do but I prefer prawns and mussels. There's no reason, other than financial, why you shouldn't add scallops or lobster. Parmesan is not added to or served with seafood risotto in Italy – but, if you like it, why not?

Serves 4

1.8 kg (4 lb) live mussels, soaked in cold fresh water for 30 minutes

200 ml (7 fl oz) white wine

Fish Stock (see page 237), if necessary

75 ml (2½ fl oz) olive oil, plus extra to serve

1 onion, finely chopped

2 cm (¾ in) piece of root ginger, peeled and finely chopped

200 g (8 oz) arborio or other risotto rice

Freshly ground sea salt and freshly ground pepper

50 g (2 oz) butter

25 g (1 oz) Parmesan cheese, grated, plus extra to serve

3 large fresh scallops, white meat sliced (optional)

100 g (4 oz) cooked, peeled langoustine tails

2 tomatoes, diced

2 tablespoons roughly chopped fresh coriander, plus extra to serve

1 teaspoon lemon juice

To clean the mussels, scrub them well, scrape off any barnacles and pull out the beards protruding from the two halves of the shells. Discard any that won't close when lightly tapped on the work surface.

THE QUICK METHOD

Heat a large pan until very hot and then put in the mussels and a quarter of the wine. Cover with a tight-fitting lid and cook for 3–4 minutes, until the mussels open. Discard any mussels that do not open. Shell the rest, leave them to cool and then store in the fridge until ready to finish the risotto.

Drain off the mussel cooking liquid into a measuring jug and reserve. You need 1 litre (1¾ pints) so, if it's a little short, add a little fish stock or water.

You can prepare the risotto base up to a day in advance. Heat 50 ml (2 fl oz) of the olive oil in a large frying pan, add the onion and ginger and sweat for about 8 minutes, until soft. Then add the rice and stir well over a medium heat until it has absorbed the oil and become translucent. Stir in the remaining wine and pepper to taste. Keep stirring for about 4 minutes, until the wine has been absorbed. Now add 850 ml (1½ pints) of the reserved mussel cooking liquid and bring up to simmering point. Simmer for 3 minutes, stirring from time to time. Then pour the contents of the pan into a large sieve set over a bowl to separate the rice from the cooking liquid. Quickly transfer the rice to a baking tray and spread flat. Cool this as quickly as possible, then put it into a plastic tub and refrigerate. Keep the cooking liquid in a bowl and refrigerate as well.

To finish the risotto, put the rice, the reserved cooking liquid and the remaining mussel cooking liquid into a large saucepan. Bring slowly to a simmer, stirring

from time to time. As soon as the risotto starts to thicken (after about 4 minutes), add the butter and beat in well with a wooden spoon. Once this is fully incorporated, add the grated Parmesan and keep beating.

Heat the remaining olive oil in a small frying pan and sear the scallops on one side only for 30 seconds. They should be slightly undercooked.

Stir the langoustine tails, scallops, mussels, tomatoes, coriander and lemon juice into the risotto. Taste for seasoning – the mussel stock will be fairly salty. Warm through for about 2 minutes. The consistency should be midway between soupy and stiff. If it is too thick, add a bit more stock. Now divide the risotto between warm serving bowls and sprinkle with Parmesan shavings, olive oil and chopped coriander. It will have been worth it.

THE CLASSIC METHOD

Once you have made the mussel and fish stock, have it at a constant, very gentle simmer in a pan beside your risotto pan – the stock must be at the same temperature as the rice. Have a ladle to hand.

Heat the olive oil in a large pan. Add the onion and ginger and stir-fry over a medium heat for about 8 minutes, until the onion has become translucent. Add the rice to the pan and stir it around for a couple of minutes until it has become well coated in the oil and is beginning to toast and turn chalky, but not colour. Add the white wine and boil rapidly for 1 minute, stirring, until it has almost evaporated. This boils off the alcohol, leaving the concentrated flavour of the wine in the rice.

Begin to add the stock a large ladleful at a time, stirring constantly until each ladleful is absorbed into the rice. The creaminess of your risotto comes from the starch in the rice, and the more it is stirred the more starch is released. Continue until the rice is tender and creamy, but the grains still firm and on no account chalky in the centre. (This should take 15–20 minutes, depending on the type of rice used.)

Just before the rice is cooked, stir in the Parmesan, then remove the pan from the heat. Cover the pan with a lid and leave to stand for a minute, to let the risotto relax. (You may have to add another ladle of stock: you're looking for a texture that is yielding but not stiff.) Cook the scallops and stir into the risotto with the langoustine tails, mussels, tomatoes, coriander and lemon juice. Warm through again and serve as above.

langoustine salad with hot garlic butter

With langoustines, freshness is of the utmost importance. If you intend cooking them yourself, it is imperative that you buy live ones. Look for lively, claw-waving prawns with a beautiful deep orange colour and translucent glow. Dead langoustines turn a dull yellow and release an enzyme that breaks down the flesh in the tail, turning it into cotton wool. If you don't want to cook them yourself, buy them precooked from a fishmonger you can trust. Good-quality, large, fresh, cooked tiger prawns are a good substitute.

Serves 4 as a starter

1.8 kg (4 lb) langoustines or 350 g (12 oz) tiger prawns, cooked and peeled

100 g (4 oz) butter

1 large garlic clove (or more if you like), well crushed

Finely grated zest of 1 lemon

2 tablespoons lemon juice

Freshly ground sea salt and freshly ground pepper

200 g (8 oz) mixed salad leaves

50 g (2 oz) fresh peas or mangetout (optional)

2 plum tomatoes, roughly chopped

1 tablespoon chopped fresh parsley

Bring a large pan filled with water to the boil. Add all the langoustines or prawns to the pan, bring back to the boil and cook for 2 minutes. Remove them with a slotted spoon, refresh in cold water and allow them to cool. Then pull off the tails and shell them by squeezing the edges of the shell together until you hear a crack, then pull the edges apart, releasing the meat. Cut each tail in half lengthwise and remove the intestinal tract (the black stringy bit).

Make the garlic butter by gently melting the butter with the garlic and lemon zest. Cook very slowly for 3 minutes, to take some of the harshness from the garlic, then add the lemon juice and a little seasoning. Set aside.

Tear the salad leaves to a manageable size, if necessary, and put them in a bowl with the peas or mangetout and tomatoes. Season and mix well, and then pile up in the centre of four serving plates.

To serve, heat the garlic butter until just boiling. Add the parsley and the langoustines or prawns, mix well and heat through. Then divide the shellfish between each pile of salad and drizzle over a little extra butter. Serve with crusty bread or toast to mop up the juices.

linguine with pesto and prawns

In Scotland we are lucky enough to have what are, in my opinion, the best prawns in the world: called langoustines, they have sweet plump tails with unparalleled flavour. Here they combine with the pesto ingredients for a delicious light lunch or supper dish. To be honest, if you are lucky enough to get your hands on spanking-fresh, creel-caught langoustines, I would simply cook them as per the recipe and either serve them hot with garlic butter or cold with a dollop of mayonnaise.

Serves 4

25 g (1 oz) pine nuts

1.8 kg (4 lb) langoustines or 350 g (12 oz) tiger prawns, cooked and peeled

175 g (6 oz) dried linguine

2 tablespoons extra-virgin olive oil

1 garlic clove

25 g (1 oz) fresh basil leaves, roughly chopped

Lemon juice

4 tablespoons grated Parmesan cheese

Freshly ground sea salt and freshly ground pepper

Preheat the oven to 160°C/325°F/Gas 3. Spread out the pine nuts on a baking sheet and toast in the oven for 5–6 minutes, until lightly browned – watch them like a hawk as they burn very easily.

Bring a large pan filled with water to the boil. Add all the langoustines or prawns to the pan, bring back to the boil and cook for 2 minutes. Remove them with a slotted spoon, refresh in cold water and allow them to cool. Then pull off the tails and shell them by squeezing the edges of the shell together until you hear a crack; then pull the edges apart, releasing the meat. Cut each tail in half lengthwise and remove the intestinal tract (the black stringy bit).

Cook the linguine according to the packet instructions and drain. Keep warm.

While the pasta is cooking, pour the olive oil into a small pan and warm through. Crush the garlic with the flat blade of a heavy knife until it's like a paste. Add it to the olive oil and allow it to infuse for 5 minutes and then add the langoustines or prawns, pine nuts, two-thirds of the basil and a good squeeze of lemon juice. Mix thoroughly, pour it on to the pasta, season and toss well.

Divide the pasta between four warmed serving bowls. Scatter over the grated Parmesan and reserved basil and serve with a bowl of lightly dressed salad leaves.

scallops with oriental salad and sweet chilli dressing

Here the unbeatable quality of Scottish seafood is allied to oriental flavours – modern Scottish cooking at its best. The vegetables for the salad are made crisp by thinly slicing them and soaking in iced water. They are then combined with the sweetness of the mango and the crunch of the nuts, with the whole thing brought together by the hot, sweet-and-sour chilli dressing. I use only hand-dived Scottish scallops, as the dredged variety are often damaged by the dredging process, which can also suffocate them with sand. Certainly never buy scallop meat which has been soaked in water, as this balloons it up, ruining the flavour and texture, and you have to pay for the extra water.

Serves 4 as a starter

12 fresh large scallops, cleaned

2 tablespoons sunflower oil

Freshly ground sea salt

1 tablespoon *furikake* (Japanese seasoning), optional

FOR THE SALAD

1 small carrot

4 spring onions

1 small ripe mango

50 g (2 oz) mangetout, shredded

50 g (2 oz) fresh beansprouts

A handful of fresh coriander leaves (use these like salad leaves), washed

200 g (8 oz) mixed small salad leaves, such as mizuna, watercress or lamb's lettuce, washed

50 g (2 oz) cashew nuts, crushed

1 red chilli, halved, seeded and finely shredded

FOR THE SWEET CHILLI DRESSING

3 tablespoons sunflower oil

4 tablespoon rice wine vinegar or white wine vinegar

2 tablespoons sweet chilli sauce

1 tablespoon light sesame oil

First make the salad. Fill a bowl with iced water or water with ice cubes in it. Shave long thin strips off the carrot with a potato peeler and put into the water. Cut the spring onions into long shreds and add them to the water too. Leave to firm up and curl in the fridge for 20 minutes, then drain well and pat dry.

Halve the mango past each side of the stone and peel with a potato peeler. Slice each half into long thin slices. Put the drained vegetables into a bowl with the mango. Add the mangetout, beansprouts, coriander, salad leaves, cashew nuts and chilli and lightly toss together with your hands. Cover and keep in the fridge.

Mix the dressing ingredients and set aside.

Pat the scallops dry with some kitchen paper. Detach the corals and save them for another dish (personally, I don't like them). Heat a ridged griddle until smoking hot. Lightly brush the scallops with the oil. Quickly lay them in the pan and sear for 30 seconds – do not move them. Quickly turn them around on the same side, so that you will brand them with a criss-cross pattern. Cook for 30 seconds. Flip them over and cook for another 30 seconds. They will now be ready. Season with a little freshly ground sea salt.

Arrange the scallops on warm plates. Toss the salad with 2 tablespoons of dressing and place a mound on each plate. Drizzle round a little more dressing and sprinkle with Japanese seasoning (if using).

As I grow older and perhaps wiser, I've started eating more vegetarian dishes. Not only am I conscious of needing to eat my five portions of fruit and vegetables daily, but I've also realized that by applying the same principles I use when cooking meat and fish, that is, subjecting the very best seasonal ingredients to good cooking techniques, the results can be very tasty indeed.

Try to use ingredients only when they are in season: this not only ensures the best flavours but usually gets you a good price into the bargain. Few things come close to the heavenly simplicity of June's new-season Scottish asparagus, chargrilled and served with a poached duck egg and fresh Parmesan (see page 102). Farmers' markets mean good local seasonal produce is much easier to come by and you can be sure you are buying regional food. It still never ceases to amaze me when I find supermarkets with piles of Spanish asparagus in mid-June, and there's not a bit of local stuff in sight.

Traditional Scottish cooking isn't big on vegetarian dishes, outside of an extensive use of potatoes. However, the Scottish climate is well suited to the cultivation of all kinds of vegetables, herbs and salad leaves. Scottish farms not only produce particularly good root vegetables, including carrots, turnips, parsnips, beetroots, celeriac and artichokes, but also fabulous brassicas – cabbages, broccoli and, most Scottish of all, kale. It is this great range of top-quality vegetables that inspires my vegetarian cooking, and that I use to produce a very Scottish flavour in Braised Root Veg with Pearl Barley and Tarragon (see page 101) or a more international flavour in My Favourite Vegetable Curry (see page 94).

My favourite vegetables are free (well, that is if you're prepared to go out and find them) between June and October. There is a bewildering array of wild mushrooms growing all over Scotland, not all of them edible, so take a guide and stick initially to the best known varieties – chanterelles with their wonderful apricot scent and distinctive yellow colour, and ceps with their cartoon mushroom looks and meaty texture.

vegetarian

tomato tarte tatin

Traditionally, *tarte Tatin* is made with apples but this savoury version using wonderful
Scottish tomatoes works really well, too. Sadly, Scottish glasshouse tomato-growing is in
decline, although at home we produce a healthy crop every year. Plum tomatoes work
best here – they don't seem to have as much water in them, so they don't collapse when
they are baked. As in a traditional *tarte Tatin*, the tomatoes are peeled and arranged in
the bottom of a shallow round tin, but I use balsamic syrup instead of caramelizing them.
Great either hot or cold, this is ideal for a lunch dish and also makes a great picnic treat.
If making in advance, leave out the breadcrumbs until you are ready to serve and turn out
and sprinkle with the crumbs *in situ* – this stops the pastry from going soggy.

Serves 4

900 g (2 lb) ripe red plum tomatoes or
vine tomatoes with flavour

6 tablespoons olive oil

2 tablespoons balsamic vinegar or
1 tablespoon Balsamic Syrup
(see page 242)

Freshly ground sea salt and
freshly ground pepper

350 or 375 g packet puff pastry

FOR THE GARLIC BREADCRUMBS

3 slices of stale bread, whizzed
into crumbs

2 fat garlic cloves, finely chopped

3 tablespoons chopped fresh
parsley or basil

Preheat the oven to 200°C/400°F/Gas 6.

Plunge the tomatoes into boiling water for a couple of seconds and then
immediately lift out and plunge into cold water – this will stop them cooking
on the outside and going mushy. The skins will now slip off – with any luck.
Cut out the wee hard 'core' in the base of each tomato, and then slice in half
lengthwise. Squeeze out as much of the seeds and water as you can without
crushing the flesh. Arrange them in a 25 cm (10 in) shallow tin or (ovenproof)
cast iron frying pan, in concentric circles, slightly overlapping each other so
they completely cover the base.

Whisk 3 tablespoons of the olive oil and the balsamic vinegar or syrup
together and pour over the tomatoes. Season well with salt and pepper. Place
the pan over a high heat and cook for 5 minutes, until the dressing begins to
evaporate and the tomatoes soften slightly on the bottom. Take off the heat.

Roll out the pastry on a floured surface into a 28 cm (11 in) circle. Lay the
pastry over the tomatoes, tucking in the edges. Prick all over with a fork and
bake in the oven for 25 minutes, until risen and golden on top.

Meanwhile, heat the remaining oil in a frying pan, add the breadcrumbs and
garlic and cook, stirring all the time, until golden. Stir in the parsley or basil and
set aside to cool.

When the tart is cooked, carefully remove from the oven and pour any juices
into a small pan. Boil the juices until reduced and syrupy, and reserve to drizzle
over the turned out tart.

To serve, turn the tart over onto a plate or board, so the pastry forms the base
of the *tarte*, drizzle with the reduced dressing and scatter with the garlic
breadcrumbs. Serve hot or cold.

my favourite vegetable curry

If you're in the habit of making your own spice blends, invest in an electric coffee grinder, which is perfect for grinding small batches of spices. But once you have used it for grinding spices it will never be the same again! It's impossible to remove all traces of the ground spices, so your coffee grinder will be a spice grinder from that moment on. Producing your own spice blends may seem like a lot of trouble but the difference from commercial blends is enormous. Don't be put off by the long list of ingredients – they are all easy to find and the spice powder keeps for several weeks in an airtight jar, so you could make a larger batch by doubling the quantities listed here. This recipe makes a very hot curry, but feel free to add as little or as much chilli as you desire. Puréeing the onions before cooking is a popular Malay technique that gives a distinctive texture to the curry and frying the onion purée with the spice mix helps release all those aromatic flavours.

Serves 6

450 g (1 lb) pumpkin or butternut squash,
peeled and cut into chunks

3 large carrots, cubed

300 g (10 oz) new potatoes, halved

6 baby aubergines, or 1 medium
aubergine, cubed

Freshly ground sea salt and
freshly ground pepper

400 g can of coconut milk

3 ripe tomatoes, quartered

Chopped fresh coriander, to garnish

FOR THE SPICE POWDER

2 tablespoons coriander seeds

1 tablespoon cumin seeds

2 teaspoons fennel seeds

6 black peppercorns

6 cloves

5 cm (2 in) piece of cinnamon stick

1/4 teaspoon freshly grated nutmeg

1 teaspoon turmeric

FOR THE ONION PASTE

3 onions, chopped

4 garlic cloves, chopped

1 tablespoon peeled and chopped ginger

8 dried red chillies, soaked and
chopped (this will make it quite hot,
so feel free to add less)

1 teaspoon sweet paprika

2 tablespoons chopped or ground almonds

1/2 lemon grass stick, chopped

5 tablespoons vegetable oil

First make the spice powder. Put the coriander seeds, cumin seeds, fennel seeds, black peppercorns, cloves, cinnamon and nutmeg into a heavy frying pan and dry-roast over a medium heat until you can smell the aroma – don't let the spices change colour or the flavour will also change and become bitter. Tip the whole lot into a spice grinder and grind to a fine powder. Stir in the turmeric and set aside.

To make the onion paste, throw the onions, garlic, ginger, chillies, paprika, almonds and chopped lemon grass into a food processor. Add 3 tablespoons of the oil and blend to a paste. You may need to add a couple of tablespoons of water to loosen the mixture and make it work – don't worry if you add more, it will evaporate during cooking.

Heat the rest of the oil in a large sauté pan. Add the onion paste and fry for about 5 minutes. Stir in the spice powder and then the pumpkin, carrots, potatoes and aubergines, coating with the onions and spices. Fry until the onions begin to turn brown and then add some salt and 500 ml (18 fl oz) of water. Bring to the boil and simmer, uncovered, for 20 minutes.

Stir in the coconut milk and tomatoes and simmer for another 15 minutes, until the sauce is thickened and the vegetables are very tender. Check the seasoning, scatter the coriander over the curry and serve with Perfect Basmati Rice (see page 249).

roasted butternut squash with crispy noodles and chilli vegetables

The success of this dish lies in the contrast of the crispy noodles, the sweetness of the roasted squash and the heat of the chilli vegetables. Excellent Scottish organic greenhouse-grown squashes are now available. One of our current favourite varieties is called Crown Prince. It has a flattish shape, is pale greeny-grey on the outside and bright orange on the inside, with a wonderfully intense and sweet flavour. *Kecap manis* is a thick, dark, sweet Indonesian soy sauce with a very assertive flavour, so add it sparingly.

Serves 4

1 medium Crown Prince or butternut squash

Olive or vegetable oil

1 packet of medium dried egg noodles

2 garlic cloves

2.5 cm (1 in) piece of root ginger, peeled and cut into matchsticks

1 red chilli, seeded and chopped

1 red pepper, halved, seeded and shredded finely

100 g (4 oz) asparagus tips, trimmed

2 courgettes, cut into 2 sticks

1 bunch of spring onions, trimmed and shredded

Juice of 1 lime

3 tablespoons light soy sauce

1–2 tablespoons *kecap manis*

Fresh coriander leaves, to garnish

Freshly ground sea salt and freshly ground pepper

Preheat the oven to 140°C/275°F/Gas 1.

Halve the squash and remove the seeds. Then peel or cut off the outer skin and cut the flesh into wedges. Heat 2 tablespoons of oil in a frying pan or wok until smoking and then add the squash. Toss until coated with oil, then turn down the heat and cook on one side for 10 minutes, until golden. Flip over and cook on the other side until golden and tender. (Alternatively, roast the squash chunks spread in a baking tin in a hot oven for 20 minutes.) Keep warm.

Cook the noodles according to the packet instructions, but slightly overcook them, by a couple of minutes. Drain well and divide into twelve small piles.

Heat a tablespoon of oil in a small frying pan until hot. Add a pile of noodles. Press down to form a 'pancake' covering the base of the pan. Cook on one side for a couple of minutes, until golden and crisp, then flip over and cook until completely crisp. Drain on kitchen paper, and keep warm while you make the rest. Always add more oil to the pan so the 'pancakes' shallow-fry, or they won't crisp.

Heat another 2 tablespoons of oil in a wok or frying pan, add the garlic and ginger, swirl around for a minute (don't let them colour) and then add the chilli and red pepper. Stir-fry for 3 minutes. Then add the asparagus and courgettes and stir-fry for another 2 minutes. Then add the spring onions, lime juice, soy sauce and *kecap manis*. Stir well, cover and simmer for a few more minutes, until all the vegetables are tender. Check the seasoning – because soy sauce is salty, it probably will be OK. Stir in the roasted pumpkin.

To serve, place a noodle disc on each warmed plate. Add a spoonful of vegetables, another disc, another spoonful of vegetables and then another disc and then put a few veggies on top. Scatter with coriander and drizzle with any remaining pan juices. Eat before the noodles go soft!

wild mushroom
and barley risotto

You don't get much more Scottish than this – a risotto made with barley instead of rice!
I call this 'barlotto'. I've used a mixture of dried and fresh wild mushrooms but you can
use any sort, even button mushrooms (which don't really have much flavour, only
texture). The nutty flavour of the barley is a natural with the slightly exotic flavour of the
mushrooms – another marriage made in Scotland!

Serves 4

50 ml (2 fl oz) olive oil

175 g (6 oz) pearl barley,
washed and drained

1 small onion, finely chopped

1 garlic clove, minced

450 ml (16 fl oz) Chicken Stock
(see page 236), Marinated Vegetable
Stock (see page 239) or water

1 tablespoon light soy sauce

150 ml (¼ pint) red wine

Freshly ground sea salt and
freshly ground pepper

200 g (8 oz) chanterelles or other
wild mushrooms such as ceps,
or field mushrooms

50 g (2 oz) butter

1 tablespoon chopped fresh tarragon

1 tablespoon chopped fresh parsley

Heat a large frying pan until it's hot. Pour in the olive oil and then add the
barley and stir until it starts to turn golden – this will take about 5 minutes. Add
the onion and garlic and continue frying for 5–10 minutes, until the barley starts
to brown. Don't let it burn.

Add the stock, soy sauce, red wine and seasoning. Bring to the boil and simmer
until nearly all the liquid is gone.

Meanwhile, brush or scrape clean the mushrooms (slicing any bigger ones in
half) and heat another frying pan until it's hot. Add half the butter and the
mushrooms. Stir-fry until lightly coloured (this will take 4–5 minutes). Season
with salt and pepper.

Add the stir-fried mushrooms to the barley and mix together. When the pan is
nearly dry, remove it from the heat and cover with foil. Pierce some holes in the
foil and leave in a warm place for 15 minutes. At this stage, you could also let
the 'barlotto' cool, reheating it for serving up to 24 hours later.

To serve, pop the pan back on the heat, add the tarragon and parsley and a
little more stock or water if the mixture is too dry. Add the remaining butter. Stir
well until hot, taste for seasoning and serve.

lasagne of wild mushrooms, asparagus and chervil

In autumn the Highlands of Scotland are carpeted with wild mushrooms, if you know where to look. You can pick chanterelles from May to October and ceps from June to October. Scottish asparagus is at its best in June, so that's the best time to give this dish a go. The individual flavours of wild mushrooms and asparagus are difficult to define, but combine brilliantly in this posh vegetarian main course. If you can't get thin asparagus, peel the regular stuff and cut into 2.5 cm (1 in) slices.

Serves 4

100 g (4 oz) thin asparagus

25 g (1 oz) butter

175 g (6 oz) mixed wild mushrooms, such as chanterelles, *trompettes de mort*, ceps, *pieds de mouton*, shiitake, pleurottes or field, cleaned and sliced

Freshly ground sea salt and freshly ground pepper

A squeeze of lemon juice

175 ml (6 fl oz) Vegetable Butter Sauce (see page 240)

2 teaspoons light soy sauce

8 lasagne sheets about 7.5 x 7.5 cm (3 x 3 in) each, cooked (home-made is best, see page 250)

2 tablespoons chopped chervil

Bring a pan of salted water to the boil and throw in the thin asparagus. Cook it for 1½ minutes, then fish it out with a slotted spoon. Cool it in a bowl of cold water. Drain it and keep to one side.

Heat a frying pan until it's hot and then drop in the butter. As soon as the foaming butter browns, drop in the sliced mushrooms and stir them to coat. Cook for 5–6 minutes, until lightly browned, and then season with salt and pepper and the lemon juice. Tip everything into a bowl and keep to one side.

To serve, have a pan of simmering water ready for the pasta. Heat the vegetable butter sauce through and add the asparagus, the mushrooms and the soy sauce. Stir and warm it through. Dump the pasta into the hot water for 90 seconds, then remove it with a slotted spoon and drain it on a clean tea towel. Season the sauce and vegetable mix.

In each of four warmed serving bowls, place a sheet of pasta and, using a slotted spoon, divide half of the vegetable mixture between the bowls. Cover each with the remaining four sheets of pasta, then spoon over the remaining vegetables. Add the chervil to the remaining sauce, spoon it over and serve at once.

spinach and ricotta dumplings with goats' cheese sauce

One of the enduring memories of my childhood is of wonderful traditional stews with dumplings, which probably explains why I now love little dumplings, or gnocchi as the Italians call them, so much. These spinach and ricotta gnocchi are very light and go fantastically with a simple tomato sauce, but I love to partner them with this goats' cheese cream. We often make this in the restaurant, cooked in individual cast iron dishes and served still bubbling away. I like to make these dumplings using crowdie, an ancient Scottish cheese with a crumbly texture like cottage cheese (which could also be used in this recipe) but moister, once commonly made on farms and still widely available. Alternatively you could use best-quality ricotta. Either way, sieve the cheese to give the dumplings a light fluffy texture.

Serves 4

600 g (1 lb 5 oz) fresh spinach or 300 g (10 oz) frozen spinach, thawed

25 g (1 oz) butter, plus extra for greasing

1 shallot, finely chopped

Finely grated zest of 1 lemon

140–175 g (5–6 oz) crowdie or fresh ricotta cheese, sieved

85 g (3 oz) plain white flour, plus extra for dusting

2 egg yolks

85 g (3 oz) Parmesan cheese, grated, plus extra to serve

Freshly ground sea salt and freshly ground pepper

A little freshly grated nutmeg

FOR THE SAUCE

2 small goats' cheese logs, approximately 140 g (5 oz), with rind

150 ml (¼ pint) double cream

Strip away the stalks from the fresh spinach and wash the leaves in several changes of cold water. Drain and pile into a large saucepan. Cook over a high heat until just wilted, cool a bit, and then squeeze out most of the moisture. (If using frozen spinach, thaw then squeeze.) Chop roughly and set aside.

Melt the butter and fry the shallot until golden. Stir in the spinach and lemon zest and cook for a couple of minutes, until coated and well mixed with the butter and shallot. Tip into a bowl. Bung in the crowdie or ricotta, the flour, egg yolks and Parmesan and mix well with your hands. Taste and season with salt, pepper and nutmeg. Cover and rest for a couple of hours (or even overnight) in the fridge to firm up – this is important or your gnocchi might collapse!

When ready to cook, take large tablespoonfuls of the mixture and quickly roll into small cork shapes or balls – you'll manage this better with wet hands. Place on a tray lined with a tea towel sprinkled with a little flour or semolina flour. Grease four small gratin dishes with butter.

Bring a large pan of salted water to the boil, drop in all the gnocchi at once, wait for the water to come back to the boil and cook for 2–3 minutes (or until they float to the surface). Scoop them out with a slotted spoon as they rise to the surface and arrange in the gratin dishes.

To make the sauce, slice the goats' cheese and mix with the cream. Bring to the boil, stirring continually until you have a rich sauce. Spoon the sauce over the gnocchi, season and shove under a blazing hot grill for 2–3 minutes or until browned and bubbling. Eat straight away, with a crunchy bitter salad and some freshly grated Parmesan.

braised root veg with pearl barley and tarragon

A lot of vegetarian dishes depend on Mediterranean influences and they've become a bit clichéd. The inspiration for this recipe came from a little closer to home, with the root vegetables that have been a staple of Scottish cooking for centuries. I really don't miss the meat in this big soupy stew, which could also be served as an excellent accompaniment to game.

Serves 4

1 onion
2 carrots
2 celery sticks
2 leeks
2 parsnips
¼ swede
2 large potatoes
25 g (1 oz) butter
3 tablespoons olive oil
25 g (1 oz) pearl barley
2 teaspoons tomato purée
1 tablespoon plain white flour
Freshly ground sea salt and freshly ground pepper
600 ml (1 pint) Marinated Vegetable Stock (see page 239)
2 tablespoons chopped fresh tarragon

Cut all the vegetables into large chunks. Heat the butter and olive oil in a large saucepan. When the butter is foaming, add the vegetables and stir-fry over a high heat until well browned. Add the pearl barley and tomato purée and cook for 2–3 minutes. Stir in the flour, add a little salt and pepper, then gradually stir in the stock. Cover and simmer gently for 25 minutes.

When the cooking time is up, check that all the different types of vegetable are tender; if not, give it a few more minutes. Stir in the chopped tarragon and simmer for 1 minute. Check the seasoning and serve.

chargrilled asparagus with poached duck egg and parmesan

Although Scotland has a short asparagus season – from early May to late June – Scottish-grown asparagus is fabulous – far superior to the imported stuff available all year round. When I can get my hands on some, I always try to make Scottish asparagus the star of its own show. Here I've partnered it with a couple of its best friends: a poached duck egg with its gloriously intense orange yolk and some shavings of Parmesan. When the raw ingredients are as good as this you don't need anything fancy.

Serves 4

450 g (1 lb) fresh medium asparagus

Extra-virgin olive oil

2 tablespoons white wine vinegar

4 fresh organic hens' eggs or ducks' eggs, chilled

Freshly ground sea salt and freshly ground pepper

Fresh chervil or flatleaf parsley sprigs, to garnish

50 g (2 oz) Parmesan cheese, shaved, to serve

Preheat a griddle pan until very hot. Trim the ends off the asparagus spears. Using a potato peeler, shave the ends (if hard and woody) to a point. Toss the spears in a little olive oil, to coat lightly. Griddle for 5–7 minutes, until tender and lightly charred. Keep warm.

To poach the eggs, pour 4 cm (1½ in) of boiling water into a clean frying pan or saucepan with the vinegar and place it over a low heat – the water should show a few bubbles on the base of the pan, but no more. Break the eggs carefully into the hot water and cook for 3–4 minutes, basting the tops of the eggs with a little of the hot water as they cook. Lift them out of the water with a slotted spoon and drain on kitchen paper.

Place a pile of asparagus on each of four warmed plates. Top with the poached egg, drizzle with more olive oil, season with salt and pepper and garnish with sprigs of chervil or parsley. Sprinkle with freshly shaved Parmesan and dig in straight away.

rocket and pine nut ravioli with quick tomato sauce

We grow a variety of wild rocket in our greenhouse at home and it is sensational in these ravioli. Making your own ravioli really is much easier than it sounds, as long as you've got a pasta machine. I've stuffed the ravioli with a thick paste or 'pesto' of rocket and crunchy pine nuts, for a really punchy flavour and texture, ready for a thin coating of rich tomato sauce. Pasta isn't swamped in sauce in Italy, it is just coated to add flavour. The point is that, originally, the pasta was served at the beginning of the meal to take the edge off the appetite, so that you would only need a little meat or fish to follow, which would cut down on the housekeeping! (Thrifty, eh? Not unlike we Scots.)

Serves 4

1 quantity Pasta Dough (see page 250)

FOR THE ROCKET AND PINE NUT FILLING
85 g (3 oz) rocket leaves
2 garlic cloves, roughly chopped
50 ml (2 fl oz) extra-virgin olive oil
Freshly ground sea salt and freshly ground pepper
50 g (2 oz) Parmesan cheese, grated
85 g (3 oz) pine nuts

TO SERVE
Quick Tomato Sauce (see page 249)
Parmesan cheese, shaved
Chopped fresh herbs or rocket

First, make the filling. Throw the rocket, garlic, olive oil, salt and pepper into a food processor and whizz until thoroughly blended. Add the Parmesan and the pine nuts. Pulse a few times until well mixed but still thick and rough; it should not be a smooth purée, rather a crunchy paste that will stand on its own.

Roll out the pasta to the thinnest setting on the pasta machine. Then lay the pasta on a very lightly floured work surface. Using a biscuit or scone cutter, cut out rounds as big or as little as you like. Place a scant teaspoon of filling in the centre of each round. Dampen the edges with a very little water on a pastry brush, if necessary. Pinch the edges up and over the filling to enclose it completely. Pinch the edges firmly together, excluding all the air. You should end up with little crescent-shaped ravioli. Lay these in a single layer on a dry tea towel until ready to cook.

To cook the pasta, have a really large pot of boiling, salted water ready. Drop in the pasta, stirring until it comes back to the boil again. Cook for 2½ minutes and then remove the ravioli with a slotted spoon and toss with a little tomato sauce.

Serve immediately, with more tomato sauce if liked, shaved Parmesan, freshly ground pepper and extra herbs or rocket.

goats' cheese soufflés

Good goats' cheese from forward-thinking independent Scottish cheesemakers is becoming more accessible through specialist shops, delicatessens and even supermarkets. Its fine deep flavour and interesting texture sets it apart from factory-produced counterparts. The soft pyramid-shaped organic Califer from Forres is a particular favourite of mine. You need a ripe cheese for this recipe. If you can't find goats' cheese, however, this soufflé is excellent made with Gruyère, Parmesan or a good sharp Cheddar.

Serves 6

50 g (2 oz) butter

2 tablespoons fresh white breadcrumbs

2 tablespoons finely grated Parmesan cheese

25 g (1 oz) plain white flour

450 ml (16 fl oz) milk

Freshly ground sea salt and freshly ground pepper

Leaves from 2 small fresh thyme sprigs, finely chopped

4 egg yolks

200 g (8 oz) ripe goats' cheese, crumbled

6 egg whites

Heavily grease six deep 7.5 cm (3 in) soufflé ramekins with half the butter. Mix the breadcrumbs with the Parmesan and use to coat the inside of each ramekin – the butter will help the soufflés to rise and the breadcrumbs and Parmesan will form a nice crust. Set them aside in the fridge.

Preheat the oven to 220°C/425°F/Gas 7.

Melt the rest of the butter in a saucepan, add the flour and cook gently for 1 minute to form a roux. Meanwhile, warm the milk in another pan – it has to be warmed as cold milk can make the roux lumpy. Gradually whisk the warm milk into the roux and then add some seasoning and the chopped thyme. It is important now to cook out the flavour of the flour, so bring the mixture to the boil, stirring all the time, and then lower the heat and leave to simmer very gently for 10 minutes – the surface should be barely moving. If it is cooking too fast, it will catch and burn.

Remove the sauce from the heat, pour into a large bowl and leave to cool for 10 minutes. Then beat in the egg yolks and the crumbled goats' cheese. The base for the soufflés is now done. If you're not baking them immediately, dot the top with butter to prevent a skin from forming.

Now whisk the egg whites to make the meringue for the soufflé. This is what makes the soufflé rise. Put the egg whites into a large clean bowl with a pinch of salt and whisk until they form soft peaks. The tips of the peaks should flip over slightly, not stand upright. The meringue mixture will need to be slightly slack so do not overbeat.

Spoon a quarter of the egg whites into the soufflé base and stir in. This loosens it up a little. Then gently fold in the remaining egg whites but don't overwork them: it doesn't matter if there are a few lumps or traces of white in the mixture.

Put the prepared ramekin dishes on a baking sheet and spoon in the soufflé mixture. Tap them gently to level the tops. Slide them into the lower part of the oven – the hot-air currents at the top tend to push the soufflé down (make sure the next rack up is not too close). Bake for 12–15 minutes, until well risen and golden brown. You can check near the end of cooking but, whatever you do, don't open the oven door in the first few minutes. Serve straight from the oven. They may crack slightly on top but don't worry, this is all part of the charm.

garlic mushrooms on toast

You could use any wild mushrooms with big caps here but this is a good opportunity to use big portobello mushrooms. I'm assuming hungry people, so I'm allowing two per person. Real garlic lovers could add an extra clove or two.

Serves 4

8 large open-cup mushrooms

About 6 tablespoons olive oil, plus extra to serve

4 smoked back bacon rashers, rinded and diced

1 small onion, finely chopped

2 garlic cloves, crushed

50 g (2 oz) butter

Freshly ground sea salt and freshly ground pepper

3 tablespoons chopped fresh flatleaf parsley, plus extra to garnish

100 g (4 oz) fresh white breadcrumbs

Juice of ½ lemon

1 baguette

Preheat the oven to 230°C/450°F/Gas 8.

Remove the stalks from the mushrooms and chop the stalks roughly. Heat a frying pan, add 1 tablespoon of the olive oil and put in the bacon. Stir-fry it until crisp, and then add the mushroom stalks, onion, garlic and butter. Reduce the heat and cook for about 7 minutes, until softened. Add some seasoning, then the parsley and breadcrumbs and mix together well.

Oil a baking tray big enough to hold the mushroom caps and put them on it rounded side down. Slather with 2–3 tablespoons of the olive oil, then season generously and add a good squeeze of lemon juice. Now divide the filling between the mushrooms. If they look a bit dry, don't be afraid to drizzle on more olive oil. Place in the oven and bake for 12–15 minutes.

Meanwhile, start on the toast. Cut eight 2 cm (¾ in) slices diagonally off the baguette and lay them on a baking tray. Once again, slather with olive oil (be generous because the bread will absorb a lot). Season lightly and put the slices in the oven with the mushrooms. They should take 6–7 minutes.

Put the slices of toast on four serving plates, put a mushroom on top of each one, and then garnish with a sprig of parsley and another drizzle of olive oil.

grilled polenta with a cep and tomato stew

This dish brings Italo-Scottish traditions together nicely. Polenta, Italian porridge, is often eaten runny but I prefer it nice and thick. I let it set overnight, then cut it into slices and fry it in a cast iron griddle pan. Ceps grow all over Scotland from June until October – I love the thrill of finding a patch of perfect undisturbed ceps, which you know are going to provide you with the most magnificent feast. If you can gather them yourself, do so. Good brown mushrooms or shiitake are a passable alternative.

Serves 6

200 g (8 oz) quick-cook polenta
Freshly ground sea salt and freshly ground pepper
50 g (2 oz) butter
20 g (¾ oz) Parmesan cheese, grated
Olive oil

FOR THE CEP AND TOMATO STEW
4 tablespoons olive oil
1 garlic clove, crushed
350 g (12 oz) fresh ceps, sliced
1 teaspoon dried basil
1 fresh thyme sprig
450 ml (16 fl oz) tomato passata

TO SERVE
25 g (1 oz) Parmesan cheese, grated (optional)
175 g (6 oz) rocket
1 teaspoon olive oil

For the polenta, bring 1 litre (1¾ pints) of water to the boil in a saucepan and then pour in the polenta and stir until it thickens. Add the seasoning and cook until it gives off a nice deep plop as it cooks – about 5 minutes. Beat in the butter and Parmesan, check the seasoning and pour onto an oiled baking tray or large plate in a layer about 1 cm (½ in) thick. Leave for 3–4 hours, until cool and set.

To make the stew, heat the measured oil in a saucepan and add the garlic and ceps. Stir-fry until well browned, no more than 5 minutes. Now add the basil and thyme and some seasoning. Pour in the passata, reduce the heat and simmer for 20 minutes, until nice and thick. Check the seasoning.

Now cut out a slice or two of the polenta per person and fry in a little olive oil in a hot frying pan for 2–3 minutes on a medium-to-high heat until each side is browned and a crust has formed. Serve with a dollop of the stew, and a little Parmesan scattered on top, if you like. Season the rocket leaves, toss in the teaspoon of oil and divide them between the portions.

chanterelles and new potatoes on sourdough

One of nature's gifts to Scotland is the happy coincidence of the appearance of chanterelle mushrooms and first early potatoes in late June. On the spud front I'm particularly fond of an early variety called Epicure, which is grown extensively in Ayrshire in Scotland – as with all earlies eat them as soon as you can after they come out of the ground. When you have such wonderful raw materials, it's imperative to keep everything simple. I serve them on griddled sourdough, a bread with a slightly sour, tangy flavour that combines perfectly with the potatoes and mushrooms.

Serves 4

400 g (14 oz) new potatoes, preferably Ayrshire

4 slices of sourdough bread

50 ml (2 fl oz) olive oil

25 g (1 oz) butter

400 g (14 oz) chanterelle mushrooms, cleaned

50 g (2 oz) fresh flatleaf parsley, roughly chopped, plus a little extra to serve

Freshly ground sea salt and freshly ground pepper

25 g (1 oz) Parmesan cheese, coarsely grated, to serve

Boil the potatoes in salted water until tender. Drain and set aside.

Heat a griddle pan over a medium heat. Brush the bread slices with half the olive oil and place on the griddle for 1–2 minutes on each side, until nice and crisp. A word of warning: keep an eye on the temperature – if too hot you'll end up with scorched bread before it has a chance to crisp. If you don't have a griddle pan, don't worry, simply bake the bread in a medium oven for 3–4 minutes.

Heat the remaining oil and the butter in a medium pan, toss in the chanterelles and potatoes and sauté for 5–6 minutes. Add the parsley, salt and a generous amount of freshly ground pepper and toss.

Place the bread on a serving plate and pile on the topping. Sprinkle with a little extra parsley and some grated Parmesan and serve.

parmesan biscuits with baby leeks and home-dried tomatoes

These biscuits are so good that, whenever I make them for the restaurant, the boys in the kitchen have to hide them from the rest of the staff. Apparently they keep for up to 48 hours in a sealed container but I've never had them long enough to verify this. You really do need to use baby leeks for this recipe and they should be no bigger than a spring onion.

Serves 4

24 baby leeks, trimmed

Freshly ground sea salt and freshly ground pepper

12 Home-dried Tomatoes (see page 247)

25 g (1 oz) Parmesan cheese, shaved, to serve

25 g (1 oz) fresh basil leaves

Olive oil

Balsamic Syrup (see page 242)

FOR THE BISCUITS

50 g (2 oz) butter

40 g (1½ oz) plain white flour

85 g (3 oz) Parmesan cheese, grated

Cayenne pepper

First, make the Parmesan biscuits. Rub the butter into the flour until you have a mixture that resembles breadcrumbs. Now add the Parmesan and a generous pinch each of cayenne and salt and work with your fingers until the mixture comes together into a dough (this stage can be achieved in a food processor). Then cover in clingfilm and leave in the fridge for an hour. Preheat the oven to 200°C/400°F/Gas 6.

Roll out the Parmesan dough until it is about 3 mm (⅛ in) thick and stamp out four rounds with a 9 cm (3½ in) scone cutter. (You can freeze the remaining dough or wrap it in clingfilm and keep refrigerated for up to 5 days.) Place the biscuits on a well-oiled baking sheet (or one lined with baking parchment) and bake for about 8 minutes, until golden.

Remove the biscuits and transfer to a wire rack to cool (this stops them from steaming and going soggy). Once cool, they'll keep for 48 hours in an airtight container.

Next, poach the leeks. Bring a large pan of water to a rolling boil, add a teaspoon of salt and put in the leeks. Have ready a bowl of iced water and a slotted spoon to fish out the leeks once they're tender, probably after 2–3 minutes. Refresh them in the iced water and leave them to cool and drain.

To serve, place a biscuit on each serving plate and arrange three leeks and three dried tomatoes on top. Scatter with Parmesan shavings and more leeks.

Place the basil leaves in a mixing bowl, season with salt and pepper, add a splash of olive oil and toss well. Arrange on top of the biscuits, leeks and tomato. Don't be tempted to do this in advance because the basil will wilt. Lastly, drizzle the balsamic syrup and more olive oil around and serve at once.

Scotland has always been renowned for the quality of its wild game, and from the Northern Isles to the Borders you will find sublime venison, hare, wood pigeon, duck and in vast areas of the Highlands and Islands that most Scottish of birds, grouse. All game is by its very nature free-range and almost organic and, properly treated, provides a wonderful eating experience.

It is, however, the superb Scottish beef, lamb and pork that is more commonly found in supermarkets and butchers and many of the recipes in this section highlight the versatility, value and flavour of these meats. Scottish meat tends to come from animals that have been extensively reared, that is beasts with plenty of access to grass pasture and a minimum amount of human intervention in their rearing. For those who can afford it, free-range organic meat can provide the ultimate experience, although it is worth bearing in mind that organic isn't an absolute guarantee of quality.

It's advisable to get to know a good local butcher, who will be able to recommend the best breeds and what cuts to use, and advise you on other factors that should influence your purchase. I've been a customer of Jonathan Honeyman (see page 256), my butcher, for over 15 years now and I know when I'm making Perfect Steak and Chips (see page 137) I'll be provided with the best native, grass-fed beef, which has been properly hung and will make a simple dish like this truly sing.

meaty

terrine of chicken and leeks wrapped in parma ham

Leeks, chicken and Parma ham are an excellent combination of flavours and this is currently my favourite non-fishy terrine. This requires a fair degree of preparation and work but it can all be done well in advance, leaving just the slicing of the terrine come serving time. Take a little care when layering the terrine, since you want to be able to see all the different layers in nice straight lines. Parma ham is very carefully regulated to protect its reputation for quality: what a pity the same precautions aren't always taken with Scottish smoked salmon.

Serves 4 as a starter

FOR THE TERRINE

2 tablespoons sunflower oil, plus extra for greasing

7 thin slices of Parma ham, large enough to wrap around the terrine

12 long, straight leeks

6 chicken breasts, preferably maize-fed, weighing 140–175g (5–6 oz) each, boned and skinned

2 egg yolks

450 ml (16 fl oz) double cream

Freshly ground sea salt and freshly ground pepper

Lemon juice

FOR THE OLIVE OIL AND CHERVIL DRESSING

125 ml (4 fl oz) olive oil

2 tablespoons lemon juice

2 heaped tablespoons chopped fresh chervil

Lightly oil a 900 g (2 lb) terrine tin and line it with clingfilm (roll up a tea towel and use it to help push the clingfilm down). Take six of the Parma ham slices and line the clingfilm-covered tin with them, making sure a little overlaps the rim.

Top and tail the leeks so they fit the terrine lengthwise. Poach the leeks in boiling, salted water for 5–7 minutes, until just tender. Remove the leeks with a slotted spoon and dump them in a bowl of cold water. Allow them to cool, then drain them. Wrap them gently in the tea towel and wring the excess moisture out, trying not to squeeze too hard, since this will remove too much juice.

Place two of the chicken breasts in a food processor and whizz until well broken down (this will take 2–3 minutes). You'll have to stop once or twice to scrape chicken from the sides of the bowl. Once broken down, add the egg yolks and whizz again for about 30 seconds. Remove the bowl, complete with the chicken, egg and blade still in, and place it in the freezer for 10 minutes (this chills the mix and makes it easier for the cream to be absorbed). Replace the bowl in the food processor and whizz again. Add the cream in a steady stream until you have a nice stiff mousse. Now add a teaspoon of salt and some pepper. Take a moment to taste as you season and try to end up being able to taste the salt and feel the heat of the pepper but not so much that either dominates the mixture (in other words, season to taste). If you're worried about tasting raw chicken, then you'll just have to use your seasoning judgement. Scrape the mixture into a bowl, cover and refrigerate until needed.

Remove the fillets from the four remaining chicken breasts and then cut the remaining parts of the breasts into five long strips of chicken. Now heat a frying pan until it's very hot. Meanwhile, season the chicken pieces with sea salt and freshly ground pepper. Add 2 tablespoons of the sunflower oil to the pan and

quickly stir-fry the chicken pieces for no more than 45 seconds. The fillets should be starting to go opaque. Squeeze a little lemon juice over them, remove from the frying pan and leave to cool on a baking tray.

To assemble and cook the terrine, preheat the oven to 180°C/350°F/Gas 4. You should have to hand:

1   the chicken mousse
2   the leeks
3   the fried chicken strips
4   the terrine tin lined with clingfilm and Parma ham
5   one more piece of Parma ham

Place a tablespoon of the mousse in the bottom of the terrine tin and spread it out thinly. Place four leeks on top of the mousse, pressing them down. Season with a little salt, pepper and lemon juice. Place another tablespoon of mousse on top of this. Now place eight chicken pieces on the mousse. Repeat the process twice (it's not dissimilar to constructing a lasagne), ending with a layer of leeks on the top and a final spread of the mousse.

Place the remaining piece of Parma ham over the top of the terrine, and fold over the ham you used to line the tin, sealing the whole thing in. Now pull the clingfilm out from the edges of the terrine and stretch it over the top, enclosing the terrine in clingfilm. Finally, place the lid on the terrine, if it has one, or cover it with four thicknesses of foil.

Now place the terrine in a roasting tin and pour in hot water so that it comes halfway up the side of the terrine. Place in the warmed oven and cook for 45 minutes, then test the terrine to see if it's ready. To do this, remove the terrine from the oven, remove the lid or foil and peel back the clingfilm. Plunge a skewer in the centre of the terrine and keep it there for 10 seconds. Remove it and run the immersed part of the skewer over your lower lip. It should feel hot/warm/hot as you go from one end to the other. If it feels warm/cool/warm then the terrine needs further cooking: give it another 5 minutes and test again.

When it's ready, remove the terrine from the oven and allow it to cool. Refrigerate the terrine in the tin for 12–24 hours before serving.

When you're ready to serve, invert the terrine on a board, give it a tap on the base and ease it out. Unwrap the clingfilm. Place the terrine on a chopping board and, using the sharpest knife you have (preferably serrated), cut into 1 cm (½ in) slices.

To make the olive oil and chervil dressing, mix together all the ingredients. Place one slice of the terrine on each serving plate, pour round a little dressing and serve at once.

tarragon chicken with wild mushrooms, beans and new potatoes

This is a true marriage made in Scotland! My favourite wild mushrooms are ceps and chanterelles or girolles. These appear in woodlands from early June onwards until the first frosts. Scotland produces all sorts of edible wild mushrooms – parasols, horse mushrooms, field mushrooms and woodland bluets to name but a few. Chicken and wild mushrooms are just perfect cooked together in butter, with fresh tarragon and a dash of cream – some crunchy beans and new potatoes are all you need to complete the dish.

Serves 4

4 free-range organic chicken breasts, skin left on

Freshly ground sea salt and freshly ground pepper

50 g (2 oz) butter

450 g (1 lb) new potatoes, scrubbed

250 g (9 oz) fresh wild mushrooms or cultivated chestnut mushrooms (not shiitake as they are too strong), thickly sliced

400 g (14 oz) fresh beans (runner, French, stick beans or bobby beans), topped and tailed

150 ml (¼ pint) dry white wine

150 ml (¼ pint) double cream

1 tablespoon chopped fresh tarragon

Season the chicken breasts with salt and pepper. Melt three-quarters of the butter in a sauté pan and, when the foaming has subsided, add the chicken, skin-side down. Cook over a moderate heat for 10 minutes without moving the chicken. This will make sure the chicken has a golden crust to it.

Meanwhile, put the potatoes on to boil.

After 10 minutes, flip over the chicken and add the mushrooms. Cook over a moderate heat for another 10 minutes.

Now cook the beans, then drain and toss in the remaining butter. Put to one side and keep warm.

Remove the chicken and mushrooms to a plate and keep warm. Check the potatoes. Drain, if ready, and keep warm.

Pour the wine into the sauté pan and stir well, scraping all the sticky bits up from the bottom of the pan. Bring to the boil, reduce until nearly dry, then add the cream and return to the boil. Return the mushrooms to the pan with the tarragon, the chicken and any juices. Stir well and allow to warm through. Season to taste and divide between four warmed serving plates. Serve with the spuds and beans.

warm salad of crispy chicken thighs

Always try and use free-range poultry, as it has a superior flavour and texture out of proportion with its price premium. Chicken thighs are not only cheaper than breasts, they are also much tastier. Their secret is being able to withstand long cooking, which would leave a breast fillet dry and tasteless. When cooking thighs this way, you end up with a crispy skin, reminiscent of crackling, and succulent, well-flavoured flesh.

Serves 4

4 chicken thighs, weighing about 140 g (5 oz) each, skin left on

Freshly ground sea salt and freshly ground pepper

2 tablespoons sunflower oil

1 garlic clove, lightly crushed

1 tablespoon lemon juice

140 g (5 oz) mixed salad leaves

1/2 red pepper, seeded and diced

50 g (2 oz) green beans, sliced into 4 cm (1 1/2 in) lengths and blanched in boiling water for 3 minutes

12 cherry plum tomatoes, halved or quartered

2 tablespoons Vinaigrette (see page 241)

TO GARNISH (OPTIONAL)

Very fine shreds of carrot

Long cut fresh chives

It's a good idea to buy boned chicken thighs but, if they are not available, you can bone them yourself. This isn't essential but it means they cook more quickly and are easier to slice once cooked. To bone them, run a sharp knife down the thighbone, cutting into the meat to allow it to come away. Do this several times on each side until the bone comes free.

Heat a frying pan over a low-to-medium heat. The heat is critical here: too hot and the skin will crisp before the thighs are cooked, too cool and the skin will never crisp up. Season the boned thighs well, add the oil to the pan, and then place the thighs in it, skin-side down. Toss in the garlic clove to flavour the oil. Now cook the chicken, skin-side down, until the skin is very crisp, like crackling. This will take about 20–30 minutes.

Turn over the thighs and discard the garlic, which will be well browned by now. Continue to cook the chicken for another 2–3 minutes. Add the lemon juice and shake the pan to make sure it is evenly distributed. Cook for another 3 minutes, then remove to a warm place to rest for 5 minutes.

To serve, place the salad leaves, red pepper, beans and tomatoes in a bowl and season, then add the vinaigrette and toss well. Divide between four serving plates. Carve each thigh into six or seven pieces and place them on top of the salad. Garnish with carrot shreds and chives, if using.

my perfect roast chicken dinner

There's nothing more satisfying than sitting down to a complete roast chicken dinner, having enjoyed the smell of roasting chicken wafting through the house while it browns and crisps in the oven. It is a simple meal really, but ask any chef or cook what their favourite meal would be and for many this would be it – a roast chicken dinner. I am no exception. But there is one hard and fast rule to follow for the perfect meal: start off with the best chicken you can afford – this pays huge dividends and you do get what you pay for. Excellent organic Scottish chicken is now sometimes available and it's really worth waiting for. The difference in flavour and texture is truly amazing.

Serves 4

One 1.3–1.8 kg (3–4 lb) free-range organic chicken
1 lemon
4–5 garlic cloves
A handful of flatleaf parsley
4–5 tablespoons olive oil
Freshly ground sea salt and freshly ground pepper
8 large floury potatoes
8 medium parsnips
Vegetable oil
1 glass of white wine
½ chicken stock cube
Steamed broccoli, to serve

Preheat the oven to 200°C/400°F/Gas 6. Untruss the chicken and let it come to cool room temperature before cooking. Cut the lemon into eight wedges, and lightly crush the whole garlic cloves so that they just crack open. Feel inside the chicken cavity between the legs and pull out any large pieces of fat still clinging to the insides. Stuff the cavity with the lemon wedges, garlic cloves and a huge handful of flatleaf parsley, stalks and all. Rub the outside of the bird all over with 1–2 tablespoons of the olive oil and season with salt and pepper. Slash down through the skin between the legs so that they go floppy; this lets the heat out of the oven into the legs. Sit the bird in a roasting tin and pour in the remaining olive oil. Roast on the middle shelf of the oven for 20 minutes.

Meanwhile, peel the potatoes and par-boil in a large pan of boiling salted water for approximately 8 minutes. Peel the parsnips, trim and cut in long quarters and set aside. Drain the potatoes well, then use a fork to roughen the outside of each potato – this will make the crunchy crust. Pour a thin layer of vegetable oil into another roasting tin on top of the stove and heat until smoking hot. Carefully add the potatoes, turning them in the oil to coat, and making sure the oil has heated up again.

Open the oven door, remove the chicken and baste it with the juices in the tin. Stick in the parsnips, turning them in the pan juices. Return the chicken to the oven and put the potatoes on the highest shelf above the chicken. Roast for another 40 minutes, basting everything occasionally and turning the potatoes at least once during cooking.

When everything is looking good and golden brown, test the chicken to see if it is cooked by sticking a skewer in the thickest part of the leg. If the juices run clear, remove the chicken from the tin and set on a warm plate, covered loosely with a piece of foil, to rest for 10 minutes. Tip the excess fat out of the pan, return to the oven and let the parsnips crisp up for 10 minutes. Remove the parsnips and potatoes from the oven. Turn the oven off. Lift the potatoes out of the tin with a slotted spoon onto a warm serving dish and do likewise with the parsnips, then keep them warm in the oven with the door propped open.

Now make the gravy. Set the chicken roasting tin on the heat, and add the wine, stock cube and 150 ml (¼ pint) of water. Bring to the boil and boil furiously for 2–3 minutes, scraping up all the sticky bits from the bottom of the tin. Taste and season very well. Tip any juices that have flowed out of the chicken into the gravy, then strain into a warm jug or gravy boat. Allow to settle, then spoon off the fat from the top. Serve immediately, with some steamed broccoli.

cold roast chicken with feta, rosemary, lemon and olive oil

This recipe is perfect for using up cold roast chicken; so good is it, indeed, that I often find myself roasting a chicken specifically to eat this way. Perfect for a picnic or an *alfresco* summer lunch, or as a winter starter to remind you of summer. This relies on good ingredients to make a simple dish great. Try to get a free-range organic chicken to roast and buy the best feta you can find. This is definitely an excuse to use your top-of-the-range olive oil. You can even make this up a day in advance as the flavours improve over time.

Serves 3–4

1.5 kg (3 lb 5 oz) free-range chicken

50 g (2 oz) butter

1 lemon, cut into wedges

4–5 garlic cloves, lightly crushed

Freshly ground sea salt and freshly ground pepper

175 g (6 oz) feta cheese, crumbled into small pieces

Leaves from 1 fresh rosemary sprig, very finely chopped

50 ml (2 fl oz) olive oil, plus extra to serve

Finely grated rind of 1 lemon

3 tablespoons lemon juice

Dressed salad leaves, to serve

Slices of grilled bread or toast, to serve (optional)

Try to roast the chicken a day ahead. Preheat the oven to 200°C/400°F/Gas 6. **Untruss the chicken** before cooking. Push your fingers between the chicken breast and the skin to make two pockets. Stuff 15 g (½ oz) of the butter into each one and rub the remaining butter all over the outside of the skin. Stuff the cavity with the lemon wedges and garlic. Season very well. Slash down through the skin between the legs so that they go floppy and put the bird on a wire rack over a roasting tin. Splash 3 tablespoons of water into the tin, put it in the oven and roast until well browned, about 1 hour, basting occasionally. Depending on your oven, you might need to cover the chicken loosely with a sheet of foil after about 40 minutes to stop it browning too much.

Test with a skewer in the thickest part of the thigh: the juices should run clear. Leave until cold, preferably overnight. Pull the legs off the chicken and use a knife to cut off the breasts. Ferret out the two 'oysters' from the underside of the bird (these are little secret crackers of flesh). Using your fingers, flake the flesh off the breasts, thighs, drumsticks and oysters. Try to get nice long strands and don't forget the skin.

Pile all the flaked chicken into a large mixing bowl and add the crumbled feta. Whisk together the rosemary, olive oil, lemon zest and juice and some seasoning and add this to the bowl. Toss well, check the seasoning again and keep cold until needed.

Serve with a few dressed salad leaves and a drizzle of olive oil, or pile onto slices of grilled bread or toast.

smooth chicken liver terrine

A posh version of chicken liver pâté, this is very rich and smooth, but you need to take care not to overcook it. Fresh chicken livers are fabulously tasty and cheap, and the Cumberland sauce provides the acidity to complement the rich flavour of the terrine.

Serves 12 as a starter

FOR THE TERRINE

450 g (1 lb) fresh chicken livers

8 egg yolks

250 ml (9 fl oz) double cream

1 tablespoon port

1 tablespoon cognac

½ garlic clove, crushed

Freshly ground sea salt and freshly ground pepper

425 g (15 oz) butter, melted

Dressed green salad, to serve

350 ml (12 fl oz) Cumberland Sauce (see page 248), to serve

Preheat the oven to 180°C/350°F/Gas 4. Line a 450 g (1 lb) loaf tin with clingfilm and put it to one side. Trim the chicken livers to remove any fat, sinew or gunky bits in general. Place in a liquidizer or food processor, add the egg yolks, cream, port, cognac, garlic and seasoning, and whizz for 2 minutes. Then add the melted butter in a thin stream. The mix in the liquidizer should turn a pale pink colour. Keep whizzing for a further minute. Pour the mixture through a sieve into the lined loaf tin, letting the mixture come to the brim.

To protect the surface from burning, cover it with clingfilm, then place a double thickness of foil on top and lightly fold the edges under the top of the tin. Place the terrine in a roasting tray and pour in enough hot water to come halfway up the tin. Place in the oven and cook for 40 minutes. After this time, the top should be slightly risen.

At this stage, you need to test the mixture to see if it has set. To do this, remove it from the oven and remove the foil but not the clingfilm. Give the tin a wee shake. The centre of the terrine should wobble, but not the edges. If the edges seem at all wobbly, stick the tin back (replacing the foil) in the roasting tray in the oven and cook for another 5 minutes. If all is perfect, however, lift the loaf tin from the tray and allow to cool. Once cooled, refrigerate overnight.

Next day, take a piece of wood, polystyrene or stiff card which is the same width as the loaf tin, but 5 cm (2 in) or so longer. Cover this with foil. Remove the top layer of clingfilm from the terrine, cutting away any excess clingfilm sticking to the edges of the tin. Dip the whole tin into a basin of hot water (the water nearly touching the top). Count to 20, then remove it and place the foil-covered board on top of the tin. Turn it upside-down and lift off the tin and clingfilm lining, leaving you with the terrine sitting on a serving board.

To serve, use a metal spatula dipped in hot water to cut slices of terrine. Place each slice on a cold plate and garnish with a little dressed salad and a tablespoon of the Cumberland sauce. This is also fantastic with some bread or even better toasted Brioche (see page 230).

You can wrap any remaining terrine in clingfilm and store it in the fridge for up to a week.

chicken liver pâté

I have fond memories of chicken liver pâté from the days when I was learning to cook –
it was a staple. I made it again recently and wondered why it had fallen out of fashion –
it really is fantastic, and very easy to make. Perfect served with some pickled gherkins
or capers as a great snack or first course. It's best eaten on hot toast so that it melts a
bit. Try to use fresh livers here, not frozen.

Serves 6 as a starter

300 g (10 oz) butter, at room temperature
1 onion, finely chopped
1 carrot, finely chopped
1 celery stick, finely chopped
1 large garlic clove, finely chopped
450 g (1 lb) fresh chicken livers
1 tablespoon chopped fresh lemon thyme,
plus extra sprigs to garnish
Tawny port, Madeira, sherry
or dry vermouth
Freshly ground sea salt and
freshly ground pepper
2 tablespoons Clarified Butter
(see page 247)
Toasted fingers of ciabatta, to serve

Melt 25 g (1 oz) of the butter in a large frying pan and cook the onion, carrot,
celery and garlic over a low heat until meltingly soft (about 20 minutes).

While this is cooking, trim the chicken livers of any gristle and cut off any
discoloured bits. Pat dry on kitchen paper. Remove the softened vegetables with
a slotted spoon to the bowl of your food processor.

Heat the pan again, add the livers and 15 g (½ oz) of the butter and fry over a
high heat, turning them as they brown, for about 3 minutes, until they are nicely
browned and crisp on the outside but still pink and juicy in the middle. Add the
chopped lemon thyme and a splash of your chosen tipple, bubble for a minute
and then tip into the food processor bowl and season with salt and pepper.
Chuck in the remaining butter and blitz in pulses until *fairly* smooth – I like a bit
of texture; this is not a parfait.

Scrape out into a large earthenware bowl or spoon into individual bowls.
Smooth the top, scatter with sprigs of lemon thyme and pour over a thin layer of
clarified butter. This will now keep for ages in the fridge.

Serve with toasted fingers of ciabatta, but remember to bring it to room
temperature before serving – fridge-cold pâté will not do!

roast breast of pigeon with savoy cabbage and bacon

Tender, tasty, lean and cheap, pigeon deserves more exposure. Here, it partners Savoy cabbage flavoured with smoked bacon, all pulled together with a gamey sauce. If you're buying whole pigeons and removing the breasts yourself, use the carcasses and legs to make stock – they produce a particularly good one. This is great with mashed potatoes.

Serves 4

4 oven-ready wood pigeons, the breasts removed and skinned

Freshly ground sea salt and freshly ground pepper

2 tablespoons sunflower oil

25 g (1 oz) butter

Perfect Mashed Potatoes (see page 165)

FOR THE CABBAGE AND BACON

1 small Savoy cabbage

2 rashers smoked bacon

2 tablespoons sunflower oil

25 g (1 oz) butter

FOR THE GAME SAUCE

25g (1 oz) butter

3 shallots, finely sliced

6 button mushrooms, sliced

1 garlic clove, crushed

1 bay leaf

1 fresh thyme sprig

6 white peppercorns, crushed

1 teaspoon redcurrant jelly

3 tablespoons red wine vinegar

125 ml (4 fl oz) ruby port

350 ml (12 fl oz) pigeon stock or Chicken Stock (see page 236)

50 ml (2 fl oz) double cream

Preheat the oven to 230°C/450°F/Gas 8.

Make the sauce first. Heat a medium-sized saucepan until it's hot, then add the butter and the shallots. Add the mushrooms, garlic, bay leaf, thyme and crushed peppercorns. Gently fry for 5–10 minutes, until golden brown. Add the redcurrant jelly and allow it to melt and be absorbed. Pour in the red wine vinegar, followed by the port and boil it until the pan is dry. Then add the stock and reduce it by two-thirds. Add the cream, bring it back to the boil and pass it through a fine sieve into a small, clean pan. Check the seasoning and keep it warm until you're ready to serve. If you are making this sauce the day before, allow it to cool, then cover it and store it in the fridge until needed.

Take the cabbage, remove the coarse outer leaves and discard them. Wash the heart of the cabbage in cold water. Quarter it, cut out the stem and, using a sharp knife, finely shred the cabbage. Start to heat a large saucepan.

Cut the bacon into matchsticks. Pour the sunflower oil into the hot pan and add the bacon. Give it a stir and cook until the bacon is nice and crisp. Add the butter, then the cabbage and 3 tablespoons of water. Stir-fry for 5–7 minutes, until the cabbage is soft and tender. Remove from the heat and keep warm.

To cook the pigeon, heat a large frying pan until very hot. Season the pigeon breasts on each side with salt and freshly ground pepper. Add the sunflower oil to the hot pan, and then the pigeon breasts, with the skinned-side down. Drop in the butter and allow it to foam and brown. After 2 minutes, turn the breasts over to cook for a minute on the other side. Remove the frying pan from the heat, and leave it for 10 minutes in a warm place, to relax the meat.

To serve, heat through the mashed potatoes and warm the sauce. Check the cabbage is warm. Lay out four warmed serving plates. Pour the juice and oil from the pigeon pan into the cabbage mix and stir in well. Check the seasoning. It shouldn't need any salt but may take a little fresh ground pepper. Pop the pigeon into the hot oven for about 1 minute to reheat.

Place a bed of cabbage and bacon on each plate and put a scoop of the mash next to that. Remove the pigeon from the oven and cut each breast in half. Fan the two halved breasts (i.e. four pieces of pigeon) out on each bed of cabbage, spoon over the game sauce and serve.

roast chicken livers with poached leeks

A variation on the classic leeks vinaigrette. Of course, you could just serve the leeks with some Parmesan and the dressing, but you'd be missing out on the fabulous flavours, textures and temperature contrasts that you get when served with the warm livers (I surely do love my temperature contrasts). Try to use fresh, not frozen, livers.

Serves 4

6 long, thin, straight leeks, trimmed
3 tablespoons Vinaigrette (see page 241)
Freshly ground sea salt and freshly ground pepper
6 tablespoons olive oil
175 g (6 oz) fresh chicken livers, trimmed
3 teaspoons rocket leaves
25 g (1 oz) Parmesan shavings
1 tablespoon balsamic vinegar
Fresh bread, to serve

Have handy a bowl of iced water and bring a large pan of salted water to the boil. Cut the leeks into 13 cm (5 in) lengths and drop them into the boiling water. Poach them until tender (this will take about 8 minutes). Lift them out with a slotted spoon and put them straight into the iced water (this stops the cooking and, at the same time, retains the colour).

Once cooled in the iced water (about 5 minutes later) remove, wrap in a tea towel, and gently wring out excess water. Cut each leek into 2.5 cm (1 in) lengths, place in a shallow serving dish and pour the vinaigrette over them. Season with a touch of salt and a generous grind of pepper. Leave for at least 30 minutes to marinate. (I've even, on occasion, left them overnight, and although they lose a bit of colour, they still taste wonderful.)

To serve, heat a frying pan until hot, splash in 3 tablespoons of the olive oil and drop in the chicken livers. Fry until nicely browned, then turn and season with salt and pepper. Keep frying until the other sides have a nice bit of colour on them (this should take about 4 minutes). Pull the pan off the heat, lift out the livers and place them on top of the leeks.

Fling the rocket leaves into the frying pan and coat them in the hot juices. Tip them out on to the livers and scatter the Parmesan over the top. Finally, drizzle over the remaining oil and the balsamic vinegar.

Either serve in the dish and let the guests help themselves, or divide between four serving plates. Have plenty of fresh bread handy to serve alongside.

wood pigeon salad with crispy parsnips and lentils

This warm salad combines the earthy, autumnal flavours of lentils with wood pigeon, which is available all year round and is greatly underrated. Scottish country wood pigeon is not at all the same thing as the unpopular urban denizen of Trafalgar Square! Pigeon breasts are becoming increasingly widely available, saving you all the faff of plucking and boning. This dish was an all-time favourite at my first restaurant, Braeval.

Serves 4

50 g (2 oz) Puy lentils, soaked overnight

140–175 g (5–6 oz) parsnips, thinly sliced lengthwise (use a potato peeler)

Sunflower oil, for deep-frying, plus 1 tablespoon for the wood pigeon

4 wood pigeon breasts, skinned and boned

Freshly ground sea salt and freshly ground pepper

140–175 g (5–6 oz) mixed salad leaves

3 tablespoons Vinaigrette (see page 241)

Drain the lentils, put them in a saucepan with just enough water to cover and cook them very slowly for 8–10 minutes, until tender. Drain the lentils again and put them in a bowl. Keep them warm until required.

Heat the oil in a heavy-based saucepan or deep-fat fryer to 190°C/375°F or until a bread cube turns golden in 20 seconds and rises to the surface. Deep-fry the thin parsnip slices until golden. Drain and leave them on a sheet of kitchen paper until required.

Season the pigeon breasts with salt and pepper. Heat a frying pan until it's hot. Drop in the extra tablespoon of sunflower oil and pan-fry the pigeon breasts for approximately 2 minutes each side. Allow them to rest in the pan in a warm place for at least 10 minutes.

In a large bowl, toss the salad leaves with the vinaigrette and the lentils. Slice the pigeon breasts thinly – about a dozen slices per breast (they should still be very pink inside) – and add them to the bowl of leaves. Carefully toss together with your hands and then divide between four plates. Top each mound of leaves with a handful of fried parsnip shreds. Serve immediately, before it all goes soggy!

roast mallard breast with root vegetables and a game sauce

Mallard are leaner and tastier than farmed duck, though smaller, and are in season from September to January. However, I usually don't buy them until about the end of October, when the birds have a bit more weight on them. They are prolific in the Stirling area of Scotland – and almost tame – and are at their best and cheapest around Christmas. If I am faced with a choice between mallard and turkey, mallard wins every time. One breast weighs about 175 g (6 oz) and is a perfect-sized portion. The meat is dark and rich but not too gamey. The only drawback is that mallard fly most of the time, unlike reared ducks, and so have small, underdeveloped legs. I just bung these in with the carcasses to make seriously good duck stock. Get your butcher or game-dealer to prepare your birds for you and ask him for the bones for making a stock, which you will need for the sauce.

Serves 4

1 quantity Roasted Root Vegetables
(see page 176)

2 tablespoons sunflower oil

4 mallard breasts, boned

Freshly ground sea salt and
freshly ground pepper

Mini Potato Fondants (see page 168) or
Perfect Mashed Potatoes (see
page 165), to serve

FOR THE SAUCE

150 ml (¼ pint) ruby port

150 ml (¼ pint) red wine

450 ml (16 fl oz) duck or Chicken Stock
(see page 236)

1 teaspoon redcurrant jelly

25 g (1 oz) cold butter, diced

To make the sauce, put the port and the red wine in a small saucepan and reduce until it's nearly disappeared. Add the stock and redcurrant jelly and reduce it by half. Add the butter and shake the pan until the butter dissolves, but don't let it boil. Keep the sauce warm.

Keep the root vegetables warm in a cool oven.

To cook the mallard, you need to heat a large frying pan until hot. Add the sunflower oil and heat it until smoking. Season the mallard breasts with salt and pepper and then add them to the pan, skin-side up. Cook for 2 minutes, then turn skin-side down and cook for a further 5–10 minutes over a medium heat, depending on how thick the breast is and how pink you like your duck. Turn skin-side up once more, remove the pan from the heat and allow the mallard breasts to relax in the pan in a warm place for 10–30 minutes.

To serve, reheat the potatoes, if necessary, and warm the sauce through. Taste to check the seasoning before popping the mallard breasts back into a hot oven for 1½ minutes. Lay out four warmed plates and divide the vegetables between them in four neat piles. Place the mini potato fondants or mashed potato garnish next to the vegetables. Carve each breast into three and place next to the vegetables. Spoon over the sauce and serve.

pan-fried mallard with stir-fried greens and a whisky, soy, honey and lemon sauce

Heather honey and whisky give this sauce a real Scottish character that brings out the flavour of the mallard wonderfully well. The secret of success is to get the sweet and sour balance in the sauce just right. If you can't get mallard, use four small Gressingham or female Barbary duck breasts.

Serves 4

600 ml (1 pint) duck stock, made from mallard carcasses, or Chicken Stock (see page 236)

2 tablespoons whisky

1 tablespoon good heather honey

1 tablespoon light soy sauce

1 tablespoon lemon juice

Freshly ground sea salt and freshly ground pepper

4 mallard breasts, boned

Sunflower oil

4 spring onions, halved lengthwise

85 g (3 oz) fine green beans

85 g (3 oz) asparagus tips

85 g (3 oz) sugar-snap peas

25 g (1 oz) cold butter, cubed

Perfect Mashed Potatoes (see page 165) or buttered noodles, to serve

In a small saucepan, boil the stock vigorously until reduced to 125 ml (4 fl oz). Add the whisky, honey, soy sauce, lemon juice and seasoning and set aside.

Season the mallard breasts well. Heat a large frying pan with a lid until hot, add a splash of sunflower oil, and then the breasts, skin-side down. Cook for 4–5 minutes, until crisp and brown. Cook on the other side for 2–4 minutes, leaving the centres pink. Remove, place on a clean plate and leave in a warm place for 10 minutes.

Add a little more oil to the frying pan, if necessary, then add the spring onions, beans, asparagus tips and sugar-snap peas and stir-fry over a high heat for 1–2 minutes. Add 2 tablespoons of water, cover and leave to sit in a warm place for 3 minutes to finish cooking. Season well.

Bring the sauce back to the boil, lower the heat and whisk in the butter. Check for seasoning.

To serve, carve each mallard breast diagonally into slices. Divide the vegetables between four warm serving plates, arrange the mallard on top, and then pour the sauce around. Serve with mashed potatoes or buttered noodles.

confit duck legs with spring greens

A great way to cook duck legs until meltingly soft. The legs are salted, to draw out excess moisture, and then they are simmered for a long time in more duck fat flavoured with herbs; my favourite means for this cooking process is a slow-cooker. The legs are then crisped in the oven, which releases more fat, and the result is golden, crispy legs with tender, flavoursome meat. In France, this was a traditional way to preserve duck for the winter months. This is an occasion to use legs from a large farmed French duck, not wild duck.

Serves 8

1 tablespoon fine sea salt

8 duck legs

1 head of garlic, roughly chopped

A couple of thyme sprigs

A couple of bay leaves

450 g (1 lb) rendered duck fat (available from supermarkets)

2 tablespoons light soy sauce

4 tablespoons runny honey

25 g (1 oz) butter

750 g (1 lb 10 oz) cabbage or spring greens, shredded

½ teaspoon ground cumin

Freshly ground sea salt and freshly ground pepper

The day before, prepare the duck. Take a small roasting tin and cover the base with the tablespoon of fine sea salt. Lay the duck legs on top and rub the salt into them all over. Turn the legs skin-side up. Tuck the garlic, thyme and bay leaves among the legs. Cover with clingfilm and pop in the fridge overnight.

The next day, heat the duck fat in a pan large enough to accommodate the legs or heat a slow-cooker to high for 20 minutes and add the duck fat. Meanwhile, take the duck legs from the fridge, rub the excess salt off the legs and rinse under running water. Pat the legs dry, taking care to remove as much moisture as possible. If you're canny like me, pick out the garlic and herbs, rinse and pat dry. Lower the legs into the melted fat and add the herbs and garlic for more flavour. Making sure the fat covers the legs, put on the lid and cook on auto for 8 hours. If you're not using a slow-cooker, cover and cook over a low-to-medium heat for 3 hours. The surface of the fat should barely tremble during cooking.

When ready, preheat the oven to 220°C/425°F/Gas 7. Lift the legs from the pot, pat dry, and lay them on a wire rack set over a roasting tin, skin-side up. Baste with a mixture of the soy sauce and honey. Roast at the top of the oven for 5–10 minutes, until the skin is crisp and golden.

Meanwhile, melt the butter in a hot frying pan and sauté the cabbage or greens until softened but not coloured. Stir in the cumin, salt and pepper.

To serve, place a generous portion of the greens in the centre of a plate and top with a confit duck leg. Boil the remaining soy and honey mixture together and drizzle over or around the duck. Serve with Rösti Potatoes (see page 166) or Perfect Basmati Rice (see page 249).

pheasant with caramelized apples, chestnuts and cider

There are still many sporting estates in Scotland where pheasant is shot. Pheasant comes into season in October but it's best to wait to buy it until December, since the price falls dramatically then (and the birds are nice and plump). The main problem with cooking pheasant is that (like pigeon) it has very little fat and so is prone to becoming dry. This dish has a nice creamy sauce that moistens the pheasant and it's probably what I'll be having for Christmas dinner. I use vacuum-packed chestnuts – not quite as good as the real thing, but a lot easier. I like to eat this with roast potatoes.

Serves 4

2 Granny Smith apples

4 pheasant breasts, weighing 140–175 g (5–6 oz), skinned and boned

Freshly ground sea salt and freshly ground pepper

1 tablespoon sunflower oil

25 g (1 oz) butter

1 teaspoon icing sugar

16 vacuum-packed chestnuts

300 ml (½ pint) dry cider

300 ml (½ pint) game, pigeon or pheasant stock, or Chicken Stock (see page 236)

150 ml (¼ pint) double cream

2 tablespoons roughly chopped fresh chervil or a mixture of parsley and a tiny bit of tarragon

A little lemon juice

Cheat's Roast Potatoes (see page 166) or Proper Roast Potatoes (see page 167), to serve

Peel, core and quarter the apples. Season the pheasant breasts with salt and pepper. Heat a large frying pan until it's nice and hot. Add the sunflower oil and half the butter to the hot pan. When the butter is foaming, add the pheasant breasts and cook for 4–5 minutes on each side, until lightly coloured. Remove them from the pan and keep warm on a warmed plate.

Add the rest of the butter and the apples to the pan, then sprinkle over the icing sugar and gently fry the apples for 3–4 minutes, until browned and glazed. Remove the apples from the heat and keep warm with the pheasant breasts.

Now add the chestnuts to the pan, increase the heat to high and stir until the chestnuts are coated with the butter from the pan. Add the cider and reduce until it's almost disappeared. Add the stock and again reduce, this time by about two-thirds. Add the cream and bring it back to the boil.

Return the pheasant breasts, the apples and any juices they have released to the pan. Warm everything through for 2–3 minutes. Add a tablespoon of the chopped herbs and season the sauce with salt and lemon juice to taste.

To serve, distribute the roast potatoes between four warmed serving plates. Place a pheasant breast on each plate and spoon over the apple and chestnuts. Pour the sauce over and sprinkle with the other tablespoon of herbs.

Note: I like to serve this sometimes with shredded Brussels sprouts tossed with pancetta – a completely different matter from the usual soggy boiled sprouts! Just finely shred the sprouts, fry some cubed pancetta (or bacon) in a pan until the fat runs and it starts to go crisp, fling in the sprouts and stir-fry for 3–4 minutes, until just wilting. Season well and serve.

pheasant breasts with drambuie, mushrooms and tarragon

Whilst this may appear quite similar to the Pheasant with Caramelized Apples, Chestnuts and Cider (see page 134) the flavours are very different: the Drambuie, a whisky and honey liqueur, gives it a real Scottish taste. Cooking pheasant needn't be a grand affair, nor should it be reserved for Sunday lunch. You can pick up pheasant breasts very cheaply around Christmas time and this recipe couldn't be easier (you could use chicken or guinea fowl instead). Pheasant can be a bit dry, especially if overcooked, so it works very well with a sweet, creamy sauce like this one. The tarragon adds a subtle extra layer of flavour. Serve with buttered kale flavoured with garlic and some Mini Potato Fondants (see page 168).

Serves 4

4 pheasant breasts, weighing about 140 g (5 oz) each, skinned

Freshly ground sea salt and freshly ground pepper

2 tablespoons sunflower oil

25 g (1 oz) butter

175 g (6 oz) chestnut mushrooms, thickly sliced

75 ml (2½ fl oz) Drambuie

450 ml (16 fl oz) pheasant stock or Chicken Stock (see page 236)

150 ml (¼ pint) double cream

1 teaspoon lemon juice

1 tablespoon chopped fresh tarragon

Season the pheasant breasts well on both sides. Heat a large frying pan. Add the sunflower oil and half the butter and, when the butter foams, add the pheasant breasts and cook them for 4–5 minutes on each side, until nicely browned and cooked through. The breasts should still be moist in the centre; be careful not to let them dry out. Remove from the pan and keep warm.

Add the remaining butter and the mushrooms to the pan and cook for a couple of minutes, until lightly browned. Now add the Drambuie and the stock and cook over a high heat until the liquid has reduced by half. Stir in the cream and lemon juice and bring to the boil.

Return the pheasant breasts to the pan, together with any juices, and stir in the tarragon. Bring back to the boil and check the seasoning.

Place one breast on each of four warmed serving plates and spoon the sauce over to serve.

perfect steak and chips

With a dish as simple as this, it's important to use the very best ingredients. For the steaks, I use rib-eye, which comes from the end of the sirloin and has a swirl of white fat through it – this not only imparts flavour but also keeps the meat moist during high-temperature cooking. The steaks must come from the best-quality carcasses, preferably native-bred, grass-fed, Scottish beef, that's been hung for at least 21 days. For the chips, I like the dense, floury texture of Golden Wonder or Kerr's Pink, two traditional Scottish potato varieties, but others seem to prefer chips made from Maris Piper potatoes.

Serves 2

2 rib-eye steaks, weighing about 200 g (8 oz) each

Freshly ground sea salt and freshly ground pepper

2 tablespoons sunflower oil

25 g (1 oz) butter

Chips (see page 167), to serve

The Perfect Mixed Salad (see page 178), to serve

Make the chips first, then tip them into a bowl lined with kitchen paper, dab them dry and keep warm in the oven with the door slightly ajar.

Place a large heavy frying pan on a high heat. Season the steaks well. Add the sunflower oil to the hot pan. When it starts to smoke, add the steaks, and then fling in the butter and allow it to foam and cover both steaks. It's important to leave the steaks: resist the temptation to move them around! After 2–3 minutes, blood will start to appear on the top; they're now ready to turn. Cook for another 2–3 minutes. If your steaks have a particularly fatty edge, use a set of tongs, hold the steak on its side and press the fatty edge into the pan to allow it to colour.

Remove the steaks and place on a metal tray in a warm place for 2–3 minutes to rest. Take the chips out of the oven and place on warm serving plates. Serve the steaks with the chips and a mixed salad.

Enjoy with a glass of gutsy, fruity red wine.

warm salad of roast beef with mustard greens and new potatoes

My wife, Holly, has her own organic salad and vegetable garden next to our cookery school, and she grows a huge variety of different salad leaves, including several different kinds of mustard greens. These peppery leaves highlight the wonderful flavour of good Scottish beef in the same way as a dollop of mustard. The addition of a few new potatoes makes this into a perfect main course.

Serves 4

450 g (1 lb) trimmed sirloin of beef
Freshly ground sea salt and freshly ground pepper
2 tablespoons olive oil
25 g (1 oz) butter
450 g (1 lb) baby new potatoes
2–3 tablespoons mayonnaise
1 tablespoon horseradish sauce
200 g (8 oz) mustard greens or spinach
1 tablespoon balsamic vinegar

Preheat the oven to 230°C/450°F/Gas 8.

Heat an ovenproof frying pan until very hot. Season the beef well, add the oil to the pan and pop in the beef. Brown well on all sides and then add the butter. Now put the frying pan into the oven, making sure that the beef is fat-side down. Cook for 12–15 minutes. Remove the beef from the oven and leave to stand in a warm place until it has relaxed and released some of its juices into the pan. This will take at least 30 minutes, but you could leave the beef to stand for up to 2 hours, provided it's not in too hot a place.

Meanwhile, cook the potatoes in boiling, salted water until tender. Drain and leave to go cold.

Thickly slice the potatoes and put them in a mixing bowl with the mayonnaise, horseradish sauce and some seasoning. Mix well to coat the potatoes.

Finely shred the mustard greens, add to the potatoes and mix well again. Divide the mixture between four serving plates.

Lift the beef onto a carving board. Use a very sharp carving knife to cut it into very thin slices. Fold these and pile them on top of the potato and mustard greens mixture.

Keep the juices that are released and scrape them back into the frying pan. Add the balsamic vinegar (do not heat the pan) and mix well. Now spoon the hot oily juices over the beef and serve at once.

roast fillet of beef with shallots, mushrooms and red wine gravy

Without a doubt, pure-bred, grass-fed, Scottish beef is the best there is. In Scotland, these hardy wee beasts spend most of the time outdoors feeding on grass, which makes some of them not far from being organic. Aberdeen Angus, Highland, Shorthorn or Galloway are my preferred breeds. Properly treated and hung for at least 21 days, this is the tastiest beef you can buy. However, even the meat from a continental cross animal, when properly hung, will be fine for this dish. But do make the effort to get native beef if you can. Ask your butcher to cut the steaks from the centre of the fillet and get him to trim off the gristle and 'chain' and give you the meaty trimmings.

Serves 4

2 tablespoons sunflower oil

4 slices of beef fillet, trimmings reserved, weighing 140–175 g (5–6 oz) each

12 whole peeled shallots, trimmings and skins reserved

1 thyme sprig

1 bay leaf

5 black peppercorns, crushed

300 ml (½ pint) red wine

400 ml (14 fl oz) Chicken and Beef Stock (see page 238)

85 g (3 oz) butter

1 tablespoon icing sugar

Freshly ground sea salt and freshly ground pepper

A squeeze of lemon juice

20 nice mushrooms (preferably chanterelles or morels, but whole brown buttons will do)

Mini Potato Fondants (see page 168), to serve

To make the gravy, heat a large frying pan, add half the sunflower oil and fry the beef trimmings until browned. Add the shallot trimmings and skins, thyme, bay leaf and crushed peppercorns and cook them on a medium heat until nicely coloured. Pour in the wine and slosh it about a bit (this 'deglazes' the pan), before reducing it until all the liquid has gone. Add the chicken and beef stock and gently simmer until thickened. This will take approximately 30 minutes.

Pass everything through a fine sieve and allow the gravy to stand. (It could be made a day in advance and left to stand overnight in the fridge.) Skim any fat off the top.

Now poach the shallots in boiling, salted water until tender (approximately 10 minutes) and drain them. Fry them in a third of the butter with the odd dusting of icing sugar (to help caramelization) and continue cooking over a low-to-medium heat until the shallots are golden brown and tender (there is nothing worse than an undercooked shallot); this will take 15–20 minutes. Keep them warm, or allow them to cool and reheat them in a hot oven when needed. Season and add a squeeze of lemon juice just before serving.

To cook the mushrooms, heat a large frying pan until it's hot and add another third of the butter. Fry the mushrooms for 4–5 minutes, until browned. Season with salt, pepper and the lemon juice. These can also be cooled and reheated.

Now for the beef fillet. Season the steaks well with salt and freshly ground pepper. Heat an ovenproof, heavy-based frying pan until very hot and add the rest of the sunflower oil – the oil should smoke. Quickly add the steaks and the rest of the butter and get some good colour on them: 2 minutes on each side for good and rare. For medium or more well done, place them in a hot oven for further cooking. Approximate cooking times are: medium rare, 2–3 minutes; medium, 4–5 minutes; well done, at least 10 minutes. Allow the meat to relax in a warm place for a minimum of 10 minutes or up to 30 minutes (after which the steaks will need 1½ minutes or so in a hot oven to reheat). Reheat the potatoes, shallots and mushrooms, if necessary. Reheat the gravy.

To serve, place the meat on one side of warmed serving plates and the mini potato fondants on the other. Arrange the shallots and mushrooms around them. Pour the sauce over and around the meat and mushrooms.

beef and mushroom stew with mustard mash

This is the kind of food that I was brought up with, and a good stew is still one of my favourite things to eat. When I'm making stews at home I always make a huge batch, so I can freeze portions, which is my version of fast food.

Serves 4

50 g (2 oz) butter

2 onions, sliced

450 g (1 lb) shoulder steak, trimmed and cut into 2 cm (^{3}/$_4$ in) cubes (or larger)

25 g (1 oz) plain flour, seasoned with salt, pepper and 1 tablespoon paprika

I tablespoon sunflower oil

100 g (4 oz) streaky bacon in one piece, cut into lardons (short strips) 5 mm (^{1}/$_4$ in) thick

200 g (8 oz) chestnut mushrooms, halved

400 ml (14 fl oz) bottle of Scottish ale or 200 ml (7 fl oz) red wine and 200 ml (7 fl oz) water or Chicken and Beef Stock (see page 238)

Freshly ground sea salt and freshly ground pepper

2 tablespoons chopped fresh parsley

Preheat the oven to 150°C/300°F/Gas 2.

Melt half the butter in a flameproof casserole dish. Add the onions and fry over a medium heat for about 10 minutes, until nicely golden.

Meanwhile, put the beef steak into a polythene bag with the seasoned flour and toss together so that it becomes well coated.

Heat a large frying pan until very hot. Add the sunflower oil, then the bacon, and stir-fry for a few minutes, until a rich golden colour. Remove with a slotted spoon and add to the onions in the casserole. Now add the mushrooms to the frying pan and brown for a couple of minutes, then add to the casserole. Add the remaining butter to the frying pan and brown the beef well on all sides. Transfer to the casserole.

Now add the beer or wine and water or stock mix to the frying pan, bring to the boil and scrape up all the browned bits from the bottom of the pan – these will help to flavour the sauce. Pour this into the casserole, add plenty of seasoning, especially pepper, and mix together well.

Cover the casserole with a tight-fitting lid and bake for 1–1½ hours. Now all you have to do is stir in the chopped parsley, check the seasoning and serve with lots of Perfect Mashed Potatoes (see page 165) with a tablespoon of wholegrain mustard stirred through and some green vegetables.

peppered fillet of beef with whisky sauce

This simple dish is a real masterpiece. A prime fillet steak is coated in cracked pepper and carefully cooked, then coated in rich meaty juices with more than a hint of whisky. Just that. Heaven. Serve with home-made Chips (see page 167) and a big bowl of The Perfect Mixed Salad (see page 178).

Serves 4

3 tablespoons black peppercorns

4 fillet steaks, weighing about 175 g (6 oz) each

4 teaspoons Dijon mustard

Freshly ground sea salt and freshly ground pepper

2 tablespoons sunflower oil

50 g (2 oz) butter

50 ml (2 fl oz) blended whisky

4 tablespoons Chicken and Beef Stock (see page 238) or 1 beef stock cube dissolved in 4 tablespoons boiling water

4 tablespoons double cream

Crush the peppercorns coarsely in a coffee grinder. Tip the pepper into a fine sieve and shake out all the powder – this is very important because the powder will make the steaks far too spicy. (Alternatively simply grind enough pepper to coat the steaks using a pepper grinder.) Now spread the peppercorns over a small plate. Smear both sides of the steaks with the Dijon mustard and coat them in the crushed peppercorns. Only season with salt now, because salting first would draw the moisture out from the steak, thus preventing the pepper from sticking to the meat. Set aside.

Heat a large frying pan until hot. Add the sunflower oil and then the steaks and give them a couple of minutes on either side (a bit longer if you don't like your meat so rare). Do not move them around once they are in the pan or the peppercorn crust will fall off – the aim is to produce a good crusty coating on each surface.

Now add the butter to the pan and allow it to colour to nut brown, basting the steaks with the buttery juices as you go. Transfer the steaks to a baking tray and leave in a warm place.

Add the whisky to the pan and boil over a high heat for 1 minute – the alcohol must be boiled off. A word of warning – the whisky is liable to burst into flames. If this worries you, have a large lid handy to whack on the pan. Then add the stock, bring back to the boil and pour in the cream. Scrape and stir together any gooey bits from the bottom of the pan. When it boils fiercely, it's ready. Pour any juices from the steak back into the sauce and place a steak on each plate. Spoon the sauce over the steaks and serve.

braised oxtail

I cook this in a slow-cooker, but you can just as easily cook it conventionally in a big casserole dish or, for speed, use a pressure-cooker. This is a really simple braising dish made with a fantastically well-flavoured cut of beef – oxtail. Get your butcher to prepare the oxtail for you. Not only is it cheap but, when slow-cooked for hours, it becomes incredibly tender, with a rich gravy. Oxtail is best served with a generous dollop of creamy mash and a crisp green vegetable, such as Savoy cabbage or kale.

Serves 6

2 kg (4 lb 8 oz) oxtail pieces, 1 cm (½ in), on the bone

4 tablespoons plain white flour, seasoned

3 tablespoons olive oil

3 carrots, peeled and chopped into 1 cm (½ in) pieces

1 large onion, chopped

4 celery sticks, chopped

2 leeks, chopped

1 large thyme sprig

1 bay leaf

1 garlic clove, crushed

125 ml (4 fl oz) red wine

1.2 litres (2 pints) boiling hot Chicken and Beef Stock (see page 238) or stock made from water and 2 beef stock cubes

400 g can of chopped tomatoes

Chopped parsley, to serve

Preheat the slow-cooker, if using, on high for 20 minutes.

Toss the oxtail pieces in the seasoned flour. Heat half the olive oil in a hot frying pan and fry the oxtail pieces in batches until brown on all sides. Add to the slow-cooker or casserole dish.

Heat the remaining oil in the same frying pan and add the vegetables. Fry these until they're just colouring and then add the thyme, bay leaf and garlic and fry for a minute or so more. Add to the oxtail in the slow-cooker or casserole dish.

Deglaze the frying pan with the red wine, loosening the sediment from the bottom of the pan, and then add half the stock and the tomatoes and bring to the boil. Pour over the meat and vegetables in the slow-cooker or casserole dish and then pour in the remaining boiling stock. Cover with the lid and cook undisturbed on auto for 7–10 hours, or cook conventionally for 2–3 hours.

Spoon any fat off the braised oxtail before serving. For a hearty family meal, serve as it is, sprinkled liberally with chopped parsley, or with Perfect Mashed Potatoes (see page 165) and Wilted Greens (see page 175).

casseroled lamb with red wine and rosemary

Scottish lamb shoulder represents fabulous value for money and when it comes to braising it is my cut of choice. This dish partners Scottish lamb with some of its best friends – tomatoes, rosemary and garlic – with excellent results. If you have a large enough casserole dish, it is just as easy to make a double quantity and freeze half for a future feast. Have a good red Rioja on standby to complement the rich juices of the sauce.

Serves 4

650 g (1 lb 7 oz) boned shoulder of lamb, cut into 2 cm (³/₄ in) cubes

2 tablespoons plain white flour, seasoned

1 tablespoon olive oil

25 g (1 oz) butter

1 tablespoon tomato purée

300 ml (¹/₂ pint) red wine

300 ml (¹/₂ pint) Chicken and Beef Stock (see page 238)

Leaves from 1 sprig of fresh rosemary, finely chopped

1 garlic clove, crushed

1 carrot, cut into 1 cm (¹/₂ in) dice

1 onion, cut into 1 cm (¹/₂ in) dice

2 celery sticks, cut into 1 cm (¹/₂ in) dice

Freshly ground sea salt and freshly ground pepper

Preheat the oven to 180°C/350°F/Gas 4.

Put the cubes of lamb in a plastic bag with the seasoned flour and give the bag a good shake so that the meat becomes well coated with the flour. Heat a large frying pan until very hot. Add the oil and the butter, and then the lamb and fry over a high heat, stirring now and then, until all the pieces of lamb are well browned. Don't crowd the pan; cook in batches if necessary. Transfer to a casserole dish and set aside.

Add the tomato purée and red wine to the pan and bring to the boil, scraping up all the little bits that have stuck to the bottom. Pour this into the casserole dish and add the stock, rosemary, garlic and diced vegetables. Add a little seasoning, cover with a tight-fitting lid and bake for 1¹/₂ hours or until tender. (If using a slow-cooker, cook on auto for about 8 hours.)

Remove from the oven and check the seasoning. Serve with penne pasta or new potatoes and Wilted Greens (see page 175).

roast leg of lamb with garlic and rosemary

Choose dark-fleshed lamb with a good covering of firm white fat that will add flavour and help keep the roast moist in the fierce heat of the oven. In Scotland we are blessed with a preponderance of hill lamb, much of it almost organic, save for one bath in a sheep dip. Personally, I am not overly fond of spring lamb as I find it a little bland although very tender. I like my lamb to be approaching its first birthday, when it is known as 'hogget' and has had time to develop real flavour. When we cooked this for the photograph, we were driven crazy by the smell of lamb, garlic and rosemary wafting out of the oven! It really is one of cooking's great combinations.

Serves 6

2–3 large branches of rosemary

4 large garlic cloves

1.8 kg (4 lb) leg of lamb

Olive oil

Freshly ground sea salt and freshly ground pepper

4 tablespoons red wine or water

Baby Plum Tomato and Broad Bean Stew (see page 180), to serve

Dauphinoise Potatoes (see page 164) or Perfect Mashed Potatoes (see page 165) or new potatoes, to serve

Preheat the oven to 220°C/425°F/Gas 7.

Pull small sprigs off the rosemary. Cut the garlic into thick slivers or sticks. Be bold and score the meat deeply in a wide criss-cross pattern using a sharp knife (about 2 cm/¾ in deep). Rub the whole leg with a good slug of olive oil and set in a roasting tin. Then tuck as much rosemary and garlic into the criss-cross cuts as you like. Grind over some salt and loads of pepper. If you've got any rosemary left over, tuck it well under the meat where it will give out all the flavour and won't burn. Add the red wine or water and bung it in the oven and sear for 15 minutes.

Then turn the oven down to 180°C/350°F/Gas 4 and roast for a further hour, basting from time to time. The meat should be well cooked on the outside, with crunchy bits, and rosy-pink near the bone. Remove the meat from the oven, transfer to a warm carving dish, cover loosely with foil and leave to rest in a warm place for 15 minutes before carving.

While the meat is resting, you can, if you like, spoon the fat from the juices left in the pan, add a little red wine or water, and deglaze scraping all the sticky bits up from the base of the tin. Taste and season; this will be a terrific concentrated 'God's gravy' to spoon over the carved meat.

Serve with the tomato and broad bean stew and dauphinoise, mashed or new potatoes.

roast loin of lamb with tomato and basil sauce

Scottish lamb is wonderful. Try to get the native organic black-face breeds or Shetland lamb. It's at its most tender from the end of May until midsummer, after which it develops a deep flavour; personally I like to sacrifice tenderness for flavour. I've chosen to use loin here, which is a long strip of meat from alongside the backbone and, in fact, is the meat from the 'eye' of a lamb chop (i.e. with no bone or gristle). Ask the butcher for one loin from the saddle of the lamb with all the fat and sinew trimmed away, leaving you with a nice piece of lean meat. Keep the meaty trimmings and some rib bones for the sauce. My favourite potato accompaniment to this dish is a gratin dauphinoise.

Serves 4

450 g (1 lb) skinless, boneless loin of lamb

Freshly ground sea salt and
freshly ground pepper

2 tablespoons sunflower oil

2 tablespoons softened butter

1 tablespoon olive oil

250 g (9 oz) spinach

4 portions Dauphinoise Potatoes
(see page 164)

FOR THE SAUCE

5–6 rib bones

25 g (1 oz) butter

50–80 g (2–3 oz) lamb trimmings

2 shallots, sliced

2 garlic cloves, crushed

1 bay leaf

1 thyme sprig

1 tablespoon tomato purée

150 ml (¼ pint) red wine

400 ml (14 fl oz) Chicken and Beef Stock
(see page 238)

1 teaspoon arrowroot

8 large fresh basil leaves

2 ripe tomatoes, roughly chopped

Preheat the oven to 230°C/450°F/Gas 8. To make the sauce, put the rib bones in a roasting tin and roast for 20 minutes, until browned. Heat a frying pan until hot. Add half the butter and, when foaming brown, add the lamb trimmings, shallots, garlic, bay leaf, thyme and some pepper and cook until they are all are well browned.

Add the tomato purée and cook until dry. Slosh in the wine to deglaze the pan. Reduce it until all of the liquid has gone. Add the bones and stir to coat and then add the stock and 200 ml (7 fl oz) water. Bring to the boil and simmer very slowly until thickened (this will take approximately 45 minutes).

Pass the sauce through a fine sieve and skim off any fat. Thicken with the arrowroot and keep warm.

Now roast the lamb. Season the loin with salt and freshly ground pepper. Heat a frying pan until it's hot. Heat the sunflower oil and butter and then add the loin. Fry until well coloured all over and place in the preheated oven for 3–4 minutes, depending on how pink you like your lamb – it should just start to become firm to the touch. Allow the meat to relax in a warm place for a minimum of 10 minutes before serving.

To serve, heat a large saucepan and add the olive oil. Add the spinach and cook quickly. Season the spinach and divide it between each plate. Cut three to five rounds of meat per person and place them on top of the spinach. Chop the basil and add it, along with the chopped tomatoes, to the sauce. Check the seasoning before pouring the sauce over and around the lamb. Serve with the dauphinoise potatoes.

roast loin of lamb with spicy couscous and an apricot and mint sauce

The wonderful flavours of spices in North African cookery have a strange fascination for me. I love the combination of spice and sweetness without the heat of chillies and this combination brings out the best in Scottish lamb. Cinnamon should be the dominant flavour in this dish but look out for the clean taste of mint, too. The sauce and the couscous can be made well in advance, if covered and chilled in the fridge.

Serves 4

450 g (1 lb) skinless, boneless loin of lamb

4 tablespoons olive oil

Leaves from 1 large fresh rosemary sprig, chopped

2 garlic cloves, crushed

Freshly ground sea salt and freshly ground pepper

Balsamic Syrup (see page 242), to serve

Flatleaf parsley sprigs, to garnish

FOR THE APRICOT AND MINT SAUCE

25 g (1 oz) butter

85g (3 oz) onion, very thinly sliced

1 garlic clove, crushed

1 teaspoon ground cinnamon

1 teaspoon ground coriander

1/2 level teaspoon ground turmeric

1/2 level teaspoon ground cumin

1 teaspoon light soft brown sugar

50 g (2 oz) no-need-to-soak dried apricots, diced

300 ml (1/2 pint) Chicken Stock (see page 236)

1 tablespoon chopped fresh mint

Place the loin of lamb in a shallow dish. Mix together the olive oil, rosemary and garlic. Pour this over the lamb, cover and chill to marinate for up to 12 hours.

Now make the sauce. Melt the butter in a small pan, add the onion and garlic and fry gently for about 4 minutes, until softened. Add the spices and sugar and cook for 2 minutes, then stir in the dried apricots and stock, cover and simmer gently for 15–20 minutes.

Add the mint and then either give everything a quick blitz with a hand-held blender or liquidize until smooth. If the sauce looks too thick, thin to a pouring consistency with a little more stock. Check the seasoning and keep warm. This can be made ahead and reheated when ready to serve.

For the spicy couscous, melt the butter in a large pan. Add the spices and fry gently for 1 minute. Stir in the sugar and stock and bring the mixture to the boil. Add the raisins, pine nuts and then the couscous, stirring constantly. Remove the pan from the heat, cover with a tight-fitting lid and set aside for 5 minutes, then use a fork to fluff up the grains of couscous.

Lightly stir in the olive oil, lemon juice and chopped coriander. Cover and keep warm. This can also be made ahead and reheated in the microwave before serving.

Heat a large frying pan until hot. Lift the lamb out of the marinade, season with salt and pepper on both sides and then add to the pan and fry for 3–4 minutes on each side, until well browned. Set aside somewhere warm and leave to relax for 10 minutes.

FOR THE COUSCOUS

25 g (1 oz) butter

1 teaspoon ground cinnamon

1 teaspoon ground coriander

½ teaspoon ground cumin

1 tablespoon light soft brown sugar

250 ml (9 fl oz) Chicken Stock (see page 236)

25 g (1 oz) raisins

3 teaspoons pine nuts, toasted

250 g (9 oz) couscous

4 tablespoons olive oil

1 tablespoon lemon juice

2 tablespoons chopped fresh coriander

To serve, put a large scone cutter on a serving plate and spoon some couscous into it, pressing it down well. Remove the scone cutter and repeat with the other three plates. Carve the lamb into thin slices and arrange, slightly overlapping, on top of the couscous. Pour a little of the apricot and mint sauce around the couscous and then trickle the balsamic syrup over, to form an attractive pattern. Garnish with a sprig of flatleaf parsley.

pan-fried lambs' kidneys with mustard sauce and saffron basmati rice

You either love kidneys or you don't. Personally I do – my favourites are lambs' kidneys, and I want them pink inside, not grey. I adore that squidgy texture and heavenly flavour. Mustard is a natural partner and here it is highlighted by a warming aroma of whisky. Basmati rice has a lovely perfume that blends well with the saffron.

Serve 4

175 g (6 oz) Perfect Basmati Rice (see page 249)

Pinch of saffron strands

6 fresh lambs' kidneys

Freshly ground sea salt and freshly ground pepper

1 teaspoon sunflower oil

25 g (1 oz) butter

2 teaspoons whisky

300 ml (½ pint) Beef and Chicken Stock (see page 238)

125 ml (4 fl oz) double cream

1 tablespoon wholegrain mustard

1 tablespoon snipped fresh chives, to garnish

First, follow the recipe for Perfect Basmati Rice on page 249, but add the saffron to the cooking water along with the rice. Drain the rice, once cooked, and keep warm.

Have a large warmed plate handy and heat a large frying pan until it is hot. Halve the kidneys lengthwise, through the gristly bit. Remove the skin and gristle and season the kidney halves. Heat the sunflower oil and half of the butter in the frying pan and put in half the kidneys, cut-side down. Fry until brown. Turn over and repeat (this should take about 4 minutes). Lift the kidneys out and onto the warmed plate. Add the remaining butter to the frying pan and cook the rest of the kidneys.

When all the kidneys have been fried, slosh the whisky into the pan. It should boil off straight away. Add the stock and reduce quickly by about two-thirds. Add the cream and bring back to the boil. Pour the kidney juices from the warmed plate into the frying pan and check the sauce for seasoning. You can hold off serving here, and have a glass of wine and a chat to your pals (I presume you are not eating them all yourself!).

When you're ready to serve, put the kidneys back into the sauce, add the mustard and warm everything through gently until the sauce bubbles. Divide the rice between four plates, making a nice pile in the centre. Place three kidney halves on top of each pile, spoon over the sauce, scatter the chives over and serve immediately.

roast saddle of rabbit with orange and thyme

Readily available all over Scotland, wild rabbit is relatively cheap, lean and, if cooked properly, has a flavour similar to a proper free-range chicken. Most supermarkets sell fresh farmed rabbit portions, which are tender and easy to cook. I prefer the saddle meat cooked on the bone, as it results in a better flavour and texture. Here the rabbit is rubbed with a mixture of orange rind and thyme, to add their perfume to the meat. The saddle is then wrapped in pancetta for extra flavour and to keep it moist, and served with a mustard mash. John Webber, the tutor at Nairns Cook School, adds prunes soaked in whisky for even more flavour.

Serves 4

4 saddles of rabbit, wild or farmed, trimmed

1 teaspoon fresh thyme leaves, plus extra to garnish

2 tablespoons olive oil

Finely grated rind of 1 orange

8 rashers thinly sliced pancetta

1 carrot, peeled and chopped

1 onion, chopped

1 celery stalk, chopped

1 bay leaf

Fresh parsley sprigs, leaves picked and chopped, stalks retained

250 ml (9 fl oz) dry white wine

4 tablespoons Chicken Stock (see page 236)

100 ml (3½ fl oz) double cream

12 prunes, soaked overnight in 4 tablespoons of whisky (optional)

2 tablespoons Dijon mustard

250 g (9 oz) dried tagliatelle

15 g (½ oz) butter

Freshly ground sea salt and freshly ground pepper

If you've got time, do this the day (or even a couple of hours) before. Trim the rabbit saddles of all of the silvery skin on the back, using a small sharp knife (if you leave this on, it will toughen the rabbit). Rub the saddles with half of the thyme leaves and 1 tablespoon of the oil, cover and refrigerate.

The next day, preheat the oven to 220°C/425°F/Gas 7. Sprinkle the saddles with the orange zest and roll 2 rashers of pancetta around each saddle.

Heat a shallow, flameproof casserole and add the remaining oil. Lightly brown the rabbit all over in the oil and then add the vegetables and cook for 1 minute. Add the bay leaf, parsley stalks, the remaining thyme leaves and half the wine. Transfer to the oven and roast for 6 minutes.

Add the remainder of the wine to the casserole, return to the oven uncovered and cook for 6–8 minutes more. Remove from the oven, lift the rabbit onto a plate and keep warm.

Place the casserole on the heat and add the chicken stock. Bring to the simmer and then strain the juices into a clean pan, pressing the vegetables lightly to extract all of the juices. Reduce the stock and juices by half. Then add the double cream and prunes and simmer for 1 minute. Whisk the mustard into the sauce and keep warm until needed.

Cook the tagliatelle according to the packet instructions. When cooked, toss in the butter and season. Place a small pile of pasta on each plate and set a saddle on top of each pile, pouring the sauce over and around the meat. Sprinkle with a little extra chopped fresh thyme.

loin of venison with a game and chocolate sauce

Roe are the smallest and the most tender deer; here I recommend the loin or saddle, which provides a very tender and virtually fat-free piece of meat. Get your butcher to prepare it for you, giving you the two loins and the meaty trimmings. Ask him to chop the rib bones into 2.5 cm (1 in) pieces. The chocolate may seem an odd flavour for a savoury sauce, but bitter chocolate (with 60% or more cocoa solids) complements gamey flavours well, and also gives the sauce a dark gloss. It's not really worth making a smaller quantity of the braised red cabbage, but it freezes well and is delicious with most game.

Serves 4

650 g (1 lb 7 oz) trimmed venison loin, plus saddle bones and trimmings

Freshly ground sea salt and freshly ground pepper

1 tablespoon sunflower oil

25 g (1 oz) butter

Braised Red Cabbage (see page 174), to serve

4 portions Dauphinoise Potatoes (see page 164), to serve

FOR THE GAME SAUCE

Rib bones, chopped, and meaty trimmings

25 g (1 oz) butter

4 shallots, finely sliced

50 g (2 oz) button mushrooms, thinly sliced

1 bay leaf

1 thyme sprig

6 white peppercorns, crushed

¼ bottle red wine

850 ml (1½ pints) Chicken and Beef Stock (see page 238)

1 teaspoon arrowroot

1 tablespoon bitter chocolate, grated

Preheat the oven to 230°C/450°F/Gas 8.

For the sauce, roast the chopped bones in the hot oven for 20 minutes, until nicely browned. Drain off any fat and put the bones to one side. Heat a saucepan (large enough to hold all the bones) and add the butter. Add the meat trimmings and fry until browned. Now add the shallots, mushrooms, bay leaf, thyme, and peppercorns and fry everything until golden.

Add the red wine and reduce until it's nearly gone. Add the bones and the stock (and a little water, if necessary, to ensure the bones are covered) and simmer for approximately 1 hour until well flavoured.

Strain the sauce and allow it to stand for a few minutes. Spoon off any fat, put the stock into a clean pot and reduce it until well flavoured. Then thicken with the arrowroot. You should be left with about 300 ml (½ pint) of sauce.

For the meat, when you are nearly ready to serve, heat a frying pan until it's hot. Season the loin with salt and pepper (you may have to cut them in half to fit the pan). Add the sunflower oil and butter to the pan, then the loins and lightly fry each side for 3–4 minutes, until well browned. Remove the pan to a warm place to relax the meat for at least 10 minutes (but no more than 30 minutes).

Warm four large spoonfuls of the braised red cabbage in a small saucepan. Reheat the sauce. Pour any juices from the relaxing meat into the cabbage, and then reheat the meat in the hot oven for 1½ minutes.

Place a spoonful of cabbage on each of four warmed serving plates, putting the dauphinoise potatoes alongside. Carve the meat into approximately 24 slices and lay six slices on each pile of cabbage. Add the grated chocolate to the heated sauce and whisk it. Check and adjust the seasoning before spooning it over the meat.

saddle of hare with wild rice, game sauce and red onion marmalade

Hare doesn't have a season but is at its best in winter. In the north of Scotland you can find 'winter' or 'arctic' hare, whose fur has turned white to camouflage it against the snow, and these are especially tasty. Each saddle of hare gives two loins and one loin is sufficient for one portion. Get your butcher to bone out the saddles and trim up the loins. He can then also hack up the bones for the stock while he's at it.

Serves 4

2 prepared saddles of hare
(giving you 4 loins)

Freshly ground sea salt and
freshly ground pepper

1 tablespoon sunflower oil

25 g (1 oz) butter

4 tablespoons Red Onion Marmalade
(see page 248), to serve (optional)

Olive oil, to serve

Deep-fried parsley, to garnish (optional)

FOR THE SAUCE

Hare bones and trimmings

1 bay leaf

1 fresh thyme sprig

2 shallots, roughly chopped

1 garlic clove, crushed

50 g (2 oz) button mushrooms,
roughly chopped

2 tablespoons olive oil

6 juniper berries, crushed

150 ml (¼ pint) ruby port

25 g (1 oz) butter, chilled

Preheat the oven to 240°C/475°F/Gas 9.

For the sauce, put the bones, bay leaf, thyme, shallots, garlic, mushrooms, olive oil and juniper berries in a small roasting tin. Roast for 20–25 minutes, stirring now and then, until well browned. Add the port and scrape up all the bits from the bottom of the tin. Tip everything into a saucepan, add water to cover, bring to the boil and simmer for 1 hour.

Pour into a conical strainer or a fine sieve set over another pan and press out all the liquid with the back of a ladle or wooden spoon. Spoon off any fat, then boil vigorously, skimming off any scum, until reduced to 150 ml (¼ pint).

Put the rice into a large pan with 850 ml (1½ pints) of water, the onion, carrot, bay leaf and thyme. Season well, bring to the boil, cover and simmer for about 35 minutes, until tender. Some of the grains will burst but that's OK. Drain, remove the aromatics, cover and keep warm.

Season the hare loins. Heat a frying pan until very hot, add the sunflower oil, butter and the loins and fry for 2–3 minutes on each side, until well browned but still pink in the centre. Leave to rest somewhere warm for 5 minutes.

To serve, gently warm the red onion marmalade in a small pan, if using. Cut the loins into thin slices. Put the rice on four warmed plates and arrange the hare on top. Bring the sauce to the boil and whisk in the butter. Check the seasoning and then pour the sauce around the rice and drizzle some olive oil over. Spoon the marmalade on top and garnish with parsley sprigs, deep-fried in sunflower oil, if using.

FOR THE RICE

200 g (8 oz) wild rice

1 small onion, quartered

1 carrot, sliced

1 bay leaf

1 fresh thyme sprig

pappardelle with hare sauce

In Scotland we are lucky to have a year-round supply of hare from our butchers and game dealers, most of it coming from the sporting estates where the interest is in shooting rather than cooking the hares. Hare is not the nicest of things to prepare – quite bloody – but the resulting slow-cooked sauce is fabulous, so ask your game dealer or butcher to prepare the hare for you. You could substitute rabbit, for a much lighter sauce. This really rich wintry sauce has its origins in Tuscany, where hare is really prized. Tuscans are not famed for making their own pasta, but they will make it specially for this dish.

**Serves 4–6,
depending on the size of the hare**

1 hare, weighing about 1.5 kg
(3 lb 5 oz), jointed

3 tablespoons olive oil

50 g (2 oz) butter

1 onion, finely diced

1 carrot, finely diced

1 celery stick, finely diced

2 garlic cloves, chopped

85 g (3 oz) unsmoked pancetta, diced

Freshly ground sea salt and
freshly ground pepper

300 ml (½ pint) dry red wine

2 tablespoons plain white flour

About 1 litre (1¾ pints) game stock or
Chicken Stock (see page 236)

2 bay leaves

1 teaspoon chopped fresh rosemary

1 tablespoon chopped fresh sage

450 g (1 lb) dried egg pappardelle
or flat noodles

The Perfect Mixed Salad (see page 178),
to serve

There are two ways of preparing this dish. You can take all the meat off the hare with a sharp knife, remove the sinews and cut the meat into small dice-like mince. Alternatively, you can brown the whole joints and simmer in the sauce until well cooked, then remove the meat from the bones and flake it at the end, mixing it into the cooking juices.

Heat the oil and half the butter in a sauté pan and add the chopped onion, carrot, celery and garlic. Stir well and cook gently for about 10 minutes, until soft and beginning to brown.

Add the pancetta and diced or jointed hare, stir well and cook for a couple of minutes over a high heat, until the meat is browned. Season well. Stir in the wine and boil hard to evaporate. Then add the flour and half the stock. Mix well, scraping any sediment lodged on the base of the pan.

Add the herbs and bring to the boil. Turn down the heat, half cover and simmer gently for at least 2 hours, topping up with more stock as necessary, until the meat is very tender and the sauce thick and reduced.

Cook the pappardelle or noodles according to the packet instructions and drain. Toss with the remaining butter and season.

Taste the sauce, season as necessary, and remove the bay leaves. If the meat has been cooked in joints, lift out the joints, flake the meat from the bones with a fork and stir it back into the sauce. The sauce is sometimes liquidized to make it finer. Toss the sauce with the noodles and serve at once. This only needs some dressed salad leaves for a splendid meal.

pork fillet with ham and sage

Purists froth at the mouth at the thought of using anything other than veal to make these delicious little escalopes. However, I am assured by an Italian cook that the Italians often make them with turkey at home. Here I'm using pork fillet, as it is more accessible and cheaper than veal. These really do jump into your mouth as the Italian name, *saltimbocca*, literally 'jump mouth', implies!

Serves 4

450 g (1 lb) pork fillet
Freshly ground sea salt and freshly ground pepper
4 slices Parma ham, halved
16 fresh sage leaves
Plain white flour, seasoned, for dusting
1 tablespoon olive oil
50 g (2 oz) butter
Buttered tagliatelle, to serve
Rocket and Parmesan salad, to serve
Lemon wedges, to serve

Trim the pork fillet of any fat and gristle. Slice crosswise into eight even-sized pieces. Put each piece between sheets of clingfilm, end grain facing up, and beat out thinly, use a rolling pin or a meat mallet to flatten without tearing.

Season each escalope with a little pepper. Lay half a slice of ham on each escalope, put a sage leaf on top and secure through the middle of the whole lot – as if you were making a large stitch – with a cocktail stick. They are *not* rolled up. Dust each of the escalopes with flour on both sides.

Heat the oil in a frying pan, add the butter and wait until foaming. Fry the escalopes four at a time over a high heat, for 1½ minutes, sage-side down. Flip them over and fry for another 30 seconds, until golden brown and tender. Remove and keep warm while you cook the next four.

Serve piping hot, with buttered tagliatelle and a simple rocket and Parmesan salad, and plenty of lemon to squeeze over.

fresh pea and ham risotto with mint

An Italian classic using the best of Scottish ingredients. We grow our own peas and they seem to be well suited to the Scottish climate. My butcher dry cures his own streaky bacon, which I use for this dish. Italian pancetta is a good substitute (most supermarkets now sell it in packets ready-cubed). As always with risotto, use the best risotto rice available – no other rice will do (my preference is for Vialone Nano, but arborio is easier to find). Equally, choose the best Parmesan you can get (Parmigiano Reggiano is the one to look for – Grana Padano is a cheaper alternative). The stock, however, is just dandy made from a good-quality cube. Use a deep heavy-based pan for the risotto as it will allow you to beat in the butter, cheese and mint, without spraying rice all over the kitchen.

Serves 4

About 1.2 litres (2 pints) Chicken Stock (see page 236) or Marinated Vegetable Stock (see page 239)

4 tablespoons olive oil

140 g packet cubed streaky bacon or pancetta

1 onion, finely chopped

1 garlic clove, finely chopped

400 g (14 oz) risotto rice

150 ml (¼ pint) dry white wine

200 g (8 oz) peas, fresh or frozen

50 g (2 oz) butter

Parmesan cheese, finely grated, plus extra to serve (optional)

Freshly ground sea salt and freshly ground pepper

50 g (2 oz) chopped fresh mint, plus extra to serve (optional)

Have the stock at a constant, very gentle simmer in a pan beside your risotto pan – the stock must be at the same temperature as the rice. Have a ladle to hand. Heat the olive oil in the risotto pan. Add the pancetta, onion and garlic and stir-fry over a medium heat, until the pancetta has lightly browned and the onion has become translucent.

Add the rice and stir it around for a couple of minutes until it has become well coated in the oil and is beginning to toast and turn chalky, but not to colour. Add the white wine and boil rapidly for 1 minute, stirring, until it has almost evaporated. This boils off the alcohol, leaving the concentrated flavour of the wine in the rice.

Begin to add the stock a large ladleful at a time, stirring constantly until each ladleful is absorbed into the rice. The creaminess of your risotto comes from the starch in the rice, and the more it is stirred the more starch is released. Continue until the rice is tender and creamy but the grains still firm and on no account chalky in the centre (this should take 15–20 minutes, depending on the type of rice used).

After 15 minutes, add the peas. Just before the rice is cooked, stir in the butter, Parmesan, seasoning and mint, beat well until creamy, then remove the pan from the heat. Cover the pan with a lid and leave to stand for a minute to let the risotto relax (you may have to add another ladle of stock – you're looking for a texture that is yielding but not stiff). Then serve immediately, sprinkled with a little more Parmesan and chopped mint if you wish.

I have an obsession with potatoes, which I am sure I inherited from my father. At home we grow some 20 different varieties every year, which provide us with the most wonderful spuds from mid-June to November. From the tiny floury 'earlies' such as Duke of York, through to the knobbly late-harvester Pink Fir Apple, we have a potato to suit every occasion.

I love the versatility of potatoes and the not-so-humble spud has many guises, from the haute cuisine of creamy, bubbly, golden Dauphinoise Potatoes (see page 164) to the simplicity of new season Ayrshire potatoes served with a little butter and parsley.

I firmly believe there is a best potato variety for every dish. Roast potatoes and chips, for example, need a floury spud with a high potato mass, such as Golden Wonder. Mash, on the other hand, needs a potato that won't fall apart during boiling and here the King Edward excels.

Traditionally, and still the rule for some today, a Scot's plate would be incomplete without potatoes of some form or another piled on the side. Luckily, when it comes to the tattie we Scots have always been inventive. Potato dishes such as Kailkenny (made with kale or cabbage), Clapshot (a blend of mashed spuds and turnip), Rumbledethumps (mashed potato layered with cabbage) and Stovies (see page 173) are just some of the many resourceful and tasty Scottish potato dishes.

We have some of the best weather for growing veg (the worst weather for many other things) and this chapter also includes some ideas for vegetables accompaniments. There's a wide range, from the light summery side dish of Steamed Carrots and Savoy Cabbage (see page 174) to the wonderfully rich, intense flavour of Braised Red Cabbage (see page 174). From Roasted Root Vegetables (see page 176) to The Perfect Mixed Salad (see page 178), there's a vegetable accompaniment for every dish.

potatoes
and vegetables

dauphinoise potatoes

The creamy, garlicky layers of this dish demonstrate the potential of the humble spud.
Potato variety is all-important and I have found that Maris Pipers produce the best result.
This method may not be orthodox but it almost guarantees a good result: the secret of
success is pre-cooking the potato slices in the garlic cream until they release enough
starch to thicken the cream. Watch the first cooking stage carefully. Cook it for too
long and the potatoes fall to bits; too short a time and you've got a runny dauphinoise;
get it just right and it's heaven on a plate! Either serve bubbling and golden straight
from the cooking dish or allow to cool, cut out individual portions and reheat in a low
oven when needed.

Serves 8

25 g (1 oz) butter
1 garlic clove, crushed
Freshly ground sea salt and
freshly ground pepper
300 ml (½ pint) full-cream milk
300 ml (½ pint) double cream
1.25 kg (2 lb 12 oz) potatoes, preferably
Maris Piper or similar

Preheat the oven to 150°C/300°F/Gas 2.

Use the butter to coat a large ovenproof dish. Using the flat side of the knife,
crush the garlic and mash it with a teaspoon of salt. Place in a large pan with
the milk, cream and a good few grindings of pepper and bring to the boil slowly.

Peel and thinly slice the potatoes using a mandolin slicer or in a food processor
– you really can't get them thin enough by hand and, even if you could, you'd
die of boredom doing all this lot! Do not rinse them. Add the potatoes to the pan
and give them a good stir to coat them evenly with the cream and milk, as the
slices often stick together. Bring back to the boil and simmer on a low heat until
the potatoes are almost tender and the potato starch has thickened the milk –
about 15 minutes.

Turn the potatoes into the buttered dish, being careful to leave behind any that
have burnt and are caught at the bottom of the pan. Bake in the oven for 1 hour,
until nicely browned on top. Serve immediately or leave to cool overnight.

To reheat, if necessary, cut the potatoes into squares or use a scone cutter to
make rounds. Lift them out of the cutter, place on a buttered tray and pop into
the oven at 140°C/275°F/Gas 1 for 45 minutes before serving.

perfect mashed potatoes

This is one of my ultimate comfort foods and probably the potato dish I cook most often at home. Mash is essential for fishcakes, gnocchi and potato scones, and the only thing to have with stew, bangers, baked cod and mince, of course! The secret of success in this dish lies in the quality and type of potatoes used (preferably King Edward, Maris Piper or a similar starchy potato). Older spuds work better than new. Mash is great for carrying flavours – try wholegrain mustard, pesto, olive oil, Parmesan and any herb that takes your fancy and, if you're a Lottery winner, try some freshly grated truffle (or truffle paste or even a tiny drizzle of truffle oil).

Serves 4

450 g (1 lb) Maris Piper potatoes, peeled and cut into even-sized pieces

Freshly ground sea salt and freshly ground pepper

3 tablespoons warm milk

25 g (1 oz) butter

Place the potatoes in a pan of salted cold water and bring to the boil. As soon as the water comes to the boil, reduce to a simmer (it's important not to cook the potatoes too quickly), and cook for approximately 20 minutes.

Check the tenderness – the point of a sharp knife should feel little resistance when pushed into the potato. Drain in a colander and return the spuds to the pan to dry out over a low heat for a few minutes.

Mash the potatoes with a potato masher, or pass them through a mouli or ricer into a bowl. Using a wooden spoon, vigorously beat in the warm milk and then, if you're serving them straight away, beat in the butter, making the mash light and fluffy. Alternatively, let the mash cool and then reheat gently when needed, using a little more milk and beating in the butter. Season with salt and pepper before serving.

rösti potatoes

Slightly tricky to make, but worth it, these should be crispy on the outside and soft and buttery on the inside. You should always make them in advance and reheat them, since trying to do them to order can be a tense experience! Use traditional Scottish Golden Wonder potatoes, or another floury variety.

Serves 4

450 g (1 lb) Golden Wonder, Kerr's Pink, Maris Piper or Cyprus potatoes, peeled

75 ml (2½ fl oz) Clarified Butter (see page 247), or olive or vegetable oil

Freshly ground sea salt and freshly ground pepper

Grate the potatoes (using a box grater) onto a clean tea towel. Wring out the excess moisture by twisting the towel tightly. Tip the potatoes into a bowl, add 30 ml (1 fl oz) of the clarified butter or oil and season. You will need to do this quickly or the potato will start to discolour.

Heat the rest of the clarified butter in a medium-sized frying pan. Add the potato mix, pushing down with a spatula to ensure that it evenly covers the pan. Cook at a medium temperature for 8–10 minutes, until you see traces of colour at the edges. Then turn over and cook until the rösti is golden-coloured on both sides (5–6 minutes). Transfer to a wire rack to cool.

When cooled, cut into quarters. Rösti potatoes can be made up to 6 hours in advance and left at room temperature until ready to use. They should be reheated in a moderate oven (180°C/350°F/Gas 4) for 5 minutes.

cheat's roast potatoes

I always feel a bit cheated if I'm given boiled and then deep-fried 'roast' potatoes in a restaurant. However, I have discovered that, if you bake rather than boil them, before deep-frying, the roasties have a fluffier texture inside and are much more like the real thing – in fact my mum prefers them, and always makes them this way.

Serves 4

4 large Golden Wonder or similar floury potatoes

Sunflower oil, for deep-frying

Freshly ground sea salt and freshly ground pepper

Preheat the oven to 200°C/400°F/Gas 6. Place the potatoes on a baking tray and bake for 1½ hours.

Cool, peel and cut into 7.5 cm (3 in) pieces.

Heat the oil in a deep-fat fryer or heavy-based saucepan to 180°C/350°F. Deep-fry the potato pieces for about 8 minutes, until crisp and golden.

Drain on kitchen paper, season with salt and pepper and serve immediately.

proper roast potatoes

My wonderful wife Holly, a great cook and a wizard at roast dinners, taught me how to make proper roast spuds – the secret is in roughing up the par-boiled spuds with a fork. I like to use dry, floury, traditional Scottish potato varieties – Golden Wonder or Kerr's Pink – but it's generally agreed that Maris Piper potatoes produce the best roasties.

Serves 4

6 tablespoons sunflower oil

4 large Golden Wonder or similar floury potatoes, peeled

Freshly ground sea salt and freshly ground pepper

Preheat the oven to 200°C/400°F/Gas 6 and put in a large roasting tin, with the oil, to warm through.

Cut the potatoes into 7.5 cm (3 in) square pieces and par-boil for 5 minutes. Drain and rough up the potatoes with a fork to give a flaky, crispy surface.

Remove the roasting tin from the oven, toss the potatoes in the hot oil (take care in case the hot oil splashes) and then return to the oven and cook until crisp and golden, turning every 15 minutes. This should take approximately 1 hour.

Remove from the oven and drain on kitchen paper for 1 minute. Sprinkle with a little salt and pepper and serve immediately.

chips

Properly made, thick-cut chips, if cooked in clean vegetable oil at the right temperature, not only taste fantastic but have far less fat than the chip shop variety. As for roast potatoes, I prefer the old Scottish traditional varieties – Golden Wonder and Kerr's Pink – but again Maris Piper is the usual spud of choice.

Serves 4

Sunflower oil, for deep-frying

600 g (1 lb 5 oz) Golden Wonder, Kerr's Pink or Maris Piper potatoes, peeled

Freshly ground sea salt and freshly ground pepper

Heat the oil in a deep-fat fryer to 180°C/350°F. While the oil is heating, cut the potatoes. I find it best to cut a slice 1 cm (½ in) thick off the potato lengthwise and then, using the flat side as a base, cut the potato into 1 cm (½ in) slices. Then cut each slice into 1 cm (½ in) fingers, resulting in square-cut chips. Wash the chips in cold water and pat dry on a clean tea towel.

Add the chips to the hot oil and deep-fry them for 12–15 minutes, until the chips are a lovely golden colour. Don't overcrowd the pan or the temperature of the oil will drop and you'll end up with soggy chips.

Lift the basket clear of the oil and shake off any excess. Tip the chips into a bowl lined with kitchen paper and dab them dry. Season with salt and pepper and serve.

mini potato fondants

I shudder at the amount of butter in this recipe, but it really doesn't work with less, so keep these for a once-in-a-while treat. These are easier to prepare than the traditional large fondants. Any new potato about 5–6 cm (2–2½ in) in length will do; I use our home-grown Charlottes. I usually allow 4 or 5 per portion but people invariably want more.

Serves 4

20–24 even-sized small new potatoes, Charlottes or similar

175 g (6 oz) butter

Freshly ground sea salt and freshly ground pepper

Preheat the oven to 190°/375°F/Gas 5.

You need an ovenproof frying pan, preferably non-stick, which will hold all the potatoes in a single layer. First slice the tops and bottoms off the potatoes, which should leave you with unpeeled cylinders around 2.5 cm (1 in) long. Now cut the butter into strips about 3 mm (⅛ in) wide and line the base of the frying pan with them. Set the potatoes, cut-face down, on top of the butter to fill the pan. Season well. Pour in enough cold water to come to the tops of the potatoes. Put the frying pan over a low-to-medium heat and keep an eye on it as the butter melts. It should just bubble gently but don't allow it to get too hot or you'll burn the bottoms of the potatoes and the water will evaporate without cooking them. They should be nicely browned underneath after 20–35 minutes, and all the water should have evaporated.

If the potatoes are still a bit undercooked on top, turn them brown-side up before placing in the oven. Put the pan into the oven for 10–15 minutes to finish cooking.

Remove from the oven and let them stand in a warm place until you're ready to serve. They need 5–10 minutes more for the butter to be absorbed but will keep warm in a hot oven for up to 1 hour.

To serve, lift them out of the pan, turn them over and place on the plate with the richly coloured side up, or cool and reheat in a hot oven when required.

crushed potatoes with olive oil, parmesan and basil

This is a kind of textured mash, so don't be tempted to make it too smooth. Use the finest new potatoes and the best olive oil you can find. You don't have to add the basil and Parmesan, but they do impart a wonderful flavour. Experiment with other herbs and cheeses.

Serves 4

450 g (1 lb) new potatoes, scrubbed

Freshly ground sea salt and freshly ground pepper

75 ml (2½ fl oz) olive oil

3 tablespoons roughly chopped fresh basil leaves

25 g (1 oz) Parmesan cheese, shaved

Cook the potatoes in simmering, salted water until tender. Drain and place in a large mixing bowl. Add the oil and, with the back of a fork, gently crush each potato until it just splits. Season, then add the basil and Parmesan. Mix carefully until all the oil has been absorbed. Don't overwork it or you'll lose the texture.

You can serve the potatoes in a pile or use a 7.5 cm (3 in) scone cutter to shape them into nice little cakes.

The mixture can be made in advance and cooled, and then reheated as potato cakes. Put them on an oiled baking sheet and bake at 200°C/400°F/Gas 6 for 20 minutes, until golden brown on top.

potato, herb and olive oil stacks

The beauty of these is that these can be made up to 4 hours in advance and popped into the oven 45 minutes before you need them.

Serves 4

4 large Maris Piper potatoes

75 ml (2½ fl oz) fruity olive oil, plus extra for greasing

2 tablespoons roughly chopped fresh rosemary

1 tablespoon roughly chopped fresh thyme

Freshly ground sea salt and freshly ground pepper

Preheat the oven to 180°C/350°F/Gas 4.

First slice the potatoes (no need to peel them) about 2 mm (1/16 in) thick, either by hand, if you can trust your hand and knife co-ordination, or on a mandolin slicer. Dump the potatoes into a large bowl, without washing, and add the olive oil and herbs. Toss well with your hands, making sure the potatoes are evenly coated. Season with a little salt and pepper and toss again to mix.

Brush a heavy baking sheet with a little olive oil and start to build eight stacks of the potato slices. Try to make them look random, and incorporate as many of the herbs as you can. Sprinkle any remaining herbs and olive oil left in the bowl around and over the potato stacks.

Bake for 35–45 minutes or until golden brown at the edges and tender all the way through. You can test this by inserting a thin skewer through the middle of a stack – it should slip through easily. Serve immediately or turn the oven to low and keep warm for up to 30 minutes.

stovies

Stovies are a very Scottish dish traditionally eaten as a main course, but I prefer to eat them as an accompaniment. They're a great way to use up leftover boiled potatoes and gravy. Traditionally made using beef dripping, I now use sunflower oil, which is nearly as tasty and considerably healthier.

Serves 4–6

50 g (2 oz) beef dripping, rendered bacon fat or vegetable oil

2 large onions, thickly sliced

900 g (2 lb) King Edward potatoes, cooked, cooled and cut into 5 cm (2 in) pieces

Freshly ground sea salt and freshly ground pepper

225 ml (8 fl oz) Chicken and Beef Stock (see page 238) or the gravy or meat jelly left over from a roast, diluted with a little water

2 tablespoons of chopped fresh parsley

Melt the dripping in a good heavy saucepan and add the onions. Stir them around a bit to coat with the dripping and cook over a medium heat for about 10 minutes, until beginning to go floppy and starting to colour around the edges. **Chuck in the** potatoes and give the whole lot a good stir. Season with salt and pepper and then pour in the stock. Bring to the boil, turn down the heat and simmer, half-covered, for 15–20 minutes. Give the potatoes a good stir once or twice during cooking, to help them break up a bit.

When cooked, the stovies should look pretty lumpy, with a thickened 'sauce' of gravy and potatoes. Taste and adjust the seasoning, stir in the parsley and take the steaming pan to the table.

skirlie

Unfortunately there is no substitute for animal fat here so this traditional Scottish dish should be regarded as an occasional treat. This is traditionally served with grouse but I've successfully partnered it with everything from lamb to scallops.

Serves 4

50 g (2 oz) bacon fat, or beef or duck dripping

1 onion, finely chopped

140 g (5 oz) medium or coarse oatmeal

Freshly ground sea salt and freshly ground pepper

Melt the dripping or fat in a frying pan and add the onion. Cook over a gentle heat for about 10 minutes, until just beginning to turn golden.

Stir in the oatmeal and 'skirl' around the pan for a couple of minutes. Traditionally this is left quite pale; however, I prefer to cook it until the oatmeal starts to darken in colour, the fat has been absorbed and the oatmeal is smelling 'toastie'.

Season and serve immediately.

steamed carrots and savoy cabbage

Thin strips of sweet carrot partner green Savoy cabbage very well and look nice into the bargain. Steaming the two together retains more vitamins and minerals than conventional boiling and, I think, gives them a fresher taste as well.

Serves 4

2 large carrots, peeled

1 small Savoy cabbage

Freshly ground sea salt and freshly ground pepper

Using a potato peeler, cut the carrots into julienne strips or thin matchsticks (or spaghetti-like strings if you are lucky enough to have a mandolin slicer). Cut out the hard core from the cabbage and cut into 1 cm (½ in) wide strips.

Toss the two together and place in an electric steamer or a steamer basket set over a pan of boiling water for about 10 minutes, until cooked but still bright in colour. Season with a little salt and pepper. Serve immediately.

braised red cabbage

Red cabbage, whilst not strictly Scottish, makes one of the best partners for our wonderful Scottish game. This dish takes some time to prepare, so it's worth making a large quantity and freezing the remainder for future use. It keeps well for up to 3 months in the freezer.

Serves 8

50 g (2 oz) butter

750 g (1 lb 10 oz) red cabbage, cored and thinly sliced

About 2 tablespoons redcurrant jelly

3 tablespoons red wine vinegar or sherry vinegar

Finely grated zest and juice of 1 orange

250 ml (9 fl oz) ruby port

Freshly ground sea salt and freshly ground pepper

85 g (3 oz) raisins

Melt the butter in a large ovenproof saucepan. Add the cabbage and stir to coat in the butter. Add the redcurrant jelly and stir until it is melted. Add the vinegar, orange zest and juice, the port and some seasoning. Bring to the boil, cover and simmer gently for approximately 1 hour or cook in an oven, preheated to 160°C/325°F/Gas 3.

Stir in the raisins and bring back to a simmer. Cook gently for another 30 minutes. Check that the cabbage is tender. Either serve straight away, keep warm in a low oven for up to 1 hour or cool and reheat.

bashed neeps and chappit tatties

These are the classic accompaniments to haggis if you want to celebrate Burns Night properly. 'Chappit tatties' are just mashed potatoes (see page 165) and 'neeps' are mashed turnips, or swedes as they say in England, highly seasoned with salt and freshly ground pepper and enriched with a knob of butter.

Serves 4

450 g (1 lb) turnip or swede, peeled and cut into even-sized pieces

25 g (1 oz) butter

Freshly ground sea salt and freshly ground pepper

Place the turnip pieces in a pan of salted cold water and bring to the boil. As soon as the water comes to the boil, reduce to a simmer and cook for approximately 20 minutes.

Drain in a colander and return the turnip pieces to the pan to dry out over a low heat for a few minutes.

Mash the turnip with a potato masher or pass through a mouli or ricer into a bowl. (At this stage you can let the turnip mash cool and reheat gently just before serving.) Using a wooden spoon, vigorously beat in the butter, season with lots of salt and pepper and serve.

wilted greens

Probably my most versatile vegetable accompaniment but best with white meat and fish. Make this with a selection of whatever greens are available, in season and in peak condition. Cut everything up into even-sized pieces, so they all cook in the same time.

Serves 4

600 g (1 lb 5 oz) mixed greens (spinach, bok choi, courgettes, Savoy cabbage and/or spring greens)

2 tablespoons olive oil

Freshly ground sea salt and freshly ground pepper

Wash and dry your chosen greens. Slice courgettes thinly on a mandolin slicer or use a potato peeler. Cut down the bok choi, removing the hard core. Roughly shred any leafy greens.

Heat a medium frying pan or wok until hot. Add the oil and toss in the greens. Stir well and then add 3 tablespoons of water, continuing to stir-fry until the greens have wilted and all the water evaporated. Remove from the heat, season and serve immediately.

roasted root vegetables

All root vegetables (those that grow under the soil) contain varying levels of sugar, and it's this sugar that caramelizes during roasting in a hot oven imparting such a wonderful flavour to quite ordinary vegetables, such as carrots and turnips.

Serves 4

4 tablespoons sunflower oil

25 g (1 oz) butter

600 g (1 lb 5 oz) root vegetables (turnip, swede, potato, celeriac, carrot, parsnip, celery and/or fennel), all cut into 4 cm (1½ in) chunks

Freshly ground sea salt and freshly ground pepper

Preheat the oven to 190°C/375°F/Gas 5.

Heat the oil and butter in a large roasting tin on top of the stove. Fling in the vegetables and stir-fry for 5–6 minutes over a high heat, until well coloured. Season and add just enough water, about 300 ml (½ pint), to half-cover the vegetables. Bring to the boil and reduce the liquid by half.

Transfer to the oven and cook for 15–20 minutes, until the water has evaporated and the vegetables are just tender. Give a good stir and return to the oven for 5–10 minutes, until the vegetables are well coloured.

Season with a little salt and pepper. Either keep warm for up to 1 hour until you need them or cool and reheat up to 12 hours later.

the perfect mixed salad

I am lucky enough to have a wife who has her own organic salad and herb garden producing the most wonderful flavoured leaves and herbs, which has somewhat spoiled me when it comes to selecting the raw materials for the perfect salad. I like to choose a mixture of sweet leaves (Little Gem, oak leaf, iceberg or Cos), peppery leaves (mustard, rocket or cress) and bitter leaves (radicchio, endive or dandelion), adding some sweet cherry tomatoes, ripe avocado, crunchy carrot and a generous handful of fresh mixed herbs. However, supermarket salad mixes are continually improving and it is possible now to find some interesting mixes prepacked in bags. Having got such a wonderful variety of flavours and textures, the salad needs the simplest of dressings – olive oil, vinegar or lemon juice and a little seasoning.

Serves 2

100 g (4 oz) mixed salad leaves

25 g (1 oz) fresh mixed herbs, whatever is in best condition

25 g (1 oz) fresh shelled peas

1 ripe avocado, peeled, stoned and cut into 1 cm (1/2 in) chunks

6 cherry tomatoes, quartered

1 small carrot, coarsely grated

FOR THE DRESSING

30 ml (1 fl oz) extra-virgin olive oil

1 teaspoon balsamic vinegar or
1 teaspoon lemon juice

Freshly ground sea salt and freshly ground pepper

First prepare the salad. Pick over the leaves and place them in a shallow bowl. Add the remaining salad ingredients and toss with your hands. Keep the salad refrigerated until you're ready to serve.

In a small bowl, mix the olive oil, balsamic vinegar or lemon juice, and seasoning, add to the salad and toss it to coat. There's no need to drench the salad in dressing; it's important just to coat the leaves in it – a pool of dressing at the bottom of the bowl means you've added too much. Eat as soon as it is dressed.

baby plum tomato and broad bean stew

Baby vegetables can be tasteless, but these little tomatoes are packed with flavour and don't hold too much water, so won't explode in the oven! Roasting concentrates the flavour and draws out the juice. Baby broad beans add the finishing spring touch, with a dash of green and their sweet young flavour. Serve with roast lamb or with some buttered pasta.

Serves 6

600 g (1 lb 5 oz) baby plum tomatoes

4 tablespoons olive oil

Freshly ground sea salt and freshly ground pepper

2 fresh thyme sprigs

700 g (1 lb 9 oz) broad beans in the pod, to give about 350 g (12 oz) podded beans, or 350 g (12 oz) frozen broad beans

Preheat the oven to 200°C/400°F/Gas 6.

Scatter the tomatoes in a roasting tin and pour over the olive oil. Mix them around and season. Tuck in the thyme and roast in the oven for about 20 minutes or until the tomatoes have collapsed slightly and the skins are beginning to brown.

Meanwhile, take the beans out of their furry pods. Blanch in boiling water for 1 minute. Drain and plunge into a bowl of cold water to cool them down quickly. Drain again and pop them out of their skins. (If using frozen beans, cook in boiling water for 2–3 minutes and do exactly the same as for the fresh ones.)

Whip the tomatoes out of the oven and mix in the beans. Pop back in the oven for a few minutes only to heat up the beans. Serve immediately.

tomato salad

This will only be as good as the tomatoes used – if you can't get good ones, don't bother.

Serves 6

1 garlic clove, lightly crushed

Freshly ground sea salt and freshly ground pepper

8–10 ripe plum or vine-ripened tomatoes

30 ml (1 fl oz) extra-virgin olive oil

1 teaspoon good-quality balsamic vinegar

25 g (1 oz) fresh basil leaves, roughly chopped or torn

Take a serving plate and rub the crushed garlic clove over it, until it releases a thin film of oil. If little or no oil is releasing, sprinkle a little sea salt on the plate and rub again; this will help release the oil.

Slice the tomatoes crosswise into 3 mm (⅛ in) slices and arrange in overlapping circles on the plate. Season with a little salt and plenty of pepper. Drizzle over the olive oil and balsamic vinegar. Scatter over the basil.

Set aside for 15 minutes before serving, to allow the flavours to combine.

celeriac purée

Most root vegetables make good purées. Celeriac is my favourite and, strangely, goes equally well with fish or game. The basic principle, with a few adjustments, is the same for all variations.

Serves 8

1 celeriac, weighing about 450 g (1 lb)
900 ml (1½ pints) milk
Freshly ground sea salt and freshly ground pepper
50 g (2 oz) butter

Cut the top and bottom off the celeriac, then cut it into quarters. Use a small knife to peel it – take off slices about 5 mm (¼ in) thick – and cut each quarter into eight pieces.

Put them in a saucepan and pour in the milk so that it just covers the celeriac. Season with salt and pepper and bring to the boil, then simmer very gently for 15–20 minutes, until the celeriac is very tender.

Pour the contents of the pan into a sieve set over a bowl and reserve the cooking liquid.

Put the hot celeriac in a food processor with the butter and about 4 tablespoons of the milk and purée for 3–4 minutes, until very smooth. Check the seasoning and then you're ready. This can be made the day before and gently reheated with a knob of butter.

Note: For carrot purée use water instead of milk. Cook for 30–40 minutes, or until very tender and add a tablespoon of lemon juice to the cooking water. For beetroot purée wear rubber gloves to peel the beetroot, then cook it in water instead of milk for 45 minutes–1 hour. For spinach purée remove the stalks from 1.5 kg (3 lb) of spinach and cook slowly in a covered pan with 3–4 tablespoons of Marinated Vegetable Stock (see page 239) for 15–20 minutes. Remove the lid towards the end of cooking to allow some of the liquid to evaporate.

As inventors of the accursed deep-fried Mars bar, it is fair to say that we Scots have a sweet tooth. We devour a vast amount of sweets, pastries, cakes and biscuits and still enjoy recipes inherited from our ancestors, such as fudge, tablet, shortbread and Dundee cake. Most of these traditional recipes make use of store cupboard ingredients, as there was limited access to luxurious or fresh ingredients for poor Scots. But there are some delights that make the most of seasonal fruits, such as Cranachan (see page 186), a traditional pudding combining cream, oatmeal, raspberries and whisky. Cranachan was the traditional celebration dessert in the late summer when raspberries were aplenty and cows were producing lots of milk for cream. For a communal celebration, the oatmeal, fruit and cream were put onto the table and everyone made their own mix, lubricating it with whisky and honey. Of course these days, with all the imported fruits on our supermarket shelves, it's possible to make cranachan all year round, but try it in late July when the first Scottish raspberries are appearing on the shelves and the results are sublime.

The secret of successful puddings is to weigh and measure all the ingredients carefully. Get to know your oven too, as temperatures can vary from one cooker to the next. Armed with these basics and a little bit of practice, you'll be serving up Hot Caramel Soufflés with Caramel Ice-cream (see page 188) in no time at all!

puddings

orange water ice with strawberries

Water ices (or *granite*, as the Italians call them) are a kind of crunchy sorbet. They are very easy to make and don't require any fancy equipment. This recipe has no added sugar, making it a good pudding for diabetics. The water ice needs a little patience but, once made, will keep for up to three weeks in the freezer. Make this when fabulous Scottish strawberries are in season, from June to September.

Serves 4

4 juicy oranges
450 g (1 lb) ripe strawberries, preferably Scottish

Squeeze the juice from the oranges and pour it into a shallow metal bowl. Place this in the freezer and remove at 30-minute intervals, giving it a good mix with a fork. Do this over a 4-hour period. Each stirring will break the ice crystals down into even smaller particles, until you end up with a crunchy sorbet texture.

If you forget one of these stages, the best way to recover the texture is to remove the mix from the freezer, let it partially thaw and then bung it into the food processor for a quick whizz. Then carry on freezing and stirring as above.

To serve, slice the strawberries in half lengthwise, leaving the green top in place. Lay them round the edges of four cold serving plates or glasses, cut-side up. Pile some water ice in the centre, dividing it equally between the plates or glasses, and serve.

cranachan

This is my favourite way to make this classic Scottish dessert. Over the years I have encountered many different variations, which have produced an array of results, from the awful to the sublime! I have decided that although it's a bit of a pain, it's best to toast the oatmeal and sugar together to give a crunchy texture and caramel flavour. In the recipe I've recommended doing this under the grill. If you are a confident cook, however, it is possible to do this in a dry, non-stick frying pan set over a medium heat, taking care to toss frequently to coat the oatmeal in caramel.

Serves 4

50 g (2 oz) pinhead oatmeal

25 g (1 oz) soft brown sugar

300 ml (½ pint) double cream

200 g (8 oz) raspberries, plus extra to decorate

2 tablespoons whisky, plus extra to serve mixed with a little warm honey (optional)

3 tablespoons heather honey, warmed

Line a grill pan with foil. Spread the oatmeal in an even layer over the foil and sprinkle evenly with the soft brown sugar. Place under a medium grill for 3–4 minutes, until the sugar begins to caramelize. Stir well and grill again until golden brown. Do not allow to burn! Cool completely and then peel off the foil and break the toasted oatmeal into chunks.

Softly whip the cream. Toss the raspberries with the whisky and the warm honey. Starting with the oatmeal, layer these three ingredients in tall glasses, ending with a layer of cream.

Top with extra raspberries and serve immediately, before the oatmeal goes soggy. Serve drizzled with extra whisky mixed with warm honey for true Scottish indulgence!

hot caramel soufflés with caramel ice-cream

First, a note of warning about the caramel: too dark will be too bitter, too pale will be too sweet. Get it right and you deserve a drumroll! The beautiful texture and spot-on aroma make this my favourite soufflé, be it savoury or sweet. Slide a couple of scoops of the ice-cream through a slit in the top of each soufflé for a lovely contrast in temperature and texture. Plan this dish well in advance.

Serves 6

FOR THE CARAMEL ICE-CREAM
140 g (5 oz) caster sugar
600 ml (1 pint) milk
6 egg yolks

FOR THE SOUFFLÉS
Soft butter, for greasing
325 g (11 oz) caster sugar, plus extra for dusting
300 ml (½ pint) milk
3 egg yolks
3 teaspoons cornflour
3 teaspoons plain white flour
6 egg whites

First, make the ice-cream. Put 100 g (4 oz) of the caster sugar into a large heavy-based pan and cook over a medium heat, stirring from time to time, until it has dissolved and cooked to a brown caramel. Take the pan off the heat, stand back and add 50 ml (2 fl oz) of water. It will hiss and splutter alarmingly, so be careful. Return to a low heat and stir until any pieces of hardened caramel have dissolved. Set aside and leave until cool but not set.

Bring the milk for the ice-cream to the boil in a saucepan. Whisk the egg yolks and remaining caster sugar together in a bowl until pale and creamy, then whisk in the hot milk. Return the mixture to the pan and cook over a gentle heat, stirring constantly, until it is thick enough to coat the back of the wooden spoon lightly. Stir in the cool caramel, strain the mixture into a bowl and leave to cool. Cover and chill well, then freeze as for Honey and Whisky Ice-cream (see page 189).

For the soufflés, preheat the oven to 220°C/425°F/Gas 7. If you have made the ice-cream some time in advance, transfer it from the freezer to the fridge about 30 minutes before serving, to allow it to soften slightly.

Lightly butter six 7.5 cm (3 in) ramekins and then dust with some caster sugar. Place on a baking sheet and set aside in the fridge. Pour the milk into a pan and bring to the boil. Meanwhile, beat the egg yolks, 50 g (2 oz) of the caster sugar, the cornflour and plain flour together in a bowl until smooth. Whisk in the hot milk, return the mixture to the pan and bring back to the boil, stirring. The mixture should be quite thick. Reduce the heat and simmer gently for about 10 minutes to cook the flour. Pour the custard base into a large mixing bowl and set aside.

Meanwhile, put the remaining caster sugar into a large heavy-based pan and cook to a brown caramel, as for the ice-cream. Take the pan off the heat, add 100 ml (3½ fl oz) water, then return to a low heat until smooth. Beat half the liquid caramel into the custard base and set aside. Cover with clingfilm to prevent a skin forming.

Whisk the egg whites in a large bowl until they just begin to form peaks. Very gradually pour the remaining hot caramel into the egg whites in a slow, steady stream, whisking all the time, until you have a stiff, glossy, caramel-coloured meringue. Now whisk one quarter of the meringue into the custard base, then very gently fold in the remainder. Spoon the mixture into the prepared ramekin dishes and place these on a baking sheet.

Bake the soufflés for 12–13 minutes. They should be well risen, browned and doubled in height but still slightly wobbly. Don't take them out too soon but don't be afraid to open the oven door to check them after the first 5 minutes.

Serve immediately. Have the ice-cream ready at the table to allow your guests to slide a scoop into the top of their soufflé.

honey and whisky ice-cream

Use a good sherry-cask-matured malt, such as a Macallan 10-year-old, and you'll end up with the silkiest, sexiest ice-cream you have ever come across. It's basically a hot toddy that thinks it's a pudding and is marvellous with Mincemeat Tart (see page 215).

Serves 6

600 ml (1 pint) milk
6 egg yolks
2 tablespoons caster sugar
85 g (3 oz) heather honey
2 tablespoons whisky
1 teaspoon lemon juice
100 ml (3^1/$_2$ fl oz) double cream

Pour the milk into a pan and bring to the boil. Meanwhile, whisk the egg yolks and sugar together in a bowl until pale and creamy. Whisk in the hot milk and then return the mixture to the pan and cook over a gentle heat, stirring constantly with a wooden spoon, until it thickens enough to coat the back of the spoon lightly.

Pour the mixture into a bowl and stir in the honey, whisky, lemon juice and double cream. Leave the mixture until cold. Then cover and place in the fridge until well chilled.

Now you can either churn the mixture in an ice-cream maker or pour it into a shallow plastic box and freeze until almost firm. Scrape the mixture into a food processor and whizz until smooth. Pour it back into the box and repeat once more. Return the ice-cream to the freezer and freeze until firm.

If the ice-cream has been made in advance, transfer it from the freezer to the fridge about 30 minutes before serving, to allow it time to soften slightly.

hot raspberry soufflés

Unfortunately the Scottish raspberry-growing industry is currently under threat. However, as the fruit has world-class flavour and is brimming with health-giving antioxidants, we should all eat more raspberries, not just to support Scottish soft fruit growers, but for our own delectation and well-being. The intensity of flavour in these pretty pink soufflés is amazing, a result of the sugarless raspberry 'jam'. This works equally well using passion fruit purée. When serving soufflés, always make sure your guests are back at the table when the soufflés are ready to come out of the oven to avoid the frustration of watching your perfect soufflé slowly sink.

Serves 6

500 g (1 lb 2 oz) fresh or frozen raspberries

Soft butter, for greasing

140 g (5 oz) caster sugar, plus extra for dusting

350 ml (12 fl oz) milk

3 egg yolks

3 tablespoons cornflour

3 tablespoons plain flour

6 egg whites

Icing sugar, sifted, to decorate

Press the raspberries through a sieve or blitz in a food processor and then sieve to remove the seeds. Bring to the boil and boil rapidly for approximately 10 minutes, stirring frequently towards the end of the cooking, until you are left with a thick 'jam'. Take care towards the end of cooking and reduce the heat to stop it catching on the bottom of the pan. This 'jam' can be made up to 2 weeks ahead and kept in the fridge in an airtight container.

Slide a baking sheet onto the middle shelf of the oven and preheat it to 200°C/400°F/Gas 6. Lightly butter six 7.5 cm (3 in) ramekins and dust them with a little caster sugar. Refrigerate until needed.

Pour all but 1 tablespoon of the milk into a pan and slowly bring it to the boil. Meanwhile, beat the egg yolks, 40 g (1½ oz) of the caster sugar, the cornflour, plain flour and remaining milk together in a bowl, until smooth. Whisk in the boiling hot milk, return the mixture to the pan and bring to the boil, stirring all the time. Reduce the heat and leave the mixture to simmer very gently for about 10 minutes, beating it every now and then, until you have cooked out the taste of the flour.

Pour 6 heaped tablespoons of the custard into a bowl and beat in the raspberry 'jam'. Whisk the egg whites into soft peaks and then whisk in the remaining caster sugar. Take care not to over whisk meringue – it should stay at the soft peak stage. Lightly whisk one quarter of the whites into the custard to loosen it slightly, then carefully fold in the remainder.

Spoon the mixture into the prepared ramekins and level the tops. Slide the ramekins onto the baking sheet and bake for 10–12 minutes, until the soufflés are well risen, browned on top and almost doubled in height but still slightly wobbly. Quickly lift them onto small dessert plates, sprinkle with icing sugar and serve straight away before they've got time to sink!

apple soufflés with apple sorbet

There are two very different flavours at work here: the intense, cooked sweet apple flavour of the soufflé and the light zing of the sorbet. The apple sorbet is one of the easiest puddings you'll ever make, and possibly the cleverest. Leave the skins on the Granny Smiths and it will have a lovely pastel colour.

Serves 6

FOR THE APPLE SORBET

4 Granny Smith apples, cored and diced

Juice of 1 lemon

100 ml (3½ fl oz) Stock Syrup (see page 255)

FOR THE APPLE SOUFFLÉS

4 Cox's apples, peeled, cored and diced into 1 cm (½ in) pieces

125 ml (4 fl oz) cider

2 tablespoons Calvados

Soft butter, for greasing

65 g (2½ oz) caster sugar, plus extra for dusting

300 ml (½ pint) milk

3 egg yolks

3 teaspoons cornflour

3 teaspoons plain white flour

6 egg whites

First, make the apple sorbet. Toss the apple dice in 1 tablespoon of the lemon juice and then spread them over a baking tray and freeze for 3–4 hours, until hard. Remove from the freezer and leave them to thaw slightly at room temperature for 10 minutes. Then scrape them into a food processor, add the remaining lemon juice and the stock syrup and process until smooth. You will have to stop and scrape down once or twice with a plastic spatula. If you want a smoother texture you could sieve out the skin at this point. Transfer the mixture to a plastic box, cover and freeze for 3–4 hours, until firm.

For the apple soufflés, put the diced apples, cider and Calvados into a pan and cook over a low heat for about 30 minutes, beating with a wooden spoon now and then if necessary, until most of the liquid has evaporated and you are left with a very thick purée. Set aside. Preheat the oven to 220°C/425°F/Gas 7.

Lightly butter six 7.5 cm (3 in) ramekins, paying particular attention to the rims as the soufflé will catch an unbuttered rim as it rises, causing a lopsided rise. Dust with a little caster sugar and set aside in the fridge on a baking tray. If you have made the sorbet some time beforehand, transfer it from the freezer to the fridge now to allow it to soften slightly.

Bring the milk to the boil in a pan. Meanwhile, beat the egg yolks, 25 g (1 oz) of the caster sugar, the cornflour and plain flour together in a bowl until smooth. Whisk in the hot milk, then return the mixture to the pan and bring back to the boil, stirring. Reduce the heat and simmer gently for about 10 minutes. (If you are preparing the soufflés in advance, it is possible to make them up to this stage; however, you must cover the mixture with clingfilm to prevent a skin from forming.)

When ready to serve, put 6 heaped tablespoons of the mix (there won't be much left over) in a large mixing bowl and stir in the apple purée. Whisk the egg whites to soft peaks, then very gradually whisk in the remaining caster sugar to make a soft meringue, taking care not to overwork. Stir a quarter of the meringue into the apple custard to loosen the mixture slightly, then very gently fold in the remainder. Spoon the mixture into the prepared ramekins, taking care to smooth down the tops. Then slide the baking tray and ramekins into the middle of the oven and bake for 10–12 minutes, until brown and risen but still slightly wobbly. The mixture won't quite double in height because of the extra weight of the apple.

Serve immediately, with a scoop of the apple sorbet.

The sorbet also keeps well in the freezer for up to 2 weeks. Leave to soften in the fridge for 30 minutes before eating.

strawberry fool

This is an incredibly easy pudding, best made in the summer when Scottish strawberries are cheap and at their best. You can jazz it up a bit by adding four crushed Amaretti biscuits. Serve this in four of your nicest glasses.

Serves 4

300 g (10 oz) ripe strawberries, hulled

25 g (1 oz) caster sugar

1 tablespoon Grand Marnier

4 Amaretti biscuits, crushed (optional)

300 ml (½ pint) double cream

Place the strawberries, sugar, Grand Marnier and biscuits, if using, in a medium-sized mixing bowl and crush everything together with a fork. Don't overwork this – you want a nice stodgy mass, not a purée.

In a separate bowl, lightly whip the cream and then fold it into the strawberry mixture.

Pour the fool into serving glasses and refrigerate for an hour before serving.

strawberry pavlova with raspberry sauce

This is easy-peasy and the pavlova bases can be made up to 7 days ahead. I make a big pavlova and then cut it into rectangles – which is not only easy to do but looks different from the common-or-garden round variety. I make the most of whatever Scottish berries are in season, not just strawberries and raspberries. Ideally, the meringue base should have a texture like marshmallow.

Serves 6

6 egg whites
200 g (8 oz) caster sugar
1 tablespoon lemon juice and 1 heaped teaspoon cornflour, mixed
Vegetable oil, for greasing
350 g (12 oz) raspberries
25 g (1 oz) icing sugar
450 ml (16 fl oz) double cream
350 g (12 oz) strawberries, hulled and halved

Preheat the oven to 160°C/325°F/Gas 3.

To make the meringue, whisk the egg whites (a hand whisk or electric mixer will make this easier) and continue whisking until they reach soft peak stage. At this point, add the sugar a little at a time until fully incorporated. But be careful – add the sugar too soon and the meringue won't bulk up enough, too late and it will separate.

When all the sugar has been added, pour in the lemon juice and cornflour mix. Whisk again on full speed for 6–8 minutes, until the meringue is thick and shiny.

Brush a shallow baking tin 30 x 20 x 2.5 cm (12 x 8 x 1 in) with a little vegetable oil and then line with greaseproof paper. Spoon the meringue into the tin and smooth it down with a palette knife. Bake for 45 minutes, until slightly risen and browned on top.

To make the raspberry sauce, place the raspberries and icing sugar in a blender and whizz for 45 seconds. Pass the mixture through a fine sieve into a bowl. Refrigerate until required.

When the meringue is baked, remove it from the oven and allow to cool for approximately 2 hours. Then turn it out onto a tray (the same size if possible) so that the greaseproof paper is top side and the brown crust is on the bottom. If you want to store the base, wrap it in clingfilm and keep at room temperature for up to 4 days.

To serve, whip the double cream until it holds soft peaks but be careful not to overbeat it. Now remove the greaseproof paper from the meringue and, using a spatula, spread the cream over the pavlova. Smooth it with a palette knife to form a clean shape with a flat top – the cream should be approximately 3 mm ($\frac{1}{8}$ in) thick. Using a thin, sharp knife, divide the pavlova into 6 x 10 cm ($2\frac{1}{4}$ x 4 in) rectangles. Lift them out and decorate them with the halved strawberries. Place the pavlova on six serving plates and pour round the raspberry sauce. Serve.

vanilla cream with caramelized blueberries

One of the best ends to a meal I know, this dessert has the benefit of being totally pre-prepared, leaving only the vanilla cream to be unmoulded and the berries to be spooned around before serving. I like to use wild Scottish blaeberries during their season from late June till September. Although they are smaller than blueberries, they are packed with flavour and have the added advantage of being free. You can gather them all over Scotland in their season; the traditional implement to use is a blaeberry rake, but juice-stained fingers do the job perfectly if slowly!

Serves 6

FOR THE VANILLA CREAMS
300 ml (½ pint) milk
1 vanilla pod, split
50 g (2 oz) caster sugar
3 gelatine leaves, soaked in cold water for 5 minutes
500 ml (18 fl oz) double cream

FOR THE CARAMELIZED BLUEBERRIES
200 g (8 oz) caster sugar, sifted
450 g (1 lb) fresh blueberries or blaeberries

To make the vanilla creams, put the milk, split vanilla pod (scraping out the seeds) and sugar into a saucepan and bring to the boil. Remove the gelatine from its soaking water and squeeze out the excess liquid. Drop the gelatine into the mixture and stir until dissolved. Pour in the cream and leave the mixture to cool. Then place in the fridge until it just begins to thicken.

At this stage, whisk the cream to distribute the vanilla seeds and lift out the vanilla pod. Pour into six individual moulds, set on a tray and refrigerate for at least 5 hours or until set.

To make the caramelized blueberries, melt the sugar slowly in a small saucepan over a medium heat. Don't muck about and stir the sugar or you will get lumps – just swirl it around the base as it melts. You can add water to dissolve the sugar, but I really don't think you need to once you are practised at making caramel. Once the sugar has melted and starts to boil, cook until the caramel starts to turn dark brown and the surface is covered in bubbles. Now whack in the blueberries or blaeberries and stir like crazy over the heat, until they are broken down and jammy. You may need to bring the mix back to the boil to melt any lumps of caramel. Keep on cooking and it will all eventually melt to give a smooth, fruity sauce. Cool, cover and refrigerate until needed.

To serve, press the top of the vanilla creams and gently pull away from the edge of the moulds (this breaks the seal). Carefully invert onto cold dessert plates. If they still won't budge, dip them very briefly into warm water and then unmould them. Spoon the blueberries alongside.

frozen whisky cream with prunes and earl grey syrup

This simple, elegant dish is basically an ice-cream that doesn't need to be churned. It is the ultimate standby dessert to have in the freezer – but it has to be prepared at least 12 hours in advance and the prunes have to be soaked for at least 24 hours before you begin. The cleverness of this dish lies in the fact that not only does the whisky flavour the frozen cream, it also acts as an anti-freeze, allowing you to serve it straight from the freezer. For flavour, I prefer a blended whisky, but use whatever you have spare. It is not practical to make this dish in smaller quantities, but it does keep well (up to 28 days in the freezer), so you can serve it on several occasions.

Serves 12

Vegetable oil, for greasing

600 ml (1 pint) Stock Syrup (see page 255)

2 tablespoons Earl Grey tea leaves

32 ready-to-eat, stoned Agen or California prunes

Lemon juice

75 ml (2½ fl oz) blended whisky

5 egg yolks

300 ml (½ pint) double cream

85 g (3 oz) caster sugar

Lightly oil twelve 125 ml (4 fl oz) dariole moulds, ramekins or yoghurt cartons.

For the Earl Grey syrup, bring the stock syrup to the boil. Add the tea leaves and allow to infuse for 6 minutes. Pass the syrup through a sieve (basically, using it as a big tea strainer) and add the prunes to the still-hot liquid. Add lemon juice to taste and 30 ml (1 fl oz) of the whisky. Place the mixture in a tub with a well-fitting lid, allow it to cool, and then store in the fridge. This could be used after 24 hours but will improve the longer you leave it, keeping for up to 8 weeks.

For the frozen whisky cream, whisk the egg yolks in an electric mixer until very pale and much increased in volume. Whip the double cream with the rest of the whisky until it just thickens. Boil the caster sugar and 3 tablespoons of water until it reaches the soft ball stage (dip in a cold spoon, coating it, then dip this into cold water to set and pinch a little between finger and thumb – when it can be rolled into a soft ball, it's ready).

With the mixer running on full speed, slowly pour the hot sugar syrup in a continuous steam onto the yolks. Reduce the speed by half and whisk for a further 5 minutes. Fold the yolk and syrup mix and the whipped cream together and pour it, using a large jug, into the moulds. Freeze immediately.

To serve, heat 4 prunes per person in enough Earl Grey syrup to cover. Remove the frozen creams from the freezer, run the tip of a knife around the top of each one, invert the moulds and give them a good tap on a hard surface to help release them. Turn the frozen creams out onto chilled dessert plates. Arrange 4 prunes around each one and drizzle a little hot Earl Grey syrup over. Serve at once.

Alternatively you could just pour the whisky cream mix into a tub, freeze it and use an ice-cream scoop to serve it. Not as pretty but just as tasty.

raspberry mousse
with raspberry sauce

This is a template recipe for making the best mousses I've tasted. You could use apricots, brambles, passion fruit, mangoes or (if they're sweet and ripe) strawberries instead of raspberries; alternatively quality shop-bought purées are very good. The mousse keeps for up to 48 hours in the fridge.

Serves 8–10

Vegetable oil, for greasing
850 ml (1½ pints) raspberry purée or 1.6 kg (3 lb 8 oz) fresh raspberries, puréed
200 g (8 oz) sugar
125 ml (4 fl oz) egg whites
5 gelatine leaves
450 ml (16 fl oz) double cream
150 ml (¼ pint) Stock Syrup (see page 255)
Juice of 1 lime

Lightly oil eight or ten 125 ml (4 fl oz) dariole moulds or ramekins.

If using fresh raspberries, put them into a liquidizer and whizz until you have a nice smooth purée. Pass this through a sieve and measure out 600 ml (1 pint) of purée.

Dissolve the sugar in a little water over a high heat and boil the resulting syrup to the soft ball stage (dip in a cold spoon, coating it, then dip this into cold water to set and pinch a little between finger and thumb – when it can be rolled into a soft ball, it's ready). Remove the syrup from the heat.

Whisk the egg whites and, when they start to thicken, slowly pour on the sugar syrup. Continue to whisk for 3 further minutes – this produces an Italian meringue, which holds more air and gives the mousse a really light texture.

Soak the gelatine leaves in cold water for 5 minutes (any more and they might just disappear!) Remove the leaves from the water and squeeze to remove excess water. In a medium-sized saucepan, warm the measured raspberry purée (do not let it boil) and, using a whisk, dissolve the gelatine in it. Transfer to a mixing bowl and allow to cool for 30 minutes.

Add a spoonful of meringue to the purée and mix well to loosen the mixture; then fold in the remaining meringue until it's fully incorporated. Now whisk the cream to soft peaks and fold it into the meringue mix. This is the mousse. Pour it into a large jug – this makes it easier to pour it into the individual moulds – or pour into an ice-cream tub and serve with a scoop. Leave it to chill overnight in the fridge.

To serve, mix enough stock syrup and lime juice into the remaining raspberry pureé to make a well-flavoured sauce. Dip the moulds in warm water for 5–10 seconds, then turn them out onto chilled dessert plates. Spoon the raspberry sauce around them. Serve at once.

rhubarb and ginger mousse with rhubarb sauce

This is a variation on a classic mousse with a Scottish accent!

Serves 8

Vegetable oil, for greasing

900 g (2 lb) fresh pink rhubarb

4 pieces of stem ginger in syrup, drained (keep 4 tablespoons of the ginger syrup for the sauce)

200 g (8 oz) sugar, plus 3 tablespoons for the sauce

4 egg whites

4 gelatine leaves, soaked in cold water for 5 minutes

300 ml (½ pint) double cream

Lightly oil eight 125 ml (4 fl oz) dariole moulds or ramekins.

Trim the rhubarb and cut into 2.5 cm (1 in) pieces. Put into a pan with a couple of tablespoons of water and simmer for 10–15 minutes, until soft and pulpy. Put the rhubarb into a liquidizer with half the stem ginger (this is best done in two batches) and whizz until you have a nice smooth purée. Pass this through a sieve. Measure out 600 ml (1 pint) of purée. You will have enough purée left over to make a sauce.

Dissolve the sugar in a little water over a high heat and boil the resulting syrup down to the soft ball stage (dip in a cold spoon, coating it, then dip this into cold water to set and pinch a little between finger and thumb — when it can be rolled into a soft ball, it's ready). Remove it from the heat.

Whisk the egg whites and, when they start to thicken, slowly pour on the sugar syrup. Continue to whisk for 3 further minutes, until doubled in bulk, and you have a firm meringue.

Remove the gelatine leaves from the cold water and gently squeeze out the excess water. In a medium-sized saucepan, warm the measured rhubarb purée (do not let it boil) and dissolve the gelatine in it. Allow to cool for 30 minutes.

Pour the rhubarb onto the meringue and fold it in until fully incorporated. Now whisk the cream into soft peaks and fold it into the meringue mix. This is the mousse mix. Pour it into a large jug — this makes it easier to pour it into the individual moulds. Leave the filled moulds to chill overnight in the fridge.

Take 8 tablespoons of the remaining rhubarb purée and add the 3 tablespoons of sugar and the 4 tablespoons of the ginger syrup. Bring to the boil, boil for 1 minute, then cool and chill. Cut the remaining ginger into fine shreds, cover and set aside.

To serve, dip the moulds in hot water for 15–20 seconds, then turn them out onto chilled dessert plates. Spoon the rhubarb and ginger sauce around them and top with some shredded ginger.

crème fraîche mousse with caramel poached pears

Scots have a very sweet tooth and I think of caramel as a very Scottish thing – maybe it's the memory of caramel toffees. Soft vanilla mousse with ripe pears poached in red wine and a delicious caramel syrup – who needs more? Use Comice pears and don't eat too much in one sitting!

Serves 6

FOR THE MOUSSE
1 vanilla pod
200 g (8 oz) crème fraîche
50 g (2 oz) caster sugar
Finely grated zest of 2 lemons and the juice of 1 lemon
1⅓ gelatine leaves, soaked in cold water for 5 minutes
200 ml (7 fl oz) double cream

FOR THE CARAMEL PEARS
500 g (1 lb 2 oz) granulated sugar
500 ml (18 fl oz) red wine
1 vanilla pod, split
6 small, ripe Comice or Conference pears

To make the mousse, split the vanilla pod and scrape out the seeds, keeping the pod for flavouring your sugar jar. Place the seeds, crème fraîche, sugar and lemon zest in a bowl and mix thoroughly. Warm the lemon juice, add the soaked gelatine and stir over a gentle heat to dissolve. Leave to cool slightly and then stir into the crème fraîche mixture. Whip the cream to soft peaks and fold into the crème fraîche mixture.

Spoon the mixture into six lightly oiled dariole moulds or mini pudding moulds, cover with clingfilm and chill overnight.

For the pears, put the sugar in a saucepan over a gentle heat until it melts and finally turns to a caramel. When the caramel is a good colour, remove from the heat and *quickly* pour in the red wine. It will hiss and splutter, so watch out! Place over the heat again, and scrape in the vanilla seeds from the pod. Stir until the lumps have dissolved.

Peel the pears, leaving on the stalks. Using a melon baller, scoop out the seeds and pith from the bottom of the pears before placing them in the boiling syrup, stalks upwards. Cover with a circle of greaseproof paper. Bring back to the boil and simmer for 10 minutes.

Remove from the heat and allow to cool in the syrup. Do this 24 hours in advance for the best results, ensuring the pears are covered by the syrup.

Next day, lift out the pears and boil the syrup rapidly until it forms a thick sauce. Cool.

To serve, dip the moulds briefly into warm water and then invert onto chilled serving plates. Serve a pear with each mousse, drizzled with a little of the reduced syrup.

hot whisky cream with frozen berries

This is my standard brûlée custard, flavoured with the heavenly combination of whisky and honey. It is very rich and luxurious and needs the acidity of a sharp fruit to contrast with it. I love the juxtaposition of hot and cold, so I serve this custard cream warm with chilled berry purée, studded with fresh whole frozen blueberries. I've used blueberries here, but feel free to use your own favourite or try the packets of mixed berries available in the freezer section in most supermarkets.

Serves 4–6

450 g (1 lb) frozen blueberries
400 ml (14 fl oz) double cream
200 ml (7 fl oz) milk
6 egg yolks
25 g (1 oz) caster sugar
50 ml (2 fl oz) whisky
100 g (4 oz) heather honey

Defrost half the berries (keep the rest frozen) and pass through a sieve, using a wooden spoon to press them through. Skim off any foam, cover and chill the purée while you make the cream.

Pour the cream and milk into a pan and slowly bring to the boil over a medium heat. Put the egg yolks and caster sugar into a bowl and whisk until pale and creamy. Pour the boiled cream over the egg yolks, stirring all the time. Pour this back into the pan and place over a very low heat, stirring with a wooden spoon for 2–3 minutes, until it begins to thicken (don't let it get too hot or it may curdle). Add the whisky and honey and mix through. Remove from the heat and stir for a couple of minutes more. Set aside.

To serve, mix the frozen berries with the berry purée and spoon into four serving bowls. Ladle the warm cream over the frozen berries and serve. Heaven!

crème brûlée

I know that everybody has a recipe for crème brûlée, but this version isn't the usual custard set-in-a-bain-marie-in-the-oven-routine, which I find can make the brûlées heavy. My method involves incorporating air into the egg yolks, giving lightness to the mixture; plus, it's quicker. Use the best-quality vanilla pods – Bourbon, if you can get them. The custard cooks very quickly, as the eggs are partly cooked and the cream ready at the boil, so pay particular attention while stirring the custard to avoid any scrambled eggs. It pays to stir from side to side – not round and round, which tends to leave the custard in the centre of the pan unmoved, so that it scrambles! Remember that you can eliminate any unfortunate lumps using a sieve.

Serves 6

600 ml (1 pint) double cream
1 vanilla pod, split
6 egg yolks
85 g (3 oz) caster sugar

Heat the cream, vanilla pod and scraped out seeds together in a pan to just below boiling. Place a whisking bowl over a separate pan of simmering water. Add the egg yolks and caster sugar to the bowl and whisk until they become thick and foamy. This should take 5–6 minutes.

Bring the cream to the boil and, just as it starts to rise up through the pan, pour two-thirds into the whisking bowl with the eggs. Whisk them together thoroughly, then pour the custard back into the pan with the remaining cream. (Another pair of hands would be useful here – ask a friend.) Place the bowl back on the heat and stir the mixture with a wooden spoon for 1–2 minutes, until it thickens. Remove from the heat and continue stirring for a further couple of minutes to distribute the residual heat in the pan evenly.

Divide the mix evenly between six 150 ml (¼ pint) ramekins, filling them to the brim. Allow the mixture to set in the fridge for at least 6 hours or, preferably, overnight.

To serve, dust the surface of the brûlées with some icing sugar (a tea strainer is good for this). Then apply the heat of a blow torch to glaze. Alternatively, if you aren't brave enough, place the brûlées under a hot grill, but watch them like a hawk because they burn very easily. When glazed, they should be a nice mahogany brown colour – but don't touch the brûlée topping as it will be extremely hot. Place the brûlées in the fridge for 5 minutes before serving, allowing the caramel to cool.

Note: For raspberry crème brûlée, use a punnet of good Scottish raspberries. Place a tablespoon of raspberries in each ramekin, crush very lightly with a fork, and proceed as per the recipe above.

passion fruit pots

One of my all-time-favourite desserts: a ramekin of passion fruit mousse topped with passion fruit jelly. This can be made up to 3 days in advance and is easy to serve as a lovely fresh end to a meal. I use frozen French passion fruit purée, which is available in most good delicatessens. A good alternative is pasteurized purée, which is sold in jars. If you can't get hold of any purée, you will need to use 36 ripe passion fruit. Halve them and scoop out the pulp into a sieve set over a bowl. Work out the juice with a wooden spoon and keep the seeds separately.

Serves 10

450 ml (16 fl oz) milk
1 vanilla pod, split
6 egg yolks
125 g (4$\frac{1}{2}$ oz) caster sugar
4$\frac{1}{2}$ gelatine leaves
300 ml ($\frac{1}{2}$ pint) passion fruit purée
450 ml (16 fl oz) double cream
5 whole passion fruit, cut in half, seeds scooped out, to decorate

FOR THE JELLY GLAZE
1 gelatine leaf
125 ml (4 fl oz) passion fruit purée
85 ml (3 fl oz) Stock Syrup (see page 255)

Put the milk in a pan with the vanilla pod and scraped out seeds and bring to the boil. Meanwhile, whisk the egg yolks and sugar together in a bowl, until pale and creamy. Lift out the vanilla pod and whisk the milk into the egg yolks. Pour the mixture back into the pan and cook over a gentle heat, stirring constantly, until the custard mixture thickens enough to coat the back of the wooden spoon lightly. Set aside.

Soak the gelatine leaves in cold water for 5 minutes. Pour the passion fruit purée into a pan and warm through over a low heat; then add the soaked gelatine and stir until dissolved. Leave to cool slightly and then stir this mixture into the custard. You can now do one of two things – either leave the mixture in the fridge for 3–4 hours, until it begins to show signs of setting, then give it a good mix with a whisk, or leave it to set completely and then whisk with an electric hand whisk until smooth and runny. If you were to pour the mix into the cream now you would lose air from the mix, making it heavier.

Lightly whip the cream into soft peaks and fold it in to the mix. Pour the mixture into ten 7.5 cm (3 in) ramekins or a 1.2 litre (2 pint) soufflé dish, leaving a little space at the top for the jelly glaze, and chill until set.

When the custard bases have set, make the glaze. Soak the gelatine leaf in cold water for 10 minutes. Pour the passion fruit purée and stock syrup into a pan and warm through over a gentle heat. Add the soaked gelatine and stir until it has dissolved.

Pour a thin layer on the top of each ramekin, add a spoonful of the passion fruit seeds and chill once more until set, then serve.

caramelized rice pudding with blueberry compote

At primary school I was force fed the most revolting glop masquerading as rice pudding, which traumatized me to the extent that I could no longer bear to eat rice pudding. Twenty years later I was converted by this recipe! This is a light, unusual rice pudding with an impressive, crunchy, caramelized top, which tastes twenty times better than it sounds and bears no resemblance at all to school dinners. The blueberries need poaching to bring out their flavour. Their deep colour contrasts nicely with the rice pudding.

Serves 4

1 vanilla pod, split
600 ml (1 pint) milk
85 g (3 oz) caster sugar
50 g (2 oz) pudding rice
125 ml (4 fl oz) double cream
Icing sugar, sifted, to decorate

FOR THE COMPOTE
200 ml (7 fl oz) Stock Syrup (see page 255)
Juice of ½ lemon
1 tablespoon crème de myrtilles or cassis (optional)
200 g (8 oz) blueberries

For the rice pudding, put the split vanilla pod, milk and sugar into a pan and bring slowly to the boil. Stir in the rice, bring back to the boil and simmer very gently for about 1 hour, stirring from time to time, until thick and gooey. Take off the heat, leave to cool and then chill.

For the compote, place the stock syrup, lemon juice and crème de myrtilles or cassis, if using, in a pan and bring to the boil. Add the blueberries and simmer for 4 minutes, then pour into a bowl and leave to cool.

To finish off the rice pudding, whip the double cream until it forms soft peaks and fold it lightly into the cooled rice mixture. Place a deep 6 cm (2½ in) scone cutter on a baking sheet. Spoon in some rice mixture, lightly level the top and then remove the cutter and repeat three times.

Dust heavily with icing sugar. Caramelize the sugar either with a blow torch or by putting the baking sheet under a very hot grill until the sugar is bubbling and has turned a dark golden brown. Set aside and leave to cool slightly.

Slide a fish slice under each pudding and transfer to a dessert plate. Spoon some of the blueberry compote around and serve.

cinnamon creams with spiced rhubarb

This cinnamon cream is really just a set cream (what the Italians call *panna cotta*), flavoured with cinnamon instead of the more usual vanilla. I like to eat them in early summer, when the first pale pink forced Scottish rhubarb arrives. If you're using the later main-crop rhubarb, increase the cooking time a little. This is a direct, simple and unfussy dessert and can be made well in advance.

Serves 8

Vegetable oil, for greasing
700 ml (1¼ pints) double cream
1 cinnamon stick
½ teaspoon ground cinnamon
3 gelatine leaves
85 g (3 oz) caster sugar

FOR THE SPICED RHUBARB
750 g (1 lb 10 oz) rhubarb
450 ml (16 fl oz) Stock Syrup (see page 255)
1 cinnamon stick
3 star anise
6 cloves
1 vanilla pod
A strip of pared lemon rind

Lightly oil eight 100 ml (3½ fl oz) dariole moulds or ramekins.

Put the cream, cinnamon stick and ground cinnamon into a pan and bring to the boil. Remove from the heat and leave to stand for about 20 minutes, to allow the flavour of the cinnamon to infuse the cream.

Meanwhile, soak the gelatine leaves in cold water for 5 minutes.

Remove the cinnamon stick from the pan and bring the cream to just below boiling point once more. Add the caster sugar and the soaked gelatine and stir until they have both dissolved. Strain the mixture into a jug and then pour it into the moulds. Leave overnight in the fridge to set.

For the spiced rhubarb, cut the rhubarb into 4 cm (1½ in) lengths (if you are using main-crop rhubarb, you may need to peel it first). Put the stock syrup in a large pan and bring slowly to the boil. Add the spices, vanilla pod and strip of lemon rind and simmer for 5 minutes. Add the rhubarb and bring back to the boil. (If using older rhubarb you may need to simmer for approximately 15 minutes.) Set aside and leave to cool. Leave the spices, vanilla pod and lemon rind in the syrup to allow the flavours to develop. Keep in the fridge until ready to use.

To serve, press the top of the creams and gently pull away from the edge of the moulds (this breaks the seal). Carefully invert onto cold dessert plates. If they still won't budge, dip them very briefly into warm water and then unmould them. Spoon the rhubarb alongside, leaving the spices behind.

caramelized apple tart

This is a really tasty marriage of apple and caramel custard. It is best served warm with a dollop of whipped cream or crème fraîche and can be reheated the next day. This is the kind of dessert that gets a lot of 'oohs' and 'aahs' both at the restaurant and round my dinner table at home.

Serves 8

300 g (10 oz) caster sugar

6 Granny Smith apples, peeled and quartered, each quarter cut into thirds

300 ml (½ pint) double cream

20 cm (8 in) Sweet Shortcrust Pastry, baked blind (see page 253)

3 eggs

Place the sugar in a large frying pan over a medium heat. Allow the sugar to melt slowly – stir it as little as possible, only to fold in the little areas of dark caramel that will start to appear. After 6–8 minutes, all of the sugar will be melted, and this is what is known as a blonde caramel. What you need is a dark caramel, so allow the sugar to cook a little further (another 1–2 minutes should do). The caramel is ready when it has large bubbles appearing on the surface and starts to release a dark, acrid smoke.

Remove the pan from the heat and carefully tip in all the apples, being careful that the caramel doesn't splash you. Hot melted sugar can give you a very nasty burn indeed so you could play safe by wearing rubber gloves for this stage. Mix everything together with a wooden spoon.

Once the apples are coated in the caramel, carefully pour in the cream (watch it, because it will boil and splutter) and place the pan back on the heat, stirring for 3–5 minutes, until all the caramel is dissolved. Pour the contents of the pan into a sieve set over a mixing bowl and allow to cool for 30 minutes.

During this time preheat the oven to 160°C/325°F/Gas 3. When you are ready to serve, arrange the apple segments in the bottom of the blind-baked tart case. Add the eggs to the caramel liquid and gently whisk them in. Place the tart on a baking sheet and strain the caramel custard through a sieve into the tart case. Bake for 35–45 minutes, until it has just risen around the edges and the centre has set.

Remove the tart and allow it to cool slightly before turning it out and dividing it into eight portions. Serve warm, with whipped cream.

chocolate tart

My enthusiasm for the flavour of evaporated milk originates from my days in the Navy when it was the only alternative to fresh milk. For some bizarre reason it was referred to as 'shaky milk'. Whatever you call it, give it a go in this recipe and be converted to the flavour of milk from a tin.

Serves 8

500 g (1 lb 2 oz) dark chocolate (at least 64% cocoa solids)

3 eggs

150 ml (¼ pint) single cream

2 x 170 g cans of evaporated milk

20 cm (8 in) Sweet Shortcrust Pastry, baked blind (see page 253)

Icing sugar, to decorate

Crème fraîche, to serve (optional)

Preheat the oven to 180°C/350°F/Gas 4. If you like, use a potato peeler to make curls from a little of the chocolate, to decorate. Break the remaining chocolate into small pieces. Put into a metal or china bowl and set over a pan of just-boiling water. Leave to melt for 10 minutes, then stir.

Whisk the eggs together in a large bowl. Pour the cream and evaporated milk into a saucepan and bring to the boil. Pour this onto the eggs and whisk together.

Strain the milk and egg mixture over the chocolate and mix well. Pour this into the blind-baked tart case. Sit the tart on a baking sheet and slide into the oven. Shut the door and immediately turn the oven off. Leave the tart in the oven for 40–45 minutes.

Remove from the oven and allow to cool completely (about 1½ hours).

Sprinkle with icing sugar and serve in thin slices, with a dollop of crème fraîche, or cover the top with chocolate curls, dredge with icing sugar and serve.

mincemeat tart

Dried fruit is popular in all kinds of traditional Scottish desserts and you don't need to wait until Christmas to enjoy this. The filling is easily made by adding a few extra ingredients to a standard jar of mincemeat. Do look for good-quality, ready-to-eat dried fruit, so you'll have a rich moist filling.

Serves 8

200 g (8 oz) luxury mixed dried fruit (figs, prunes, dates, apricots and/or raisins)

400 g jar of mincemeat

Juice and finely grated zest of 1 orange

1 Granny Smith apple, peeled, cored and grated

25 g (1 oz) caster sugar, plus extra for dusting

50 ml (2 fl oz) dark rum

2 quantities of Sweet Shortcrust Pastry (see page 253)

Crème fraîche, to serve

Chop the dried fruits into raisin-sized pieces and then stir them into the mincemeat, with the orange juice and zest, grated apple, sugar and rum. If possible, cover and leave for 2–3 days to allow the mixture to absorb the orange juice and rum.

Preheat the oven to 200°C/400°F/Gas 6. Roll out half the pastry on a lightly floured work surface and use to line a 25 cm (10 in) loose-bottomed metal tin. Spoon in the mincemeat mixture and lightly level the top. Roll out the remaining pastry to a round about 28 cm (11 in) in diameter. Brush the edge of the pastry case with a little water, lay the remaining pastry on top and press the edges together well to seal. Trim away the excess pastry. Prick the top here and there with a fork and bake for 30–35 minutes, or until pale golden.

Remove the tart from the oven, dust with caster sugar and cut into wedges. Serve warm, with crème fraîche scooped with an ice-cream scoop.

Note: You could use the pastry to line individual tartlet tins instead and bake them for 10–15 minutes – perfect mincemeat pies for Christmas!

bramble and almond tart

Bramble-picking is something of a national obsession in Scotland, at its height in October, when blackberries are there for the taking in hedgerows all over the country. A personal request to brambling Scots – please make sure your cars are parked and your car doors closed before commencing picking! This tart should be eaten warm, when the pastry will still be crumbly and light.

Serves 8–10

250 g (9 oz) softened butter
250 g (9 oz) caster sugar
25 g (1 oz) plain white flour
250 g (9 oz) ground almonds
4 eggs
25 cm (10 in) Sweet Shortcrust Pastry, baked blind (see page 253)
500 g (1 lb 2 oz) fresh blackberries or 600 g can of pitted black cherries, drained
3 tablespoons apricot jam
Crème Anglaise (see page 255), to serve (optional)

Preheat the oven to 160°C/325°F/Gas 3.

Cream the butter and sugar together in a large mixing bowl until very pale and thick. Beat in the flour and a quarter of the ground almonds until smooth. Then beat in the eggs, one at a time. Fold in the remaining ground almonds. (You can successfully freeze the mixture at this stage, if you wish.)

Spread the almond frangipane mixture in the tart case and then dot the brambles or cherries here and there over the top, pressing them into the frangipane. Protect the edges of the cooked pastry with very thin strips of foil and bake the tart for 1 hour, or until risen and golden.

Put the apricot jam in a small pan and leave to melt over a low heat. Add a little water if it is very thick. Press it through a sieve to remove any lumps and then brush it liberally over the top of the tart to glaze. Serve warm, with some cold crème anglaise, to evoke childhood memories of bramble tart with custard, or a scoop of ice-cream.

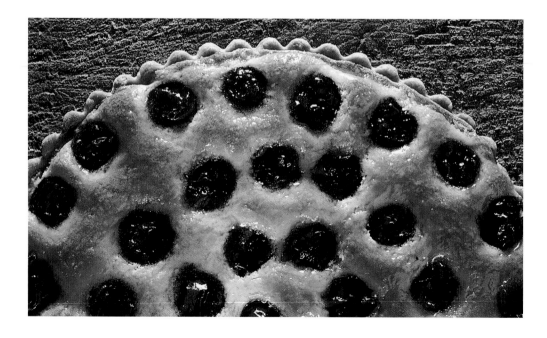

chocolate orange cups

Wonderful orange-scented chocolate is now available in selected supermarkets and is well worth searching out. Wherever you find it, you've done the hardest part of the recipe because the rest of it is so easy. However, you do need a liquidizer, not a food processor, to get the right texture.

Serves 6

125 ml (4 fl oz) full-cream milk
125 ml (4 fl oz) double cream
125 g (4½ oz) orange dark chocolate
1 egg
Double cream, to serve

Put the milk and the cream into a large pan over a medium heat. You want it to come to the boil very gently. Meanwhile, break the chocolate into small pieces – you can grate it but I prefer to chop it finely with a knife.

Put the chocolate into a liquidizer and, once the milk and cream has just come to the boil, add it to the chocolate. Leave to stand for a minute. Put the lid on the liquidizer, remove the centre and cover the hole with a clean tea towel. Whizz the chocolate and the hot creamy milk together; the heat of the milk melts the chocolate in about 30 seconds.

Crack the egg, add it to the liquidizer and whizz again for about 45 seconds.

Divide the mix between six little espresso cups and leave them in the fridge for a couple of hours to set. You can make these the night before if you like, but I wouldn't make them any further ahead than that.

Serve on the saucers that match the cups. I like to finish the pots by pouring some really cold double cream over the surface of the chocolate. As you scoop into the chocolate the cream runs into the centre, cutting through the sweetness.

chocolate soufflé, chocolate mousse and chocolate pudding

Three boffo desserts for the price of one! This mixture is extremely versatile: it can be served hot as a soufflé, or left uncooked to set in the fridge, where it becomes a fabulously rich, dark chocolate mousse. Your third option, should you desire, is to leave the soufflés to stand for 5 minutes once they're out of the oven, allowing them to sink back into the ramekins. They can then be turned out and served with hot chocolate sauce and whipped cream to make the most excellent warm chocolate puddings! The uncooked soufflé mixture can be prepared up to 45 minutes in advance and kept at room temperature before baking. If you do this, they won't rise quite as well, but are just as delicious.

Serves 6

FOR THE SOUFFLÉS

Soft butter, for greasing

100 g (4 oz) caster sugar, plus extra for the ramekins

300 g (10 oz) dark chocolate (at least 60% cocoa solids)

4 egg yolks

8 egg whites

TO SERVE

1 teaspoon icing sugar, plus extra for dusting

150 ml (¼ pint) whipping cream, whipped

1 tablespoon whisky

FOR THE CHOCOLATE SAUCE (OPTIONAL)

100 g (4 oz) dark chocolate, grated

3 tablespoons milk

Preheat the oven to 220°C/425°F/Gas 7. Butter and sugar six ramekins and place them in the fridge.

Melt the chocolate in a mixing bowl placed over a saucepan of simmering water. When completely melted, beat in the egg yolks with a wooden spoon until the mixture becomes thick and stiff.

In a food mixer, whisk the egg whites until they start to thicken. At this point add all of the sugar and continue to whisk for about 3 minutes, until the meringue becomes thick and smooth. Take care not to over-whisk; it should just come to soft peaks.

Whisk about one-fifth of the meringue into the chocolate-and-egg-yolk mixture and then carefully fold in the remaining meringue. You need to retain as much volume as possible, since it is the trapped air that makes the soufflés rise.

Divide the mixture between the ramekins and give each one a good tap to flatten the surface. There is no need to smooth the top. Bake for 12–13 minutes, until they have risen well.

Dust each one with icing sugar. Mix the whipped cream with the whisky and icing sugar and serve a dollop of the flavoured cream with each soufflé.

If you want to serve them as warm puddings instead, make the sauce by melting the chocolate with the milk on a low heat, stirring continuously with a wooden spoon until it is smooth and glossy. Turn the puddings out onto dessert plates, pour over the sauce and serve with the flavoured whipped cream.

soft chocolate cake

You might as well ask me to list the moons of Jupiter as name my favourite pudding. This one comes close, though: it's as rich and moist as any chocolate cake I've ever tasted. A good dollop of crème fraîche is the only partner it needs.

Serves 8

200 g (8 oz) good-quality plain chocolate (at least 65% cocoa solids)
200 g (8 oz) butter
140 g (5 oz) caster sugar
6 egg yolks
8 egg whites
Icing sugar, sifted, to decorate
Crème fraîche, to serve

Preheat the oven to 160°C/325°F/Gas 3. Lightly butter a 25 cm (10 in) springform cake tin and then line the base with a circle of baking parchment.

Break the chocolate into a bowl and add the butter. Rest over a pan of simmering water, making sure that the bowl does not touch the water. Leave to melt, stirring until it is smooth and glossy. Remove and set aside.

Put the sugar and egg yolks into a large bowl and whisk together until the mixture becomes pale and thick and leaves a trail on the surface for a few seconds. Gently fold this into the melted chocolate.

Now whisk the egg whites into soft peaks – the tips of the peaks should just fold over, not stand upright. Very gently fold the whites into the chocolate mixture. Pour into the tin and bake for 45 minutes. It will soufflé up during cooking and just crack when it's ready but then collapse once you bring it out of the oven. Don't worry, this is just the way it should be. Leave to cool in the tin.

When cold, carefully remove the cake from the tin and peel off the paper. Dust with icing sugar, cut the cake into wedges and serve with dollops of crème fraîche.

clootie dumpling

Clootie dumping is traditionally made in an old pillowcase or 'cloot', although a square of muslin will suffice. A few years ago I judged a clootie dumpling competition and I learned that a perfect pudding should be as spherical as possible, have an unblemished shiny coating and a dense, moist, flavoursome interior. Real custard is the perfect accompaniment but I really don't mind the stuff out of a can for this, or perhaps a couple of scoops of ice-cream.

Serves 8

200 g (8 oz) plain white flour, plus 25 g (1 oz) for sprinkling

1 teaspoon bicarbonate of soda

1 teaspoon ground mixed spice

1 teaspoon ground cinnamon

1 teaspoon ground ginger

¼ teaspoon freshly ground sea salt

175 g (6 oz) caster sugar, plus 1 tablespoon for sprinkling

100 g (4 oz) shredded suet

100 g (4 oz) sultanas

85 g (3 oz) currants

85 g (3 oz) chopped stoned dates

50 g (2 oz) muscatel raisins

1 apple or carrot, coarsely grated

1 tablespoon black treacle

1 egg

About 150 ml (¼ pint) buttermilk

Sift the flour, bicarbonate of soda, spices and salt into a bowl and stir in the sugar, suet, dried fruits, and the grated apple or carrot. Mix the black treacle with the egg and enough of the buttermilk to give a soft mixture with a cake-like dropping consistency when mixed into the dry ingredients.

Dip a large piece of muslin, an old pillowcase, a pudding cloth or a tea towel into boiling water, remove it and squeeze out the excess water. Lay it out on a surface and, in the centre, sprinkle the extra flour and sugar in a 30 cm (12 in) circle. Spoon the pudding mixture on top, carefully gather up the corners of the cloth to shape the pudding mix into a sphere and tie securely with string, leaving a little room for the pudding to expand.

Rest a heatproof plate in the base of a large pan, on a trivet so that it is not in direct contact with the heat, and place the pudding on the plate, knotted-side up. Pour in enough water almost to cover the pudding, cover with a tight-fitting lid and simmer gently for 3¾–4 hours. Take a peek every now and then to check the water level and top it up if necessary.

Preheat the oven to 180°C/350°F/Gas 4. Lift the pudding out of the pan and dip it briefly in a bowl of cold water – this will ensure that the outside of the pudding does not stick; unwrap the pudding and transfer it to an ovenproof serving plate. Slide it into the oven and leave it for 15 minutes, until the outside of the pudding has dried off and is dark and glossy. Allow to cool for a few minutes or allow to cool and store in an airtight container for up to seven days. The best way of reheating I've found is in a microwave, or alternatively in a low-to-medium oven covered in buttered foil.

Serve in chunky wedges, with scoops of clotted cream or custard and perhaps a small glass of whisky.

lemon and sugar crêpes

I love making crêpes, so where I say this recipe serves four, I have been quite generous but, if you're like me, gluttony and crêpes go hand in hand. The first crêpe always seems to stick – I think it's meant to! It helps 'season' the pan – after that the rest will be child's play.

I remember my mum making these crêpes. The lemon and sugar combine to make a lovely, slightly crunchy syrup, which, in turn, soaks into the pancakes. In the Nairn household, these are a great breakfast treat straight from the pan.

Serves 4

2 eggs

25 g (1 oz) caster sugar

250 ml (9 fl oz) milk

90 g (3½ oz) plain white flour

1 tablespoon sunflower oil, plus extra for the frying pan

3–4 unwaxed lemons (depending on how juicy they are)

About 6 tablespoons caster sugar

To make the crêpe batter, break the eggs into a bowl and whisk in the sugar and half the milk. Whisk in the flour and the sunflower oil until smooth, then gradually whisk in the remaining milk. Set aside and leave to rest for 1 hour.

Heat the frying pan until hot. Brush with a little oil, pour in some of the batter (about 2 tablespoons – I like to use a small ladle to help judge the correct amount of batter) and tilt the pan until the mixture covers the base in a thin, even layer. Once you have cooked a couple you will be able to judge how much you will need for the rest. Cook over a high heat for 1–2 minutes, until golden underneath, then lift up the edge with a palette knife, flip it over and cook for ½–1 minute longer, until lightly browned. Tip out onto a plate and continue like this, layering the crêpes up with squares of greaseproof paper, until you have made about 16. Either keep warm in a low oven or the pancakes can be made in advance and frozen, layered with greaseproof paper.

Squeeze the juice out of 2 or 3 of the lemons. Cut the remaining lemon into 8 wedges. If you've made them in advance, simply heat the crêpes through in the oven or microwave. Sprinkle them with plenty of lemon juice and caster sugar, fold into cones or roll up and place on four warm serving plates. Serve quickly while still warm, together with the lemon wedges.

Other good things to serve with crêpes include honey, golden syrup, chocolate hazelnut spread, jam, whipped cream and chopped fresh fruits, such as strawberries, mango or raspberries.

tablet

This is a traditional Scottish sweetie and it's like a hard crumbly fudge. Interestingly, John Webber (the maestro at Nairns Cook School) can't make this for toffee! But he does produce the most delicious fudge – I suppose it's because he comes from Birmingham. The secret of perfecting the texture is always to make it in the same pan over the same heat source to get the cooking temperature spot on. A word of warning: tablet is very sweet but beloved by anyone who's ever had it, me in particular. I've always been very vague about this recipe whenever asked, since it took me a long time to perfect it, but some things just shouldn't be kept to oneself.

Makes approximately 12 squares

400 ml (14 fl oz) can of condensed milk
1 kg (2 lb 4 oz) granulated sugar
250 g (9 oz) butter
25 g (1 oz) white chocolate, grated
(optional, but recommended)

Line a baking tin, 30 x 20 cm (12 x 8 in), with greaseproof paper.

Place all the ingredients, except the chocolate, in a large saucepan with 600 ml (1 pint) of hot water and bring to the boil before reducing to a medium heat. This temperature is very important – too cold and the tablet will turn dark brown before it's ready to set, too hot and the tablet will burn on the bottom. The temperature is about right when the tablet is simmering at just over double its original volume. Simmer for 30–40 minutes, until the tablet has darkened to a golden caramel and started to thicken. Give it a stir at this stage. It will have probably caught a bit at the bottom of the pan but don't worry – this is normal and the bits are dispersed during the beating later. You can check if it is ready by removing a teaspoonful onto a cold plate – it should set hard after a couple of minutes.

Now remove the pan from the heat and add the white chocolate, if you are using it. Apart from adding extra flavour, it helps the tablet to set. Start beating the mixture with a wooden spoon or, preferably, an electric mixer and don't stop until it starts to thicken and set in the pan. It takes about 10 minutes with a wooden spoon and less with an electric mixer.

Pour the mixture into the lined tray and allow it to set for 10–15 minutes. Then, using a thin-bladed knife, cut the tablet into 1 cm (½ in) squares. Leave it for 2–3 hours, to harden fully.

Remove the tablet from the tray, breaking it into the squares, and store it in an airtight container. Tablet stales after 4–5 days but I don't expect it will survive that long once you've started dishing it out.

Asking for a loaf of bread in Scotland was once met by the question 'Plain or pan?' These are the two types of bread offered in every shop and supermarket. The majority of Scots were brought up on plain bread, as pan bread wasn't widely introduced until the 1970s, and is nostalgically remembered as 'what your mother gave you'. The only bread for making a 'jeely piece' or jam sandwich, plain bread has characteristic thick, chewy crusts, soft sides and a dense texture. The dough is shaped in tins before being turned out and pressed together, giving each loaf a hard top and base but soft sides. Pan bread on the other hand is baked in the tin resulting in an all round crust and is perhaps the most common loaf bought today.

Bought bread has its place, but mass-produced bread contains a little more salt than is good for you. Baking your own not only allows you to control the salt content, but is altogether more satisfying than buying shop-bought bread and is much easier than you might imagine. A mixer with a dough hook can take a considerable amount of the effort out of kneading dough, although kneading by hand will lift a lot of stress out of your life!

The secret of success in achieving the perfect loaf lies in the consistency of the dough, and the quality and amount of kneading it receives. A good dough should be soft enough to require a bit of flour dusted over it during kneading, to prevent it from sticking. It then needs at least 15 minutes of kneading, most of which can be done by machine, though it is always best to finish off with a good vigorous hand-kneading as this allows you to feel the texture of the dough which, at this stage, should feel light and wonderfully elastic.

A couple of notes on proving: the ideal temperature for proving is about 20°C/68°F; any warmer and the bread proves too quickly to allow it to develop sufficient flavour and texture. It is possible to prove at lower temperatures but then you need to keep a careful eye on the dough as the length of time is fairly unpredictable. I know some people who prove their bread overnight in the fridge, ready to bake first thing in the morning.

If all of this sounds a bit too much like hard work, go out and buy a good-quality breadmaker, which gives you great results for little effort, as there really is nothing better than freshly baked home-made bread.

The majority of these recipes use fresh yeast, which is available from most bakers given 24 hours' notice, although dried yeast will work just as well too. I normally buy a block of fresh yeast (cut it into 2.5 cm/ 1 in cubes and freeze it), which works for me.

Resist the temptation to slice the bread as soon as it comes out of the oven as the trapped steam will make the bread soggy. Allow it to cool for about 1 hour and your patience will be rewarded with perfectly textured bread, still warm enough to melt butter.

bread
and baking

walnut bread

I normally make this chunky bread with a blend of equal quantities of strong white flour and strong wholemeal flour. If you like a lighter loaf, you could use 75% white flour. Due to its high oil content, this loaf keeps well and it is the perfect accompaniment to cheese. Try it toasted with ripe Gorgonzola and a drizzle of runny heather honey. Fabulous.

Makes 2 x 900 g (2 lb) loaves

25 g (1 oz) fresh yeast or 2 sachets easy-blend dried yeast

1 tablespoon runny honey

100 ml (3½ fl oz) walnut oil

2 tablespoons chopped fresh rosemary (optional)

500 g (1 lb 2 oz) strong white flour, plus extra for dusting

500 g (1 lb 2 oz) strong wholemeal flour

2 teaspoons salt

250 g (9 oz) walnuts, roughly chopped

Dissolve the fresh yeast and honey in 600 ml (1 pint) of warm water (approximately 50°C/122°F) and place it in a mixing bowl. If using dried yeast, add it to the flour. Add the oil, rosemary (if using), the two flours and the salt to the honey mixture and bring together to form a dough. Turn out onto a clean worktop and knead it for 10 minutes. Knead in the walnuts and work it for a further 5 minutes. Place the dough back in the mixing bowl, cover with a damp tea towel and allow it to prove in a warm place until more than doubled in size.

Turn the dough out onto a floured worktop and cut it in two. Roll it into sausage shapes, tapering at each end. Place them on a floured baking sheet, cover them with a damp tea towel and allow them to prove in a warm, but not hot, place for 30 minutes–1 hour, until doubled in size.

Preheat the oven to 220°C/425°F/Gas 7. Slash the tops of the loaves with a sharp knife. Place an ovenproof dish of water in the bottom of the heated oven; leave it undisturbed for 10 minutes. The water will start to steam, making the air in the oven moist, which helps the bread to rise and gives it a nice crisp crust.

Bake the loaves in the middle of the oven for 30–45 minutes. They should be golden brown on the top when ready and should sound hollow when tapped on the bottom. Remove the loaves and leave them on a wire rack to cool. You can wrap them individually in clingfilm and freeze for later use.

olive oil bread

This loaf uses olive oil instead of butter, and I prefer it not to be cooked in a tin – just rounded by hand into a loaf shape and cooked on a baking sheet. This gives it a thicker crust and has the added advantage of being less fiddly to do. It improves the crust if you put an ovenproof dish of hot water in the bottom of the oven to keep the atmosphere humid. This is also the recipe that I use for making my pizza bases.

Makes 4 x 450 g (1 lb) loaves, 2 x 900 g (2 lb) loaves or 8 x 25 cm (10 in) pizzas

1 kg (2 lb 4 oz) strong white flour, plus extra for dusting

125 ml (4 fl oz) olive oil, plus extra for greasing

50 g (2 oz) fresh yeast or 1½ sachets easy-blend dried yeast

2 teaspoons sugar

2 teaspoons salt

Place the flour and olive oil in the bowl of your food mixer with the dried yeast, if using. Fit the dough hook and switch it on to medium speed. Dissolve the sugar and the fresh yeast, if using, in 600 ml (1 pint) of warm water (approximately 50°C/122°F) and slowly pour onto the mixing flour. After a minute or so, the flour should come together to form a dough. Reduce the speed to a slow-to-medium speed and knead for a further 8 minutes. Add the salt and knead for another 2 minutes.

Tip the dough out onto a lightly floured surface and hand-knead it for approximately 5 minutes, until you feel the dough 'tighten'. Pop the dough into a large oiled mixing bowl (you could clean and use the bowl from the electric mixer) and cover it with a damp tea towel. Put it in a warm place and allow it to prove until it has doubled in size (it will take 30 minutes–1 hour).

Tip the proven dough out onto a floured surface and gently knead it for 2 minutes. Form the dough into a large ball then, using a sharp knife, cut it into quarters. Form each quarter into a smooth ball, as near as possible to a sphere.

Place the loaves on a lightly floured baking sheet, cover with lightly oiled clingfilm and put them back in the warm place to prove for a further 30 minutes–1 hour. Ten minutes before you bake the bread, preheat the oven to 230°C/450°F/Gas 8 and put an ovenproof dish of water in the bottom of the oven.

When doubled in size, remove the clingfilm from the bread. Give the loaves a quick squirt of water with a plant spray, if you like (this will give them a better crust), then bake for 20–30 minutes in the oven.

When they are ready, the loaves should be well fired on top (very dark brown). Remove them from the oven and place them to cool on a wire rack. You can scoff them as soon as they're cooled or cover them in clingfilm and freeze them until required. To defrost the loaves, see Braeval Bread (page 228).

braeval bread

This recipe is a classic, tried and tested over the years in different restaurants. The idea actually originated from a flour packet, which proves that the free recipes found on the backs of packets are actually often worth reading.

Makes two 900 g (2 lb) loaves

1 kg (2 lb 4 oz) strong white flour, plus extra for dusting

25 g (1 oz) fresh yeast or 1 sachet easy-blend dried yeast

50 g (2 oz) butter

2 teaspoons salt

1 tablespoon caster sugar

Vegetable oil, for greasing

Place the flour, dried yeast, if using, butter and salt in the bowl of an electric food mixer. Work in the ingredients with your hands until you have dispersed the butter. Dissolve the sugar and fresh yeast, if using, in 600 ml (1 pint) of warm water (approximately 50°C/122°F) and add it to the bowl. Mix everything with the dough hook running at a slow-to-medium speed. Once everything is fully incorporated, set the machine to a slow speed and leave it to work the dough for a full 10 minutes. The dough should then come cleanly away from the sides of the bowl. You could do this by hand; it just takes a bit of elbow grease.

Tip the dough out onto a lightly floured surface and work it with your hands until you feel the dough 'tighten' (this should occur after approximately 5 minutes). Replace the dough in the mixing bowl and cover it with clingfilm or a damp tea towel. Put the bowl in a warm place and leave it to prove until the dough has risen out of the top of the bowl, approximately doubling the volume. This takes 30 minutes–1 hour, depending on the temperature.

Tip the dough onto a worktop, give it a quick knead by hand and then form it into a smooth ball. Cut the dough in half and form each one into a round ball, then elongate into a loaf shape. Try to ensure a nice smooth surface as this will help the bread to prove evenly. Drop the loaves into two lightly oiled 900 g (2 lb) loaf tins and place on a baking sheet. Preheat the oven to 200°C/400°F/Gas 6.

Put the loaves in a warm place and cover them with lightly oiled clingfilm – this prevents a skin from forming (which would not allow an even rise on the loaf). Wait until the loaves are well risen (just over the top of the tin) before removing the clingfilm and leave them for up to 5 minutes before placing the tins and baking tray in the oven. Be careful not to knock the tins as, at this stage, the dough is very light and well risen and could fall, giving you a squashed loaf.

Bake the loaves for 15 minutes. Then carefully remove them from the tins, using oven gloves or an oven cloth, place them on the tray lying on their sides and cook for a further 10 minutes. Remove the tray from the oven, turn the loaves over and put them back to bake for a further 10 minutes.

The loaves are ready when they are a deep brown colour and sound hollow when tapped on the bottom. Leave them to cool on a wire rack.

You can either use the bread that day or wrap the loaves individually in clingfilm as soon as they're cool and freeze them. They will keep for 3 weeks. To defrost the loaves, place each one, still in the clingfilm, in a microwave and cook it on the highest setting for 1½ minutes. Allow the loaf to stand for 8 minutes before removing the clingfilm. Alternatively, allow the loaves to stand at room temperature for about 4 hours.

brioches

A wickedly rich, buttery loaf, much beloved of the French, and the best partner to strawberry jam I know. I find it slightly less temperamental than bread and even a 'not so brilliant' brioche tastes great!

Makes 2 x 1 kg (2 lb 4 oz) loaves or 4 x 500 g (1 lb 2 oz) loaves

50 g (2 oz) fresh yeast or 2 sachets easy-blend dried yeast

50 g (2 oz) sugar

125 ml (4 fl oz) warm milk

8 eggs

1 kg (2 lb 4 oz) strong white flour, plus extra for dusting

2 teaspoons salt

350 g (12 oz) butter, softened to room temperature and diced

Vegetable oil, for greasing

In the mixer bowl, dissolve the fresh or dried yeast and sugar in the warm milk (approximately 50°C/122°F), then whisk in the eggs. Fit the dough hook and start the mixer on a medium-to-high speed, slowly adding the flour, a spoonful at a time. As the dough starts to thicken, turn the speed back to medium and then slow-to-medium. Add the salt and work the dough for 7–8 minutes, until firm. Add the softened butter, a piece at a time, kneading again until it is fully incorporated. Then knead for a further 5–6 minutes until the dough is shiny and elastic.

Remove the dough to a floured worktop and work by hand until you feel the dough 'tighten'. This will take 3–5 minutes. Form the dough into a ball and return it to the clean mixer bowl. Cover with clingfilm or a wet tea towel and leave it in a warm place to prove for about 40 minutes, until doubled in size.

When the dough has doubled in size, tip it out onto the floured worktop and lightly knead it for 1 minute. Form the dough into a large shiny ball and cut into quarters. Roll each quarter into a ball and then form it into a loaf shape.

Place the loaves in four oiled 450 g (1 lb) loaf tins on a baking sheet and cover them with a damp tea towel or oiled cling film. Put them in a warm place and leave until the dough has risen out of the tins (about 30 minutes). Preheat the oven to 200°C/400°F/Gas 6.

Remove the tea towel or clingfilm and prove the dough for about 15 minutes, until it is fully risen. The brioches should rise about 2.5 cm (1 in) out of the tins.

Place the brioches in the preheated oven for 15 minutes, then remove them from the tins and cook for a further 8 minutes on each side. Remove from the oven and let them cool on a wire rack. Stand by with butter and strawberry jam!

Alternatively, wait until the brioches are cooled, cover them in clingfilm and freeze. They will keep for 3 weeks. To defrost the brioches, see Braeval Bread (page 228).

my mum's pancakes with a choice of preserves

Whilst these are perfect for afternoon tea, in our house they are devoured at any time of the day or night; a little clotted cream wouldn't go amiss either. The preserves make far more than you need for one sitting but also taste great on toast or warm scones. My mum has always cooked these pancakes (or drop scones, as they are known south of the border) directly on the slow ring of her Aga with wonderful results.

Serves 4 (makes about 12 pancakes)

FOR THE WHISKY AND RHUBARB PRESERVE
1.5 kg (3 lb 5 oz) cultivated rhubarb
900 g (2 lb) sugar
Finely grated zest of 1 lemon
175 ml (6 fl oz) best Islay whisky

FOR MY AUNTY ULLA'S NO-COOK MARMALADE
200 g (8 oz) dried apricots, washed and soaked overnight
1 lemon
2 oranges
450 g (1 lb) caster sugar

FOR THE PANCAKES
85 g (3 oz) self-raising flour, plus a little more for sprinkling
1 teaspoon baking powder
50 g (2 oz) granulated sugar
1 egg
150 ml (¼ pint) milk
Butter, to serve

For the whisky and rhubarb preserve, cut off the ends of each piece of rhubarb and wipe the stalks clean with a cloth – there's no need to peel them. Cut into 2.5 cm (1 in) long chunks. Layer the rhubarb and sugar in a large deep bowl or dish and leave for 24 hours. Drain the sugary liquid into a preserving pan and add the grated lemon zest. Bring to the boil briskly for 30 minutes. Add the rhubarb and boil for another 30 minutes. Take the pan off the heat and slowly stir in the whisky. Place the pan in a warm place and leave to stand for another 30 minutes. Spoon the preserve into sterilized jars, cover with waxed disks and seal.

For my Aunty Ulla's no-cook marmalade, drain the apricots and mince them with a mincer or give them a whizz in a food processor. Scrub the lemon and the oranges, then drop them into a pan of boiling water and scald for 1 minute. Remove and, when slightly cooled, cut them in half and squeeze out the juice. Mince or whizz the flesh and mix this with the juice, the sugar and the minced apricots. Pack the mixture into a sterilized jar. You can use it straight away but it's best kept for 2–3 days, to allow the flavour to mature.

For the pancakes, sift the flour and baking powder into a bowl and stir in the granulated sugar. Whisk the egg and stir it into the dry ingredients – it is very important that you don't beat it in. Then whisk in enough milk to give a batter which is the same consistency as double cream.

Heat a smooth cast iron griddle over a medium-to-high heat. Test the heat by sprinkling the griddle with a little flour. If it browns straight away, it is too hot. If it takes a few seconds before it browns, then it's perfect.

Drop 3 tablespoons of the batter, spaced a little apart, onto the griddle. After 2–3 minutes, when bubbles appear over the tops of the pancakes and they are golden brown underneath, turn them over using a palette knife and cook for another 2 minutes, until golden brown on the other side. Lift onto a plate, cover with a cloth and keep warm while you cook the rest.

Serve them spread with a little butter or clotted cream and some preserve.

oatcakes

These oatcakes are traditionally cooked on a griddle over an open fire but you can get a great result by baking them in the oven, too. They can be made well in advance, cooled and stored in an airtight container. A nice bit of Scottish cheese is all you really need with them, though you can also use them in all kinds of imaginative ways. Here are some suggested toppings, but really these should be limited only by your own imagination: goat's cheese, basil and cherry tomatoes; Mull Cheddar and chutney or pickle; hot-smoked salmon and rocket; smoked salmon and crowdie; blue cheese, walnuts and watercress; smoked ham and mozzarella.

Serves 4

200 g (8 oz) medium oatmeal, plus extra for dusting

¼ teaspoon bicarbonate of soda

A pinch of salt

3 teaspoons bacon fat, lard or butter

Preheat the oven to 180°C/350°F/Gas 4.

Put the oatmeal, bicarbonate of soda and salt into a bowl and mix well. Place the fat, lard or butter and 150 ml (¼ pint) of water in a small pan and heat until the fat has melted. Make a well in the centre of the oatmeal, add the liquid and mix together with a palette knife. The mixture will initially seem a bit wet but the oatmeal will gradually absorb all the liquid to give you a soft dough.

Divide the mixture in two and roll each piece out on a work surface lightly dusted with oatmeal to a 15 cm (6 in) circle, about 5 mm (¼ in) thick. Don't worry if the edges aren't very neat – they look better that way. Cut into quarters ('farls', as they say in Scotland), brush off the excess oatmeal and place on an ungreased baking sheet.

Bake in the oven for about 20 minutes, turning the oatcakes every 5 minutes or so to stop them from steaming and going stodgy, until they are crisp and lightly golden. Leave them to cool on a wire rack.

Either devour immediately or keep for up to 5 days in an airtight container.

This is a collection of recipes that crop up throughout the book, many being cornerstones of cooking, so rather than repeating them it made sense to have this reference chapter. The majority of these recipes can be made in advance when you have some free time on your hands and are ideal for making larger quantities for storing or freezing.

Stock-making can be a time-consuming business, so it's best to tackle it when you've got a bit of spare time. I usually make the biggest batch of stock I can, by simply multiplying up the ingredients in these recipes to fill the largest stockpot I have. Then I put it into clearly labelled 600 ml (1 pint) tubs and freeze it for future use. Not only is stock easier to make in bigger batches, but it will also have a better flavour. In the summer it's best to freeze the stock immediately but in the winter it will keep for up to 48 hours in the fridge.

basic recipes

chicken stock

Back in the old days, big hotels made rich chicken stock using whole chickens – this would produce a deep, rich stock and the added bonus of cooked chicken ready for room-service sandwiches. A fantastic if somewhat extravagant way to make stock. This method uses carcasses and produces an excellent result for all purposes.

Makes 1.3 litres (2¼ pints)

3 chicken carcasses, skin and fat removed

1 large carrot, quartered

1 leek, cut into quarters

2 celery sticks, halved lengthwise

1 onion with skin left on, quartered

1 small head of garlic, halved across its equator

6 peppercorns

1 bay leaf

1 thyme sprig

3 teaspoons parsley or tarragon stalks

Place the carcasses in a pot large enough for the bones to fill it only halfway. Just cover them with about 2.5 litres (4½ pints) of cold water (too much water will dilute the flavour of the stock) and bring to the boil. Once boiling, reduce the heat immediately to a simmer and then, using a large spoon or ladle, skim off the fat and any scum from the surface. Add the rest of the ingredients, all of which should lie on top of the carcasses. Adjust the heat to a very slow simmer and skim once more.

The simmering stock will now rise and fall through the vegetables, which act as a filter, absorbing all of the gunk from the liquid and leaving it crystal-clear. Leave it to simmer like this for 2–3 hours, tasting regularly. You should eventually notice the point at which the flavour stops improving. This means it's ready.

Remove the pan from the heat and empty the stock into a colander set over a bowl. Now pass the stock through a fine sieve into a tall container or 2.5 litre (4½ pint) jug. Cover it and allow it to cool by placing it in a sink of cold water.

When it's cool, place it in the fridge overnight. Skim off any fat that settles on top and spoon out the now-jellied stock into tubs. Freeze until ready to use.

fish stock

You should only make this when you have access to good-quality fresh fish bones, so it pays to make friends with your fishmonger. Otherwise you can substitute vegetable stock.

Makes about 1.2 litres (2 pints)

750 g (1 lb 10 oz) fish bones, preferably sole, turbot or brill

1 tablespoon olive oil

½ onion, finely diced

1 white of leek, finely diced

1 celery stick, finely diced

6 peppercorns

½ bay leaf

3 teaspoons fresh herbs (chervil, parsley, tarragon and/or coriander)

300 ml (½ pint) dry white wine

Soak the fish bones in cold water for 30 minutes. Wash, drain and roughly chop.

In a medium-sized saucepan, heat the olive oil and gently sweat all of the finely diced vegetables, the peppercorns, bay leaf and herbs until soft, but without colouring them. Add the white wine and boil until nearly dry.

Now add the fish bones and stir to coat. Pour over enough cold water just to cover the mixture – about 1.2 litres (2 pints). Bring it to the boil, skim, and then simmer for about 20 minutes (do not allow it to boil again). Remove it from the heat and allow to stand until cool (this takes 3–4 hours).

Once cooled, pour the stock through a sieve or colander, then pass it through a fine sieve into a tall container. Place in the fridge and leave it overnight to allow it to settle.

The next day, skim off any scum that has settled on the top, then spoon off all the clear jellied stock, which should then be frozen until needed. You may notice some white gunge at the bottom of the container: this should not be considered edible and should be disposed of.

chicken and beef stock

John Webber, who runs Nairns Cook School, donated this recipe, which makes simply the best meat stock I have ever tasted. It doesn't rely on the traditional veal bones but has at the heart of it a pig's trotter and a shin of beef, which any decent butcher should be able to supply. The trotter gives a gelatinous quality and the shin a wonderful flavour. Although the process is in two stages, unlike most recipes for beef stock using bones, this stock can be made in one day.

Makes 1.7 litres (3 pints)

STAGE 1

4 kg (8 lb 12 oz) chicken carcass
1 pig's trotter, around 2 kg (4 lb 8 oz), split
2 carrots, diced
2 onions, diced
2 celery sticks, diced
1/2 head fennel, diced
2 tablespoons tomato purée
2 cloves of garlic

STAGE 2

200 g (8 oz) shin of beef, diced
1 turkey thigh, diced
2 carrots, diced
1 celery stick, diced
1 onions, diced
150 ml (1/4 pint) red wine
100 g (4 oz) tinned tomatoes
1 thyme sprig

Preheat the oven to 220°C/425°F/Gas 7. Trim the chicken carcass of unwanted fat and place in a roasting tin. Roast to a golden brown. Take care not to burn the bones or a bitter flavour will result.

Place the bones and the pig's trotter in a large pot (narrow tall pots work best for stocks). Add the vegetables (not the garlic) from stage 1 of the recipe to the roasting tin. Return the tin to the oven or set over a high heat and allow the vegetables to brown, stirring from time to time. This will take approximately 30 minutes.

Once the vegetables have caramelized and browned, add the tomato purée and stir into the vegetables. Let the purée caramelize lightly, to take the redness off the mixture, then deglaze the tin with approximately 2 litres (3½ pints) of cold water. Mix well, scraping the bottom of the tin with a wooden spatula. Now add to the bones in the pot.

Cut the garlic cloves in half and then add to the pot. Then top up with water, leaving 5 cm (2 in) of bones showing above the water level; these will shrink as the stock cooks. Now bring to the boil, reduce to a gentle simmer and cook for 2½ hours, skimming the surface of the stock occasionally.

Strain the stock into a clean pot. Using a large frying pan, brown the diced meat and vegetables for stage 2 of the recipe. You may need to do this in small quantities, to avoid stewing the meat.

Add the browned meat and vegetables to the stock. Deglaze the frying pan with the red wine. Add to the stock along with the tomatoes and thyme and return to a simmer, skimming off any scum that appears. Cook the stock at a gentle simmer for another 2 hours.

Strain the stock through a fine strainer into covered containers, cool, then remove any fat from the surface and store in the fridge for up to 48 hours or freeze for later use.

marinated vegetable stock

Although this marinated vegetable stock takes 48 hours to prepare, it is relatively simple
to make, using readily available ingredients. It has a wonderful sweet, aromatic flavour,
which lifts it above other run-of-the-mill vegetable stocks. It keeps well in the freezer.

Makes 1.2 litres (2 pints)

1 large onion

1 leek

2 celery sticks

1 head of fennel (optional)

4 large carrots

1 head of garlic, halved
across its equator

8 peppercorns, crushed

1 teaspoon coriander seeds

1 star anise, optional

1 bay leaf, optional

40 g (1½ oz) mixed fresh herbs

300 ml (½ pint) white wine

Chop all of the vegetables into 1 cm (½ in) dice, place in a pot and cover
with water. Add the garlic, peppercorns, coriander seeds, star anise and bay
leaf, bring to the boil and simmer for 10 minutes.

Add the fresh herbs and simmer for a further 3 minutes. Now add the white
wine and remove from the heat. Leave covered and allow to marinate for
48 hours in a cool place.

Once marinated, strain the stock through a fine sieve. It can be used
immediately or frozen for up to 6 weeks.

vegetable butter sauce

This sauce has a delightful, fresh, buttery flavour on its own but with the addition of other ingredients (freshly chopped herbs, chilli, pesto, tomato, shellfish…) it can take on any flavour. The one essential item of equipment is a hand-held blender. Without one, it is difficult to obtain the light, smooth quality that makes this sauce so versatile.

Makes about 300 ml (¹/₂ pint)

600 ml (1 pint) Marinated Vegetable Stock (see page 239)
200 g (8 oz) cold butter, diced
1 teaspoon lemon juice
Freshly ground pepper
75 ml (2¹/₂ fl oz) double cream (optional)

Pour the vegetable stock into a small straight-sided saucepan, filling slightly more than half the pan. Place on a high heat and bring to the boil. Reduce to roughly one-fifth of the original volume. (It turns dark and looks thick and sticky!)
Turn the heat to low and plop in all of the butter. Stick in your hand-held blender and give it a good old thrash about until all of the butter has been melted and the texture is light and frothy. Add the lemon juice and pepper, tasting as you season, and keep warm (but don't let it boil) until it's needed.
If you let this sauce go cold and it solidifies, you can bring it back again by melting the sauce. It will separate and the butter will float to the top. Now boil the double cream in a small saucepan. When boiling, use the hand-held blender to whisk it and, at the same time, pour in the hot separated sauce in a steady stream. And hey presto, welcome back to a lovely light sauce.

speedy hollandaise sauce

Hollandaise should be regarded as a special occasion sauce; the heavenly combination of egg yolks, butter and lemon produces a sauce which is on the sinful side of healthy.

Serves 4

2 egg yolks
225 g (8 oz) hot melted butter
Juice of 1 lemon
Freshly ground sea salt and freshly ground pepper

Put the egg yolks and 2 tablespoons boiling water into a liquidizer and place the lid on. Remove the centre of the blender lid and cover the hole with a clean tea towel. Whizz for approximately 30 seconds until the yolks start to go fluffy.
Pour the hot butter into the hole in a continuous stream (this should take 15–20 seconds). Add the lemon juice and some seasoning
Have a small heatproof glass bowl ready, three-quarters full of boiling water. When the hollandaise sauce is ready, pour out the water and pour in the hollandaise. Taste and adjust the seasoning. Covered in clingfilm, the hollandaise will keep warm for about 1 hour (in a warm place).

shallot and tarragon butter

Flavoured butters are one of my secret weapons. They can be stirred into otherwise lacklustre sauces and stews at the last minute. Whip this one out of the freezer whenever you think a dish needs an extra touch of richness.

Makes about 350 g (12 oz)

200 g (8 oz) butter, softened
100 g (4 oz) shallots, very finely chopped
25 g (1 oz) fresh tarragon, finely chopped
Lemon juice
Freshly ground pepper

Always make this well in advance so that it has enough time to chill. Melt 25 g (1 oz) of the butter in a pan, add the chopped shallots and cook over a gentle heat for 10 minutes, until very soft but not coloured. Leave to cool.

Using a wooden spoon, beat the shallots into the rest of the butter with the chopped tarragon and lemon juice, seasoning with pepper to taste.

Spoon the mixture onto a sheet of clingfilm and shape into a roll 2.5 cm (1 in) thick. Wrap well in the clingfilm and chill in the fridge for a week or freeze for up to 2 months.

vinaigrette

This is my version of the classic French salad dressing. It has evolved over the years into this present form – a bit of an 'everything but the kitchen sink' recipe but well worth trying. After all, ten years of research and development must count for something.

Makes about 850 ml (1½ pints)

1 tablespoon smooth Dijon mustard
100 ml (3½ fl oz) white wine vinegar
100 ml (3½ fl oz) balsamic vinegar
200 ml (7 fl oz) hazelnut oil
200 ml (7 fl oz) sunflower oil
200 ml (7 fl oz) olive oil
1 garlic clove, crushed
1 teaspoon freshly ground sea salt
Freshly ground pepper

Place all the ingredients in a liquidizer and blitz them for 1 minute. Strain through a fine sieve into a jug, then pour the vinaigrette into any container of your choosing. I keep mine in an old olive oil bottle, which means that I can give it a good shake before using. A well-rinsed-out detergent bottle is also good.

Note: A simpler alternative version to this vinaigrette uses just 1 teaspoon smooth Dijon mustard, 100 ml (3½ fl oz) good-quality white wine vinegar, 400 ml (14 fl oz) olive oil, a little salt and freshly ground pepper, blitzed in a liquidizer.

balsamic syrup

Well-aged balsamic vinegars, with their intense flavour and syrupy consistency, are available in the deli section of some supermarkets or specialist Italian delis like the fabulous Valvona & Crolla in Edinburgh (see page 258), but the downside is they are extremely expensive. However, it is possible to recreate their thick syrupy consistency, by boiling and reducing a cheaper balsamic vinegar – the resulting syrup is great drizzled over an array of different foods, but sadly it lacks the subtle flavours of the real thing. When you're preparing this, make sure that the kitchen is well ventilated – the fumes make your eyes nip!

1 bottle balsamic vinegar

Bring the balsamic vinegar to the boil and simmer until reduced by half. Leave to cool. We store ours in small squeezy bottles for convenience.

herb oil

Herb oils are a great fridge standby as a replacement for sauces: they add colour, flavour and fragrance to a dish. They can be made with a variety of different herbs, either as a mixture or individually. Chive oil retains its grassy colours better than any other, while the aroma of basil oil is unmistakable and guaranteed to lift the mood in dishes with a Mediterranean slant. Feel free to experiment with different combinations of herbs. You can use the oils either filtered or unfiltered; personally I like the flecks of green and the extra flavour which come from not filtering. I recommend you use everyday olive oil here as the flavour of an extra-virgin olive oil would be lost under the herbs.

Makes about 300 ml (1/2 pint)

85 g (3 oz) mixed fresh chives, parsley and tarragon
300 ml (1/2 pint) olive oil

Drop the herbs into a pan of heavily salted, boiling water for 10 seconds. This fixes the chlorophyll and keeps them green, giving the oil a lovely rich colour. Drain and refresh under cold running water to stop the cooking process. Wring them dry in a clean tea towel or kitchen paper and then chop roughly.
Put the herbs into a liquidizer with the oil and blitz for 3 minutes, until the oil is emulsified and green. If the herbs are reluctant to give up their colour, tip the oil into a small saucepan and bring to the boil over a low heat – this should fix the colour. Cool immediately and store in a squeezy bottle in the fridge. It keeps for up to 10 days, then starts to lose its colour. Herb oils also freeze surprisingly well.

chilli oil

This chilli oil is very spicy and you have to take care not to get any in your eyes or other sensitive parts. Used sparingly, chilli oil imparts a wonderful glow to many dishes. Don't be tempted to fry anything with it, as it produces an effect similar to mustard gas.

Makes about 1 litre (1¾ pints)

200 g (8 oz) ripe red chillies
850 ml (1½ pints) sunflower oil

Slice the chillies in half lengthwise and place in a saucepan. Pour on the oil, plonk the pan on the hob and bring to the boil. Simmer gently for 5 minutes, remove from the heat and allow to cool (this takes approximately 2 hours).

Once cooled, transfer the chillies and oil to a plastic tub with a lid and store in a cool place for 2–3 weeks.

Then pour the oil through a sieve to remove the chillies before using it (or else your oil will just get too hot). I usually keep the chilli oil in an old olive oil bottle (it will keep for 3 months), but label it well – a skull and crossbones will suffice.

lobster or shellfish oil

This adds a wonderful flavour to many fish and seafood dishes. It's also a great way of making use of all those shells that are usually just discarded.

Makes about 300 ml (½ pint)

175 g (6 oz) lobster or langoustine shells
350 ml (12 fl oz) sunflower oil
1 tiny piece broken star anise
3 white peppercorns
1 carrot, diced
2 shallots, diced
1 celery stick, diced
2 garlic cloves
3 teaspoons mixed fresh herbs (parsley, thyme and tarragon are all good used here)
1 tablespoon tomato purée
50 ml (2 fl oz) dry white wine

Crush the shells and drain away any liquid. Heat 4 tablespoons of the oil in a pan, add the shells, star anise and white peppercorns and fry over a medium heat for about 15 minutes, stirring every now and then.

Add all the remaining ingredients, except the remainder of the oil, and cook until the wine has evaporated. Add the rest of the oil and leave to simmer for 45 minutes.

Remove from the heat and leave to stand for 24 hours. Strain through a muslin-lined sieve, transfer to a bottle and seal. This oil will keep in the fridge for about 1 month.

chorizo oil

This oil has a wonderful warm paprika glow and amber colour. I often add it to dishes containing pulses.

Makes about 150 ml (¼ pint)

150 ml (¼ pint) olive oil
50 g (2 oz) chorizo sausage, finely sliced
1 garlic clove, crushed
2 thyme sprigs

Put all the ingredients in a stainless steel pan and slowly bring to a simmer over a low heat. Simmer for 10 minutes, remove from the heat and cover. Leave to stand for 4 hours.

Strain and bottle the oil – it will keep for up to 6 weeks in the fridge. The cooked chorizo is great diced up in a risotto.

curry oil

This oil has a wonderful amber colour and aromatic taste, perfect for cooking dishes of a similar nature, as well as for garnishing spicy dishes. Don't be put off by the long list of ingredients – it's actually quite easy to make. Use a light olive oil, nothing fancy here.

Makes 1.2 litres (2 pints)

1 onion

3 celery sticks

1 leek

1 green apple

4 garlic cloves

2 plum tomatoes

25 g (1 oz) root ginger

2 lemon grass stalks

Pared rind of ½ lemon

1.2 litres (2 pints) vegetable oil

50 g (2 oz) raisins

3 star anise

3 teaspoons ground coriander

1 teaspoon Thai red curry paste (optional)

4 tablespoons curry powder

2 tablespoons tomato purée

600 ml (1 pint) olive oil

Freshly ground sea salt

Roughly chop the onion, celery, leek, apple, garlic, tomatoes, ginger, lemon grass and lemon rind. Heat a little of the vegetable oil in a thick-bottomed pan and add the chopped vegetables and flavourings. Cover the pan and allow the vegetables to sweat over a low heat until they are soft – this should take about 10 minutes.

Add the raisins, star anise and the coriander and continue to cook for a few more minutes. Stir in the red curry paste, if using, the curry powder and the tomato purée. Mix well and then stir in the remainder of the vegetable oil and the olive oil. Add a little salt and simmer very gently for 2–3 hours.

Strain well and bottle the oil for later use. This oil will separate slightly, so shake before using. It will keep for up to 3 months in the fridge.

natural dried breadcrumbs

This is the best use for stale bread (apart from feeding ducks).

Stale bread, crusts removed

Put the slices of bread in a food processor and whizz until you have fine crumbs. Spread out on a wide tray and leave in a warm place for 12 hours. Keep in an airtight container for up to 2 weeks, or in the freezer for up to 3 months.

clarified butter

Clarified butter is just the oily part of butter, i.e. without the buttermilk, and is wonderful for frying potatoes, giving them a rich buttery flavour. It can also be used in place of duck fat. You can buy it ready-prepared from Indian delicatessens (as 'ghee').

Makes about 200 ml (7 fl oz)

250 g (9 oz) butter

In a small saucepan, melt the butter on a low heat. Allow it to stand for a few minutes, until all the oil rises to the top, then skim off the oil into a sealable plastic container. It will keep for 2 months.

Alternatively, put the butter in a plastic jug and microwave on a high heat for 1 minute. If it is not completely melted, heat again for a further 30 seconds. Do not allow it to boil. Continue as above, discarding the watery buttermilk.

home-dried tomatoes

These are a sweet, plump version of what comes in jars labelled 'sun-dried tomatoes' and which, in my opinion, look and taste like shoe leather. Forego the supermarket shelves and make them yourself – it's worth it, they are a taste sensation. It is important to buy really good, ripe plum tomatoes. Approximately 12 hours of oven time is involved, so don't plan on using your oven for anything else. Better still, make them overnight.

Makes 24 home-dried tomatoes

12 large, ripe plum tomatoes
Freshly ground sea salt and freshly ground pepper
50 ml (2 fl oz) olive oil, plus extra for preserving (approximately 200 ml/ 7 fl oz for a 600 ml/1 pint Kilner jar)
1 basil or thyme sprig
1 garlic clove, crushed

Preheat the oven to 110°C/225°F/Gas ¼ – the lowest heat possible – you are trying to recreate the conditions of a sun-drenched Tuscan hillside!

Slice the tomatoes in half lengthwise. Then remove the green eye. Lay the tomatoes on a baking sheet, cut-side up, and sprinkle lightly with crushed sea salt and a few turns of pepper. Drizzle the measured olive oil over them.

Place the tomatoes in the oven (you may have to prop the oven door open slightly to keep the temperature down). Leave for 8 hours.

When you return, the tomatoes should be reduced to half their original size but not browned. Turn them over and leave for a further 4 hours, or until they are nice and firm.

Remove from the oven and leave until cool. Then place them in a Kilner jar, add the sprig of fresh basil or thyme and the crushed garlic clove and cover with olive oil. These tasty beauties can now be stored in your fridge for up to 3 weeks.

red onion marmalade

The natural sweetness of red onions gives this a mellower flavour than ordinary onions. The marmalade is great with cold meats, game, chicken livers and bacon. Or add a tablespoonful to a meat gravy to make a rich onion gravy.

Makes 500 g (1 lb 2 oz)

100 ml (3½ fl oz) olive oil
1.5 kg (3 lb 5 oz) red onions, finely sliced
Freshly ground sea salt and freshly ground pepper
125 ml (4 fl oz) best-quality sherry vinegar or, even better, Cabernet Sauvignon vinegar
3 tablespoons crème de cassis or 2 tablespoons redcurrant jelly

Heat the oil in a large saucepan over a medium heat. Add the sliced onions, stir well to coat with the oil and then season. Cook slowly, uncovered, stirring from time to time until the onions are very soft and the sugary juices have caramelized. This should take about 45 minutes and the onions should look thick, dark and sticky.

Now add the vinegar and crème de cassis or redcurrant jelly and cook for another 10 minutes or so, until all the harsh vinegar has been boiled off and the marmalade has a glossy texture. Leave to cool.

Store in a jar in the fridge. If you pour in a tablespoon of olive oil to seal the top it should keep for 6–8 weeks.

cumberland sauce

This traditional game accompaniment is extremely versatile, and I use it not just to lift the flavour of the odd pigeon but also drizzled over warm salads or to accompany Smooth Chicken Liver Terrine (see page 123). It should have the consistency of runny honey. I keep this zingy, fruity sauce in a plastic squeezy bottle in the fridge, where it keeps for up to 6 weeks.

Makes 700 ml (1¼ pints)

500 g (1 lb 2 oz) redcurrant jelly
250 ml (9 fl oz) ruby port
Juice and grated zest of 2 lemons
Juice and grated zest of 2 oranges
1 teaspoon ground cinnamon
2 teaspoon English mustard

Place all the ingredients in a saucepan and bring to the boil. Skim away the froth and reduce over a low heat for approximately 30 minutes. Strain the sauce through a fine sieve and cool.

quick tomato sauce

The secret of this recipe is the cooking time – for a really thick and tasty sauce a good 30–45 minutes is essential. Make a large batch, which can be stored for up to 3 weeks in an airtight jar in the fridge. It's not just a tasty pasta sauce – I use it for stuffing ravioli, as a topping for pizza or as a last-minute addition to risotto.

Makes 200 g (8 oz)

4 tablespoons olive oil
1 garlic clove, crushed
400 g can of chopped tomatoes
3 teaspoons fresh basil leaves, torn
Freshly ground sea salt and freshly ground pepper

Heat the olive oil in a wide-surfaced frying pan and add the garlic. Cook away until soft but not brown (it will taste bitter), about 1–2 minutes. Then add the chopped tomatoes and bring up to the boil and boil fast, stirring most of the time to stop it sticking. When really thick (this should take about 15 minutes depending on the speed of cooking), stir in the basil and season well.

For a wicked creamy version, stir in some double cream at the end. If storing ensure that you cover with a film of olive oil to prevent oxidation. This sauce will keep for up to 1 week in the fridge.

perfect basmati rice

I've given two ways of cooking basmati rice. The second method is the traditional one, but I find the result can be a little too sticky for my liking. My first method, on the other hand, guarantees perfect fluffy rice every time.

Serves 4

300 g (10 oz) basmati rice
1/2 teaspoon freshly ground sea salt

Bring a large pan (with a tight-fitting lid) filled with salted water (the secret of no-stick rice is to have at least 5 times as much water as rice) to the boil. Wash the rice under cold running water until the water runs clear. Throw the rice into the large pan of boiling water. Bring back to a rolling boil and stir once. Boil for exactly 7 minutes then drain the rice well, return to the pan and slam on a lid. Place the pan in a warm, not hot, spot and leave to steam in its own heat undisturbed for another 10 minutes. Fork up and serve. Perfect fluffy rice!

To cook rice in the traditional way, rinse the rice under cold water until the water runs clear. Put the rice into a really big pan with 600 ml (1 pint) of salted water. Bring to the boil and boil hard for 1 minute. Slam on a lid, turn down the heat and leave to simmer gently for exactly 8 minutes. Take the pan off the heat and leave the rice to steam undisturbed for another 10 minutes. Fork up and serve.

pasta dough

Whilst it it possible to shape pasta dough by hand, using a pasta machine makes life much easier so that's what I've used here. For best results, use Italian '00' flour (the finest grade of soft wheat flour available), though ordinary plain flour produces a more than acceptable result. A food processor makes the dough in seconds, although purists would insist that a perfect pasta dough needs the heat of your hands. Either way, this dough produces pasta with a wonderful soft yet still *al dente* texture, ideal served with fish, shellfish and vegetables. These quantities are only guidelines – depending on humidity, type of flour and so on, you may have to add more flour. The dough must not be too soft – it should be quite hard to knead. Too much extra flour will make the pasta tough and taste floury. This quantity of pasta will provide enough for 6 people.

Makes about 250 g (9 oz)

185 g (7 oz) Italian '00' pasta flour
2 whole eggs

Place the flour in a food processor and start giving it a whizz round. Add the eggs and keep whizzing until the mixture resembles fine breadcrumbs (it shouldn't be dusty, nor should it be a big gooey ball). This takes 2–3 minutes. Alternatively, roll your sleeves up and do it by hand: tip the flour onto a clean work surface, make a well in the middle and add the eggs. Use a fork to bring it all together, then knead well until you have a thick smooth dough.

Tip out the dough and form into a ball shape. Knead it briskly for 1 minute. Wrap in clingfilm and rest for 1 hour before using.

Now cut the dough in two pieces. Flatten each piece with a rolling pin to 5 mm (¼ in) thickness, then wrap one piece in clingfilm and keep to one side. With the pasta machine at its widest setting, pass the dough through the rollers. Repeat this process 10 times (the dough needs to be worked well to give it the necessary elasticity), folding over the dough until the pasta is silky smooth and shiny.

Pass the dough through the rollers and between each pass reduce the setting by one stop, until the pasta is at the correct thickness.

Once the desired thickness is reached, pass the dough through a second time at the penultimate setting on the machine, then allow it to dry for about 5 minutes. Hanging it is the best way to dry the pasta – I have used a suspended broom handle, which works well – or toss in fine semolina and lay on a well-floured (with semolina) tea towel on a basket or tray.

For lasagne, cut the pasta dough into squares (or rounds, if you prefer). For fettuccine, pass the dough through the machine's big cutters. For tagliatelle, pass through the small narrow cutters.

To cook, bring a large pan three-quarters full of salted water to a rolling boil. Chuck in the pasta and stir. Bring back to the boil and cook for 1 minute. Remove the pasta – I find a pasta lifter invaluable for this – and either use the pasta immediately or plunge into a bowl of cold water to stop the cooking. Drain and toss with olive oil.

This will give you three portions – if cooking for more people, repeat the above process with the second piece of dough. You can keep all the cooked pasta in a tub with a tight-fitting lid in the fridge for up to 12 hours before use. If, after storage, you find the pasta is stuck together, simply add a small amount of cold water. Replace the lid, shake well and – hey presto – unstuck pasta!

pesto

The traditional version of this sauce uses only basil leaves. I like to vary it by using a combination of flatleaf parsley, rocket and basil. You can double the amount of olive oil to make runny pesto, which looks good drizzled onto a plate. Whatever you do, don't forget that pesto should have a crunchy texture, which is easily lost by overworking in a food processor. During summer, when leaves are at their most plentiful and best, I like to make large batches of pesto and freeze it in an ice-cube tray – turn out the cubes and wrap in clingfilm and they keep for 6 months in the freezer.

Makes about 450 ml (16 fl oz)

3 garlic cloves, roughly chopped
200 ml (7 fl oz) extra-virgin olive oil, plus extra for covering the pesto
85 g (3 oz) fresh basil, flatleaf parsley and rocket leaves
50 g (2 oz) pine nuts
50 g (2 oz) Parmesan cheese, grated
1 teaspoon freshly ground sea salt
Freshly ground pepper

Put the garlic and oil in the food processor and whizz until you've got a really garlicky oil. Scrape down the sides with a spatula, then add the leaves and whizz until smooth.

Add the pine nuts and whizz for a few seconds, until they start breaking down but the mixture is still crunchy, not smooth. Lastly, add the Parmesan, salt and a generous grinding of pepper, and process for a couple of seconds, until thoroughly mixed. Don't overwork: pesto should have a crunchy, not smooth texture.

Scrape out into a clean jam jar, cover with a film of olive oil and keep in the fridge for up to 2 weeks or freeze.

Note: Each time you use some of the pesto, flatten the surface with a spoon and splash in some more olive oil before returning it to the fridge. This keeps the pesto sealed and stops it from darkening and losing its freshness.

savoury shortcrust pastry

The variety of fillings for savoury tarts is endless but the recipes in this book are some of my favourites. The principles of tart-making are the same in every case, just the ingredients vary. Individual tarts look great but are a bit of a faff; it's much easier and every bit as tasty to make one large one and cut slices from it. The tart case can be baked blind and the filling made a day in advance. Assemble the tart just before baking. If you don't need all this quantity of pastry, freeze any left over for later use.

Makes enough for a 25 cm (10 in) flan

175 g (6 oz) butter, plus extra for greasing
250 g (9 oz) plain white flour
A good pinch of salt
1 egg, beaten

Rub the butter, flour and salt together in a mixing bowl until the mixture has the consistency of fine breadcrumbs, or whizz in a food processor for 30 seconds. Then add the egg and bring it all together into a dough. Knead this lightly three or four times with floured hands. Cover in clingfilm and refrigerate for an hour before use. Or, if you are blessed with cold hands and a deft pastry touch, you may be able to roll it out straight away.

Preheat the oven to 200°C/400°F/Gas 6. Roll the pastry out 3 mm (1/8 in) thick and use to line a greased 25 cm (10 in) metal loose-bottomed tin, 3 cm (1 1/4 in) deep. I wrap the pastry round the rolling pin, unroll it over the baking tin, then press the pastry down well into the tin and fold the spare pastry over the edges.

Chill in the fridge for 15 minutes before baking. Rather than trimming it with a knife, this stops the pastry from shrinking back. Prick the pastry a few times with a fork to allow the steam to escape during cooking. Cover with greaseproof paper and fill with baking beans and bake blind for 11 minutes. Remove the beans and paper and bake for another 8–9 minutes, until lightly golden.

sweet shortcrust pastry

Whilst the main use for this pastry, or sweet paste as it is often referred to by chefs, is for making pastry shells for tarts and tartlets, any trimmings may be used to make the most delicious shortbread thins. Simply roll out the trimmings to 3 mm (⅛ in) thickness and use a scone cutter to stamp out rounds. Bake these on a baking sheet lined with baking parchment in an oven preheated to 200°C/400°F/Gas 6 for 8–9 minutes. Cool on a wire rack, then dust with caster sugar.

Makes enough for a 25 cm (10 in) flan

175 g (6 oz) butter
50 g (2 oz) caster sugar
A pinch of salt
250 g (9 oz) plain white flour
1 egg yolk

Cream the butter, sugar and salt at a medium speed in the bowl of a food mixer. When light and fluffy, add 50 g (2 oz) of the flour. With the mixer on a lower speed, add the egg yolk and the remaining flour a tablespoon at a time. When the flour is fully incorporated, add 1 tablespoon of cold water and mix it for a further 15 seconds.

Remove the bowl from the mixer, tip out the dough onto a floured worktop and, with floured hands, gently knead the dough three or four times until it comes together. Wrap it in clingfilm and allow it to rest in the fridge for at least 3 hours before you roll it out.

Preheat the oven to 200°C/400°F/Gas 6. Take the sweet pastry from the fridge and place it on a floured worktop. Roll out until the pastry is about 3 mm (⅛ inch) thick. Cut it into a circular shape, slightly larger than the diameter of a 25 cm (10 in) loose-bottomed flan ring. Don't worry if the pastry cracks, it can be 'repaired' by filling in with trimmings or even pressing together with warm fingers. Press the pastry down into the shape of the flan ring, folding the edges over the top of the ring, and place it on a baking sheet. Line the pastry with clingfilm (you can use clingfilm in the oven for this) or, if you prefer, use foil or greaseproof paper and fill it with baking beans (I use dried peas or butterbeans).

Place it in the fridge and leave for 15 minutes before baking it in the oven for 11 minutes. Take it from the oven, remove the clingfilm, foil or paper and the beans and then replace it in the oven. Bake it for a further 9 minutes, until the pastry is lightly browned. Remove, neatly trim away the overhanging pastry and leave it to cool until required. Use within 24 hours.

tuile pastry

This sweet pastry is spread out thinly on a non-stick baking sheet to produce a variety of thin shapes. It is ideal for making baskets, cones and cigars, which are often filled with ice-creams, sorbets or pastry cream.

Makes 8–10 servings

50 g (2 oz) caster sugar

50 g (2 oz) plain flour

2 egg whites

50 g (2 oz) melted butter, plus extra for greasing

Preheat the oven to 180°C/350°F/Gas 4. Put the caster sugar, flour and egg white into a bowl and beat together to a smooth paste. Beat in the melted butter and then cover and chill in the fridge for 20 minutes.

To make shapes, drop about 4 teaspoons of the mixture well apart onto a lightly greased non-stick baking tray. Spread the mixture very thinly into approximately 13 cm (5 in) circles. Bake for 6–8 minutes, until lightly coloured in the centre with a rich golden edge.

Remove from the oven and leave to cool for a few seconds. Then, working as quickly as you can, lift each one off the baking sheet with a palette knife and roll into your preferred shape. I find cones and cigar shapes work well or you can make a basket shape by moulding the pastry over an upturned tea cup. Leave to cool and harden. If the tuiles set before you can mould them pop them back into the oven for 1 minute to heat through again.

Any extra pastry can be kept in the fridge for up to a week or can be frozen for up to 2 months.